T0335504

# Video Game Law

Everything You Need to Know About Legal and Business Issues in the Game Industry

# Video Game Law
## Everything You Need to Know About Legal and Business Issues in the Game Industry

By

S. Gregory Boyd, Brian Pyne, and Sean F. Kane

CRC Press
Taylor & Francis Group
Boca Raton London New York

CRC Press is an imprint of the
Taylor & Francis Group, an **informa** business

CRC Press
Taylor & Francis Group
6000 Broken Sound Parkway NW, Suite 300
Boca Raton, FL 33487-2742

International Standard Book Number-13: 978-1-138-05849-1 (Hardback)

---

**Library of Congress Cataloging-in-Publication Data**

Names: Boyd, S. Gregory, author. | Pyne, Brian, author. | Kane, Sean F., author.
Title: Video game law : everything you need to know about legal and business issues in the game industry / Stephen Gregory Boyd, Brian Pyne, Sean F. Kane.
Description: Boca Raton : Taylor & Francis, 2019.
Identifiers: LCCN 2018006067 | ISBN 9781138058491 (hardback : alk. paper)
Subjects: LCSH: Video games industry. | Video games industry--Law and legislation. | Video games--Marketing.
Classification: LCC HD9993.E452 B69 2019 | DDC 794.8068/1--dc23
LC record available at https://lccn.loc.gov/2018006067

---

**Visit the Taylor & Francis Web site at**
**http://www.taylorandfrancis.com**

**and the CRC Press Web site at**
**http://www.crcpress.com**

*Greg:*

*To Stephanie, you built a 50-ton stone wall with me over three years, and our life together every day. You make the cozy.*

---

*Brian:*

*To my awesome wife, Regina, my loving parents, Nadeen and Jim, and my illiterate dog, Sam.*

---

*Sean:*

*To Jennifer, Pierce, and Marlena, for their love and endless support throughout the writing of this book and also within the rest of my life.*

---

# Contents

# Foreword

WHEN I STARTED OUT in the games industry in 1978, well, it wasn't actually yet an industry. It was a disparate assortment of people who were either game enthusiasts looking to use computers to make games, or computer programmers looking for fun projects to code; occasionally, as in my case, it was both.

My claim to fame is that I co-wrote (with Roy Trubshaw) a game called *MUD*. Don't worry, I know you haven't heard of it—it was *that long ago*. However, almost all today's MMORPGs are direct descendants of *MUD*, so it is of some historical significance. I mention this not to boast (although obviously I'm feebly attempting to do so), but to establish my credentials as someone who has been in the games industry as a designer, programmer, consultant, and academic for four decades.

Over that period, I've seen computer games descended upon and studied by people from a wide variety of different disciplines. Economists, anthropologists, dramatists, sociologists, futurologists, and many other -ists have looked at games, formulated theories about them, then in the main departed. Sometimes, when they found games lacking, they would stay to activate for changes; feminists did this. Sometimes, they took games and created a sub-discipline related to them; educationalists did this. Sometimes, they picked on very particular aspects of games to study in detail and ignored everything else; psychologists did this (in general, badly).

Only one group ever came and never went away: lawyers.

This is because if the lawyers went, so would the games industry.

It's also why, if you're interested in working in the games industry, this book should be on your (physical or digital) bookshelf.

*MUD* was written on a room-sized computer belonging to Essex University. As part of the conditions for using the computer, all software written on it was deemed as belonging to the university. Back then, this draconian measure was a perfectly defensible legal position under UK law. When the game began to take off, I approached the university to ask if they would transfer the intellectual property (IP) to me. They practically thrust it into my hands, for free, here, take it! This is because, also back then, games were regarded as not seriously worthy of respect; if word had got out that the university owned a game, well, prospective students might have applied to other universities that exhibited higher academic standards. The fact that by the late 1980s *MUD* would be making $5 million a year was neither here nor there. Stature is stature.

That was UK law. U.S. law was... different.

The reason I said earlier that "almost all" today's MMORPGs descend from *MUD* is because we weren't the only people who created a virtual world from first principles. The concept was invented independently on at least five other occasions. *MUD* took off because we made our program code available to anyone who wanted to write their own, similar game, so it rapidly developed a family tree of descendants. The other pioneers tended to keep their code secret so they wouldn't get ripped off. One of these games, Alan Kleitz's *Sceptre of Goth*, grew popular enough to lead to the formation of a company, GamBit, which enjoyed some commercial success. All went swimmingly well until one of its programmers took the game's code and set up his own server. Under U.S. law, there was absolutely nothing GamBit could do to stop this! Software wasn't yet something regarded as stealable.

Since those days, laws have been created and aligned to address some of the issues. They're not pretty, and they don't yet address everything. For example, should you be prosecuted for stealing in-game items belonging to another player that can legitimately be sold for tens of thousands of real dollars? Probably, yes—but if "stealing" is part of the game, well no, you shouldn't. Such unsolicited changes in ownership have indeed happened on multiple occasions in *EVE Online*, but it's no more theft than when someone wins money off you in poker. As for whether you should pay *tax* on your loot, OK, well I did say the laws didn't address everything... .

It's not just laws, of course: it's practice. You probably have a working knowledge of IP, and will be able to seek legal advice on how to acquire and work with it. That's fine. What you might not consider is whether you should seek to use an established IP in the first place. The reason you would is because it will garner you more players; the reason you wouldn't is because it may not cover its expense. I'm reminded of the story of three British comedians who went to the United States in the 1960s. They were offered a fee of £100 each, which sounded a lot more then than it does today. One of them engaged an agent to argue for a higher fee, and it worked: his fee was increased to £110. Then, the agent took his 10% fee and left the comedian with £99. IP is like this: you may make more money, but the license fee may take it all (and more) away.

I assure you, it's actually a lot more complex than that... .

Now you may be wondering why this is of any relevance to you if you just want to make games. What has all this business and law stuff got to do with making games? After all, degree courses in programming don't routinely teach programmers about how to set up and run their own businesses—they just teach them how to program. If it were important, surely they would?

Well, an increasing number of degree courses in game development *do* routinely teach their students how to set up and run their own businesses. You may indeed be reading this book as part of such a course! It *is* important for games. This is because there is an over-supply of would-be game developers: more people want to work in the games industry than the games industry can employ. If you take the right steps then you *can* increase your chances of landing a job, but there's no guarantee you'll triumph. If you want to make games, and for these games to be the games you want to make, then the best way to do it is as a start-up. Also, if you want to make money from games, then equity is the way to do it; another consequence of having an over-supply of people wanting to work in the games industry is that it leads to lower salaries than those of other software engineering industries (for programmers, about a third lower).

This is why game developers need to know about the practicalities of setting up and running a company, even though (as creatives) all they *really* want to do is develop games.

It's also why a book like this makes perfect sense for the games industry when other software-oriented industries might find an equivalent volume surprising.

There are a few Wild West elements to consider, too: other industries have boilerplate non-disclosure agreements from which the force majeure clause has not been accidentally omitted, and they have exclusivity agreements that explain what happens when the company assigned the exclusivity does nothing except instruct its personnel not to answer emails on the subject. Why yes, both of these have indeed happened to me.

I mentioned earlier that I've been involved in the games industry for a long time. I was there when the first legal scholars looked at games and figured that this topic was something new that required specialist knowledge. I'm telling you this because the first such specialist lawyer I ever met was Greg Boyd. The second was Sean Kane. This is not a book written by opportunistic hucksters: this is a book written by people who have more experience in this area than *pretty well anyone else.*

To summarize, then: the games industry isn't about making games. The games industry is about making companies that make games. Whether you land a job at an existing company or start up your own, the games business is just that—a business—and if you want to work in it, you need to understand it.

Fortunately, you appear to have found a book that can help you do exactly that.

**Richard A. Bartle**
*Colchester, Essex, United Kingdom*

# Acknowledgments

THE AUTHORS WOULD LIKE to gratefully acknowledge the contributions of the following people, without whom this book would not have been possible:

Professor Richard Bartle for his wisdom over many years and for writing a terrific Foreword; our agent Jennifer Chen Tran and the team at Bradford Literary; Rick Adams, Jessica Vega, and their team at Taylor & Francis; Jas Purewal and David Greenspan for their contributions to the Intellectual Property Chapter; and Marc Handelman at Frankfurt Kurnit for his valuable suggestions and proofreading. Marc may be one of the few people that ever read the whole book.

# Author

**S. Gregory Boyd** is one of the most prominent video game attorneys in the United States. He is a founding member of the Video Game Bar Association and formerly served on its Board of Directors. He co-chairs the Interactive Entertainment Group at Frankfurt Kurnit and has been featured in a variety of publications, including *Fortune*, *Forbes*, Mashable, and Gamasutra.

**Brian Pyne** is the Director of Legal Affairs and Enforcement for the Entertainment Software Rating Board (ESRB) and legal counsel to the International Age Rating Coalition (IARC). Prior to joining the ESRB, Brian was Associate Counsel at Take-Two Interactive Software, the parent company of Rockstar Games and 2K. Brian has also taught a course on intellectual property law and the video game industry and spoken on those topics at a variety of events.

**Sean F. Kane** has been practicing video game law for 15 years and *Variety* magazine named him to its 2017 Dealmakers Elite New York list and 2016 Legal Impact Report. He co-chairs the Interactive Entertainment Group at Frankfurt Kurnit, where he represents many of the most well-known names in the video game industry. Sean is also on the Board of the Video Game Bar Association and is a sought after author, speaker, and industry commentator.

# CHAPTER 1

# Introduction

## *Getting Started in the Game Industry*

E VERYONE THAT WORKED ON this book is frequently asked how to get into the video game industry. This chapter will attempt to answer that question, including some potentially interesting side questions like: Is the game industry worth working in, and are you sure you want to do this to yourself?

## THE HISTORICAL IMPORTANCE OF THE GAME INDUSTRY

It is hard to overstate just how important video games are. Certainly, they can be mindless and poorly made, but that should not disparage the art form as a whole. Books, movies, and plays can also be mindless and poorly made. Like any art form, quality games are often drowning under layers of *dreck*. Still, games are becoming humanity's culturally and economically dominant art form for the economically advanced societies on the planet. An easy and commonly made argument is that video games now account for more than 100 billion dollars per annum in global revenue. Their dominance as an art form is also shown by the many hours consumers devote to games at the expense of previously dominant media like books, film, music, and television. As suggested above, economically, games already surpass any other entertainment industry and that trend looks to continue unabated. Many other entertainment arts are moving toward games to gather some of that success as well. Art that was previously not digital and not interactive is now becoming digital and more interactive. Still, beyond the dollars and other more commonly made arguments, games themselves as an expression and human invention have an independent importance when viewed on the historical axis.

It is rare to live at a time when an entirely new art form is born. In the 2 million years of human existence, this has only happened a few times. As we develop new media and new distribution methods, art will grow to fill that gap. In terms of live entertainment, music and storytelling are probably the oldest. Ancient flutes are more than 40,000 years old and we were probably banging sticks together before that. Six hundred years before the

Common Era, people were putting on plays in Greece. Mechanically printed books and oil paintings came in before opera was invented at the end of the 16th century. Photographs came about in the late 19th century. Film and recorded music, including jazz, ushered in the early 20th century. Television and rock and roll were broadcast into households in the 1950s, demonstrating new variations on prior art forms as well as new distribution methods. All of this was passive for the audience. The audience participated in this art, but mainly in their imaginations.

The participatory nature of interactive entertainment is one of the attributes that makes it so special. In the 1970s, when *Pong* was first introduced to the public, it is hard to describe to younger audiences how different this was from all other forms of entertainment. Each passing year makes the story less personally descriptive and more of a historical curiosity. Remember that color television was not yet widely adopted in most parts of the United States, and that the remote control was a luxury as well. Suddenly, with *Pong*, you could talk to the television! Not actually talk, of course, but that is how people discussed it. Prior to games, the television, like other art forms, was a one-way entertainment device. Games fundamentally changed the device itself and entertainment forever.

Now, there are thousands of game companies in the United States alone. Those companies directly or indirectly support hundreds of thousands of jobs in games.[1] The first step to getting into the industry is finding a job with a game company and learning the business.

## GAMES: WHERE DO YOU FIT IN?

Getting a job in the game industry is easier now than ever before, but that does not mean it is easy. There are more jobs in the game industry now than at any other time in history. Sony Interactive Entertainment has 8000 employees. Many of the top publishers and game developers have thousands of employees. There is also more to do than ever before. In the early days of the video game industry, you were essentially required to have skill in programming computers. Now, people work in legal, marketing, sales, business development, production, art, audio, community management, and human resources as well as programming. The vast majority of people working in games do not have a programming background. So, the first question for you is: What are your best skills and where do they fit within a game company?

## DEVELOP CONCRETE SKILLS AND INDUSTRY KNOWLEDGE

Just because there is wide variety of jobs in the game industry does not mean they are low-skilled or easy to get. In fact, essentially every job in the game industry requires a college degree in something. It does not have to be computer science, but there are very few people without at least a college education working in games, especially at senior levels. As a first piece of advice, stay in school and get a degree, or even two. As with starting out in most other industries, you should try to find an internship at a game company while you are in school. Beyond the skill set you will bring to making games, you need a functional knowledge of how the industry works.

## STARTING A GAME COMPANY: LOOK BEFORE YOU LEAP

If you have worked in game companies for a few years and you have made several games, then you might think of starting a game company. It is even better if you have worked in a couple of different game companies, working in different roles and working on different game types. For instance, you will know more if you have done both art and production for a console game company and a mobile game company. How about working for a year at a publisher to get to know that side of the business? Publisher contacts are enormously important for the funding and development of your own games down the road.

People often want to start a game company immediately out of school. And students often ask me how long before they can or should go out on their own. If you have not worked for five years on at least three completed games, you really have no business starting a game company. You should also have worked on at least one hit game and one failed game. You learn different skills from each type of environment. I am writing this with the kindest of intentions. And I know it is hard to hear. But I am saving you a lot of pain. Please, go put the work in first, then come back and make the greatest game the world has ever seen. Think of it this way: Why learn how to do something using your own money? It is better to use someone else's money and have them train you in a skill that you can later take to found your own game company. I know you are smarter and better than everyone else you know, but this is still my advice. Everyone is teaching you something all the time, even if it is what not to do.

Playing games is not the same as making games. There is something relatively technical and mysterious about how games are made that has led to a misunderstanding on this point. Even in the early 2000s, you often heard people say that they had "an idea for a game." Over the years, there have been many great responses to this. My favorite is that I once heard Brenda Romero answer this statement during a conference and say, "Thank God, because I was fresh out of ideas."

You think you have an idea for a game? Let me tell you, confidentially, as your friend, it is terrible. Really, it is terrible. How do I know your idea is terrible? Because they are all terrible. All game ideas are terrible. Only detailed game design, writing, art, character development, programming, software tools, and execution make the game good.

When someone walks up to you and says, "I have an idea for a game," remember that the idea is the cheapest ingredient in making the game. Everyone that has had a shower has had an idea. I would almost go so far as saying an idea for a game is a detriment to actually making one. You are much better off having or developing amazing programming, art, management, or fundraising skills. Any of those is far superior to having the "best" idea for a game.

## STARTING A CAREER IN GAMES

So, how do you get this first job in games? I was fairly stupid about this for a long time. People were asking me for years and I did not know. I did not really have anyone tell me how to do it. In truth, I stumbled upon it by trial and error mixed with some good luck.

After many years of working in games and teaching about games in universities, law school, and at conferences, I am now certain I have "the formula."

Here are a few thoughts on the formula:

- The bad news is that it is hard and relatively unpleasant. Not everyone is going to do it. But, that does go a long way toward explaining why there are about 10 people who "want" to work in games for each person that actually gets a job in games.

- The good news is that it works 100% of the time. I am certain about this. I have been talking to people about versions of this for almost 15 years and have never had anyone that went through the process below fail to get a job in games.

*There are only five steps*:

1. *Meaningfully participate in industry groups in-person*: Find every game industry group that meets where you live or within a reasonable driving distance. These include the International Game Developers Association (IGDA) and every other local group you can find. This also includes conferences that meet near you or that you can get to easily. Put these meetings on a calendar. Update that calendar regularly (at least twice a month) and then go to the meetings. Find a leadership position in these groups. You don't have to be the president, but try to get on a committee or three. Aim for committees that are actually doing work and that need help doing that work. In a major game industry city like New York, Los Angeles, San Francisco, Seattle, Austin, Boston, Raleigh, or Montreal, this should give you two meetings a month or more. Importantly, you have to be willing to move to one of these cities if you want a real shot at working in games. All the industry organizations such as the IGDA are affordable. Conferences vary in cost, but some conferences will give discounted rates for students, volunteers, or press covering the event. There is no better way to meet speakers and other conference attendees than by working for the conference.

2. *Meaningfully participate in groups online*: Participate in the online forums where these groups meet as well. They almost always have some type of online area where you can productively discuss the industry. You should be reading these places daily, reading game industry news daily, and participating in online areas on a weekly basis. Posting on IGN or Gamespot does not count. The IGDA and similar places have helpful forums.

3. *Write about what you are learning*: There are literally thousands of blogs and other areas where you can write about the things that interest you most in the game industry. Take everything you are learning from all of these steps and put that down on paper. If it is good (and even if it is not very good), you can find a place to publish it. Get your work into the best publication you can. It should be better than your own blog, but it does not have to be Gamasutra.

4. *Do informational interviews*: Take everything you are learning and start to talk to people about games. You are going to meet those people by doing the steps here and

doing internet research. Do *not* ask them for a job. Only ask them for three things: AIR. A is for "advice." Do they have any advice for someone in your position? I is for "information." What can they tell you about themselves, how they got there, and what they do? R is for "referrals." You enjoyed talking to them so much, is there anyone they can introduce you to that they think would be helpful? Would they mind sending an email introduction for you, and perhaps copy you? If not, can they give you the contact information? Again, don't ask them for a job. If they have a job, they will tell you about it—I promise. Very important—if they offer you a job, take it. One of my students was talking to the CEO of a Californian game company. The CEO asked him if he would ever consider moving to California, and he said no way, he loved New York. Big mistake.

This is the other key to informational interviews—they only "count" if they are with a person that could give you a job or if they are one person removed from someone who could give you a job. Talking to junior employees or other "wannabes" is important, and you should do it, but it does not count for the purposes of this paragraph. Why am I talking about counting? I'm talking about counting because you are going to make a spreadsheet. It will include names, contact information, and notes on all of your informational interviews. You will use this to keep score and follow-up with the informational interview contacts. You will send these people "personalized" emails with articles and other things you think are interesting. Each email should include a couple of genuinely personalized sentences. You should reach out to these contacts every two to three months. The best follow-up should be important and relevant—perhaps even an article written by you. That spreadsheet should be numbered 1–100 of relevant informational interviews that "count," as I described above. I have *never* had anyone make it to 100 before they got a job. Usually, people get a real hit between 30 and 75 names. Other people worry about finding people to talk to. Trust me when I say that you will not have any problem getting to 100 if you make the effort because each person will ideally give you 1–3 referrals. The first 10 are the hardest. You will find it gets much easier to get the interviews and they will start to get easier/better because you will know a lot more after the first 10. In addition, just going through steps 1 and 2 above are going to get you near some people to do informational interviews.

5. *Start working even if you are not paid*: Look at everything above and think about what you can do. All of those organizations above and many companies need good free (or cheap) labor. Busy professionals are often part of those groups. You can impress them through your work there and turn that into a job or a warm recommendation down the road. There is a reason I mentioned joining committees that need work done. In the course of talking to people, you will discover needs. Maybe these places have internship programs, but most often they do not. What usually happens is that someone from your informational interviews, a conference, or an industry group will need help with something important—such as research on a topic, organizing another conference/meeting, or writing something. They won't have an actual

position, but they'll have a project, and you should volunteer to do it. That will give you real experience, a genuine contact for referrals, and a game industry person to review your work and act as a reference for you. The more you do this, the better. For students, a goal of—one to four of these projects per semester should be realistic.

All of the above is done with two goals in mind. First, learning everything you can about games. Second, getting to know people in the game industry. The end result is that you will be seen as (and actually become) an insider.

So, the five steps above are the entire plan. How long does it take? To do it meaningfully usually takes one to two years. Again, it has a 100% success rate if you do it properly. Most people are looking at this as students or as a career change. This plan is so good that it comes with a personal guarantee. If you demonstrably do steps 1–5 above and do not get a job, I will buy you dinner in New York. By "demonstrably doing the steps," I mean show me on a calendar that you did every step. Show me your writing and your involvement. Show me your informational interview spreadsheet and your follow-ups as well, with 100 good names on it. Talk to me about your volunteer and cheap labor work. In 15 years of doing this and sending versions of this sheet to more than 100 people, I have never had to pay out on this guarantee. Most people who really work at the items above get something within a range of three to six months.

Most of all, the other authors of this book and I wish you luck. We firmly believe the game industry is one of the most exciting areas you could possibly work in. This is a golden age, similar to film in the 1930s or comics in the 1940s. Though the game industry was founded almost 40 years ago, and now has photoreal graphics and a connected world, this is the start of something great. Hopefully, it is the start of something great with you in it.

## NOTE

1. ESA Data reported in Venture Beat "The U.S. game industry has 2457 companies supporting 220,000 jobs." Dean Takahashi. February 14, 2017.

# CHAPTER 2

# How to Make a *Bad* Licensed Game

## *A Tried and True Recipe for Disaster*

I THOUGHT ABOUT WRITING A chapter on how to make a great game, but decided against it. First, as an attorney, I am not really qualified to do that. Second, there is already a lot written on making great games.

Unfortunately, the vast majority of games are not very good. And many are downright terrible. Many more are never completed. Each year, in every development budget, there are a few shining stars, games that seem to have everything: wonderful design, artistic choices, engrossing game-play, and Midas monetization. Making those games in any price range is extraordinarily difficult and people that are qualified to write about it will tell you that, in addition to following the right path, you also have to be more than a little lucky. But the majority of games are not good.

Second, I might know something that is almost as interesting as how to make a great game. And that's how to make a *bad* game. While the right path to quality games requires careful execution and more than a little luck, making a bad game is much easier. I know *exactly* how to make a bad game. Over many years, I have been part of more than a billion dollars in game development. Some of those games have turned out to be great. Many were serviceable. But many more were horrific.

As an attorney, game deals often come to my desk partially baked. They have many or most of the parts in place and it is my job to create the documents to memorialize the deal. I have come to recognize commonly repeated elements that are part of the recipe for disaster. This chapter is not written from the perspective of the intellectual property (IP) holder, game publisher, or developer. I have been in all of those chairs at one time or another and have seen the same mistakes made. Many of the structural errors below do originate with the IP holder, financier, or publisher, and those are the clients I represent most often. However, this section is my best attempt to lay out the structural errors from wherever they may originate.

Lastly, by way of introduction, the rules below are focused on licensed games, but the reader will easily see that they apply to making bad games in general. This is because trans-media-licensed IP (film, TV, books-to-games) is one of the easiest ways to make a bad game. This is not because the underlying IP is bad. In fact, we *know* that the underlying IP is good. That is a key part of the seduction of licensed IP, and is why people enjoyed it in another medium and are investing to make a game out of it. Licensed IP makes an interesting subject to analyze because we know that the game itself is bad, not the underlying idea. Avoidable mistakes are made in the planning and execution stages that point, almost invariably, toward a bad product.

## BACKGROUND: *E.T., THE EXTRA-TERRESTRIAL*

The game industry has been making bad licensed games from the start. A seminal example of this is the *E.T. Extra Terrestrial* game. In 1982, *E.T.* was (and still is) one of the most successful films of all time and well on its way to becoming a billion-dollar franchise.

Naturally, there was an expectation that there would be a game to go along with the film. Atari paid 25 million dollars for the license and gave the developers five and half weeks to make the game. This was a massive upfront payment, but not nearly enough time was allowed for development. More cartridges were printed than Atari had consoles. The game had numerous bugs and was essentially unplayable. Most of the units sold were returned. Ultimately, almost 750,000 of those cartridges were buried in a landfill in New Mexico, making this one of the largest failures ever in the game industry. The lack of public faith that followed the launch is one of the most often-cited reasons for the industry crash in 1983.

The surprising thing is not that we messed it up so terribly in the beginning. The surprise is that we still mess it up in exactly the same way by doing exactly the same things.

Below are the rules to follow to make a *bad* game:

## RULE 1: TREAT THE GAME LIKE A MARKETING PRODUCT INSTEAD OF A GAME

Video games are high art. They are the most recently invented, technologically sophisticated, narratively complicated and intricate art form known to human civilization. Literally, games are the evolutionary frontier of human expression. If you do not immediately and intuitively understand that this is true beyond doubt, if you think of games as sales support or ancillary revenue for something else, you are going to make a horrible game. Obviously, *Angry Birds* is not *War and Peace*, but the first sentence of this paragraph is about potential and the respect for the genre required to make a good game. Losing sight of that potential is the first and most important step toward making a bad game.

This one rule is the primary reason that almost every game made by a film or television studio is *dreck*. This is the reason that almost every game associated with a brand is also *dreck*.[1] Video games are not t-shirt sales. *Video games should have a marketing department, not be run by the marketing department.* There is no overlap between the skill set of your marketing department and the skills required for managing the production of a video game.

We are still going to seek the transmedia holy grail that *Harry Potter, Game of Thrones,* and precious few others have done well (even those made great films and books, but not games).[2] People are still going to want to license non-game IP into games. At some time in the future, we may even want to stop "doing it wrong." The key to that is to treat the game as its own creative product. Give it the same serious consideration, budget, and infrastructure investment that you would the original IP.

One of the most common effects of the marketing product mentality is over-reliance on a launch date that is tied to other products. The game launch should not be tied to the launch of any other product. Remember, the game is an independent creative product. If it misses the film, TV, or baking soda launch window, that should be fine if the time is needed to make the game great. We are culturally and technologically far past the opening weekend consumption mentality. A game can have a marketing support function at the middle or end of a season. There is no data to indicate that launching a game in concert with a film or television show has any effect on the viewership of that show. Licensors still seek to do it constantly, but without evidence in support. Anyone that will guarantee to build a game on a tight schedule that is associated with the launch of another product is not going to do a good job and is likely not even capable of doing a good job.

## RULE 2: PICK DEVELOPERS/EXECUTIVES WITH A LONG HISTORY OF FAILURE OR MEDIOCRITY

There are people in the game industry that have not just worked at but led three, four, or more failed game companies. There are others that have worked on games for decades, and have never made anything good. Do not give these people another chance. They can work on another person's game. These people are good at sinking ships or driving them around in circles. Do not let them work on your boat.

You may think that this is an easy rule to follow, but it is not. These people often involve themselves in projects early on. They are a friend of a friend that happened to be "available" to work on the game or they were "consultants" early on. Worst of all, they come with access to funding dollars or a special publisher relationship. It is just not worth it. A great executive or developer with no money can do more than a bad executive with seven figures of funding.[3] Purge these people from your team as early as you can and actively prevent others like them from joining the project.

When interviewing team members, ask them about the last five projects they worked on. Look up those projects if you are not familiar with them. What was their critical reception? What was their financial reception? Was their game of a similar type to your game? People tend to make the same kinds of games as they made in the past. High-quality indie or AAA developers stay on those teams and work in those circles. These are the people to trust. A person that has worked on 10 metacritic 50 games in a row will turn your game into a metacritic 50 game. That is what they know how to do.

## RULE 3: LET SOMEONE IN MARKETING OR IT MANAGE THE GAME DEVELOPMENT, INSTEAD OF HIRING A COMPETENT GAME PRODUCTION LIAISON

The main problem is a general technological illiteracy in corporate management. They think "Computers—Ugh!" and lump everything together in their minds. IT, web development, productivity/infrastructure software development, mobile development, accounting software, and console games are all just "computer stuff" to them. This illiteracy can lead to the employment of people to make games who have no business making games.

Compare games with films. A person that likes to watch movies does not know how to make them. A person that works at a game rental store (back when such things existed) does not know how to make them. A person that makes a website to stream movies does not know how to make movies. A person that markets or advertises movies does not know how to make movies. Film directors, film talent, and film production teams know how to make movies. These other people are enormously important, but they are involved in downstream and peripheral processes. Intuitively, it is easy to grasp that these people should not actually be involved in making film. Still, every day we have game development supervised by people from equivalent backgrounds, appointed by IP holders/funding companies.

Your senior vice-president (VP) of digital media and your director of marketing are not game designers or producers. The VP of digital media has a background in web development. The director of marketing understands product positioning. Neither of these people should be allowed to touch a game design or production decision. Their job is downstream, after the game is made. This is true even if they have supervised flash web applications or small app development. Despite what they or other corporate people may say, those projects were not actual training in the competent production of larger-scale games. Those were small mistakes with limited budgetary and creative impact.

Instead of IT or marketing, pick a production liaison that has actual experience in game development. The production liaison between the IP owner and the developer should be picked and interviewed jointly by the IP owner and the developer. Ideally, the IP owner and the developer should work together to pick a person. If that doesn't work, have the IP owner pick three people with the right background and have the developer make the final decision. He or she should not come from a film and television background or any other background; he or she should arrive with extensive experience in game development and production. The person should be picked as carefully as the game developer and should have shipped multiple quality games in the past.

## RULE 4: CHOOSE THE DEVELOPER BASED ON A POWERPOINT PRESENTATION

If you are treating the game as art and not like a t-shirt, that is the best frame of mind for picking a developer. As a rule, do not pick the developer of the game based on a PowerPoint presentation. Furthermore, do your best to remove from the decision-making process around a game anyone that would choose a developer based on a PowerPoint presentation. Instead, pick the developer based on past work they have done together as a team (not at other companies). In fact, one of the most common mistakes is to fund a developer based on the fact that they were "part of the team that created" another game. You could be funding one person from janitorial services, one from the mailroom, and a server programmer. It is rare to get the magic of a prior game with a small spin-off team. Even if the creative leadership leaves that game company, that person is really only as good as his or her team. Taking a small part of the team makes re-creating that magic unlikely.

You can pick a t-shirt manufacturer from a PowerPoint presentation, but not things that require tens or hundreds of thousands of hours. The best judge of a team is their portfolio of work. This sounds obvious, but look at the developers that have done licensed IP over the past decades. Were these picked based on the quality of their work product? They were often picked based on their ability to raise money to pay for the license. In fact, as a good rule of thumb, immediately exclude the developer that pitches your brand with the highest revenue projections. They are often the most out of touch with a realistic outcome.

## RULE 5: MICROMANAGE DEVELOPMENT

The brand owner/investor should control the look and feel of the IP and the overall game bible, but all game design and development decisions should be made by the game studio. This means that the brand owner/investor puts in a lot of thought in advance and then hands things off, without going into the details. Ask yourself, as a representative of the brand, am I making a decision because it is directly related to the brand IP (i.e., this is against the canonical story bible, or the game designer is killing a character off that cannot die in the story arch) or is a decision being made because the brand is "playing" at being a game designer. It is most often the second motivation, and pride prevents people from seeing this. The self-awareness and honesty to truly answer that decision is normally impossible to muster. You are hiring the game developer for their expertise in making games. Trust in it and build the agreement in a way to prevent you, as a brand, from exercising too much authority or authority at the wrong times.

Let us also be particularly wary of the cardinal sin of making a bad game. The final decision-maker on game development should not work in the IP owner's marketing or IT departments. This additional responsibility is often assigned to someone in one of those roles on the false belief that those skills are close to game development. If this sounds far-fetched to you, you have never made a licensed game. Almost 100% of the production liaisons/creative directors for licensed video game projects in film and television come from IT or marketing, and that practices harms the final game quality.

## RULE 6: USE MINIMUM GUARANTEES TO PROTECT OUR DOWNSIDE

The recurring theme in this section is that IP holders (especially transmedia IP holders) are (1) risk averse and (2) not well equipped to make games. They cover this risk aversion by providing layer after layer of "protections" and "control" in the game deal. It turns out that what normally passes for protection and control actually provides very little of either.

The developer should not be providing any minimum guarantee (MG). I know that this sounds insane, and I wrestled with this thought a lot before placing it here. I am aware that this idea alone is so radical that it may cause people to disregard this chapter or perhaps even the entire book.

Making a game with a revenue split is not a guarantee for success, but making a game with an MG is a guarantee for failure.

The IP owner should pay for the production of the game. If you are making an independent creative product, and not t-shirts, you would not expect the creative team involved to pay the production costs. If this were a film, TV show, book, etc.—whatever the game is based on—the IP owner is used to the idea of paying for production or sharing the costs of production. That should be done here, too. Imagine calling up Peter Jackson and saying that you want him to make another *Lord of the Rings* film and that he has to pay for it. He would righteously hang up on you and so will any developer that is going to make a good game. The issue is that if an IP owner is looking for a company to finance production of the game and minimum guarantees (i.e., they are looking for a t-shirt vendor instead of a game developer), they are going to get a poor production. The reason is that great developers are in demand. There are very few of them and they are well paid. Anyone that is begging for IP licensing scraps and self-financing production is not going to be very good as a rule. A licensor should be avoiding those developers, not seeking them out.

There are two main arguments for having an MG in a deal. First, established IPs are worth a great deal and an MG is a symbol of that worth. Second, an MG is supposed to protect the IP holder's downside and provide a guaranteed return.

The MG is like a bid at auction. The raw MG number and the developer, or the developer's investors ability to pay that number, is often the key factor in selecting a licensing IP developer. The concept works on the idea that the person paying the highest MG is the person that wants that IP the most. This is the way we buy other things at auction, from potatoes to fine art. However, there are two large problems with using an MG in the game development space.

First, the entity willing to pay the highest MG is almost certainly not the entity that is going to make the best entertainment product. Instead, they are the entity that has the best access to investor capital. Historically, these companies create bad or mediocre entertainment properties at best. You should choose the developer based on their track record and ability to create quality player experiences. If the developer has great access to investor capital or large reserves from prior successes, that is a plus, but you don't want those resources as MGs. You want those resources put into the game itself.

Second, the notion of an MG is a poison that spreads, infecting the rest of the deal on paper and in day-to-day production. It changes the way people think about what they are working on. It erodes the idea of an entertainment product and replaces it with the t-shirt mentality. The MG will be used as a measure of quality. It will be used as a factor for material breach. It will take over the drafting of the document and the relationship between the parties.

## What is the Alternative to the MG?

An MG is two things in a game development deal. First, it is a risk mitigation device. Second, it is a measurement of success. Both of these can be accomplished through better mechanisms than an MG.

| MG Alternatives | Description |
| --- | --- |
| Developer investment | This generates some downside protection by reducing costs and gives the developer more incentive for the game to do well |
| Number of concurrent players, number of downloads | These are successful non-monetary game-play indicators. For film, television, book, or product licensing, this can be a measure of engagement that generates a double bottom line |
| In-game purchases | This is one of the most common modern mobile or social monetization measures to reward a developer |
| Total sales | Total sales is another more inclusive alternative to just counting in-game purchases. Total sales can even include merchandising as well as retail sales |
| Metacritic rating | Though this is linked to economic success, it is not always exactly the same. *Clash of Clans* has a metacritic rating of 74. Still, in broad terms, it is useful, especially for scores under 60 and over 80. Like player base independent of revenue, this measure can be important for game IP with a double bottom line of fan engagement |

Each item in the table above can be linked to bonus payments or an escalating royalty if certain numbers are met.

MG alternative discussions are a great time to pull out that shiny developer PowerPoint. It had that slide at the end with a graph showing how we will all be millionaires, movie gods, and rock stars. Take that slide and use it to generate the developer revenue share. We should be brutally honest here because this is especially important. Your game will most likely fail. Almost all games fail. This is not the time to be greedy. If the developer delivers on those ridiculous sales promises, they deserves to make out like bandits. On the other hand, the developer has likely over-promised in that slide, and it is time to have some accountability. I like to use that slide to build either or both cash bonuses when some of the milestones above are hit or to build an escalating revenue share as they are hit. This escalation, in my view, should be extraordinarily generous, not the 20%–30% of net developers are used to seeing in these agreements. Again, we are rewarding the developer in the very unlikely scenario of a hit and aligning the incentives so they are working out of hopeful expectation rather than fear. That will produce much better results for both parties in the long term.

## RULE 7: TIE A LOT OF SPECIFIC MILESTONES TO PAYMENT

Meet often and have few milestones. In the name of control, people often create long sheets of milestones with dates, approvals, and payments attached. Games only need three approvals. Games should have specific requirements for language, but these should not be cluttered with approval and submission language. The list of requirements should be supported by daily or weekly interaction between the developer and the funding party/IP owner. There should be substantial detail in the design documentation, setting out those requirements, and the game should be built toward that documentation, but the idea of payment based on milestone delivery is an ancient and flawed concept. Having three or four large check-point milestones makes much more sense.

## Approvals

People create game deals with weekly or twice-monthly milestone approvals. This is a failed effort to maintain control. If the game is going poorly, people often keep the developer working as long as there is funding available for the game. When things go very badly and there is a dispute down the road, a court will ask, "If you had weekly milestone approvals, why did you allow 'work to continue? You must have accepted some of these. The developer could not have been in breach the entire time." These approvals do not create control or downside protection. Instead, they create the illusion of these, and can backfire on you in a dispute.

You only need three approvals: (1) The game design document, (2) the platform submission build, and (3) the final launch build. The game design document approval is important for one obvious and one not-obvious reason. The obvious reason is that you don't want the developer to build the game based on a plan and rules that are unacceptable to the entity funding the game. The not-obvious reason is that you want everyone involved in the process to work toward the same goals with the same idea for the game in their minds. It is a good idea to spend months on this document before a line of code is written, and to build the whole game on paper, down to the UI elements. The unfortunate norm in the industry is that a game concept is funded, but not a full game design. Developers that later complain that the funding entity "changed its mind," had "feature creep," or created "moving targets" are usually just saying that they did not spend enough time in the game design documentation phase. Clearly, the game design document is a living document that changes over time during development, but having a robust version to start with is an enormous help to all sides of the deal.

The second approval is the platform submission build. Of course, the funding entity and the development team have been meeting weekly or even daily throughout the development process. So, this is just a place for everyone to take stock of what is going to be presented to the world as a representation of the game. It should be as complete and launch-ready as we can make it. The final approval is over the game before it goes out the door to the public. In truth, this approval is almost unnecessary. The fixes done between the platform submission and the final launch version are not substantive changes. The three approvals above give all the control that really matters in development. The first approval is as much to orient the funding entity as the developer and the last two are quality checks to confirm that the overall experience is faithful to the design document. Any other approvals are a wasted effort.

In this process, beware a design or management-by-committee philosophy. Milestones and milestone approval are, more than anything else, an opportunity to highlight mismanagement at the IP owner level. One person at the IP owner should be in charge of approving creative decisions. Having multiple and conflicting layers of approval is one of the keys to failure. The developer should be building toward the game design document under the direction of that person and the production liaison. The progress on that task should be communicated to the IP owner on a frequent basis. The IP owner can take input from multiple parties, but the final decisions driving the developer should be made by one competent person at the IP owner who is in constant consultation with the developer, not management by committee. The two most common ways to get this process off track are

(1) feature creep and (2) repeatedly changing direction. Having one person in charge of the decisions on the IP owner side who is constantly referring to the game design document helps mitigate these two issues.

No one from the IP owner is allowed to use the words "protect the brand" to justify anything. These words come from a place of fear and ignorance. I have heard them justify innumerable bad decisions and mark the death of quality in any number of games. It is a meaningless catch-all phrase used by the incompetent to sprinkle some power and pseudo-justification onto a decision that they are trying to make, when they are not creatively and intellectually equipped to make it.

The recurring underlying theme in this section is that both MGs and the traditional milestone approval process are poor substitutes for properly researching and selecting a game developer. They are also poor substitutes for proper management and control of the developer. The alternative is more and better work ahead of a project. Pick the developer based on similar, successful, past projects created by that team. Draw up a game development document that is robust enough to have all of the necessary components in it and then work with the developer to see how they would realize that vision.

As an alternative, consider payment based on time. Time can be attached to a schedule and can be terminated with a notice period. For instance, the team is paid $50,000 every two weeks and the IP holder is allowed to terminate the agreement at any time with four weeks' notice. This prevents any disagreement over payment and milestones, which makes the developers happy. It also allows the IP owner to terminate the agreement at any time if it is going poorly, which makes the publisher happy. Lastly, the termination notice period is negotiable between the parties to give the developer some runway to handle staffing and new project issues in the termination period.

When implementing any payment system, plan for delays, scope changes, and extensions. Almost no internal financial plans calculate this, but every game ever made has them. So, there needs to be some cushion built into the schedule. Sometimes people fear this could lead to a "blank check" mentality with the developer, where they always plan to use the additional cushion. One mechanism that can help there is to make the usage of that cushion affect developer compensation in other ways. For instance, using 20% of the cushion has no effect, because those are planned delays. However, using cushion beyond that amount has negative effects on developer compensation (reduction in bonus payments, royalty reductions, etc.).

## CONCLUSION

Are these the only ways to make a bad game? No, absolutely not. There are many more bad game rules that didn't make the top of the list. There are also exceptions to the above, just like there are exceptions to every bad rule of engineering. This is no reason to have one of these exceptions operating in your game project. The key to the mistakes above is that they (1) happen most frequently, (2) cause the most damage, and (3) seem like the "right" thing to do. As I wrote at the start of this chapter, I do not know the rules for making great games, but hopefully by placing these warning signs I will help smarter people than I am to find the right path.

A word on marketing and marketing spend: rather than spending so much money on user acquisition, think about building better games and content. Spend less time filling a leaky bucket and more time building a better bucket.

This is the most unpopular subject I write and speak about. I have given a version of this as a talk to media companies in both New York and Los Angeles as well as at conferences with hundreds of media executives in attendance. They do not deny the underlying facts on the process. They do not deny the results, nor could they because the results are obvious. Strangely, the main resistance that I get in the discussions is that (1) this is the easier way for the executives to make games and (2) they have always done it this way. Why go against the tradition and spend more money for the possibility of a high-quality game when in truth they don't care about the game and they can make a bad game, with a low budget, that still makes a tidy sum *in spite* of the quality. Basically, it is just too hard and too far outside of the film and television skill set to do it right. It challenges their industry hubris and distorts their marketing budget. Worst of all, the public is stupid enough to fall for it every time, even 30 years after *E.T.*

In 2014, an article by Kyle Orland, writing on Ars Technica,[4] estimated that games on Steam sold approximately 100,000 copies if they had a Metacritic rating of 70–79. That score indicates a competently made game. Games rated 80–89 would sell approximately 200,000 copies, while those rated 90+ sold an average of 800,000 copies. Ratings are not everything, of course. A star developer, a sequel, or a quality movie license can all move sales upward. Still, everything else being equal, nothing is better for game sales than making a terrific game.

## WHY IT WILL NEVER WORK

Being right is not enough to bring about change. After spending considerable time on this subject, both in life and in the preparation of this chapter, I would like to end by acknowledging defeat. The traditional way of making licensed games derided in this chapter has several advantages.

First, it is cheaper. No monetary outlay is usually required to make licensed games, so there is very little apparent risk to the licensor (beyond degrading the original IP with a poor product). Investors will gladly fund a game company with a valuable license. Second, the t-shirt view of licensed games requires less oversight. No additional training is needed for management. As long as the game is functional, that is going to be enough. Third, it is psychologically more comforting for a licensor to not acknowledge the complexity of games along with the renouncement of omnipotence and creative control that would be required to seek proper help in building quality licensed games. Fourth and finally, the old method has a long history of successful mediocrity. These poorly done licensed games have been making money ever since the game industry first started. As critical as I have been of the game industry in this regard, I cannot ever see that trend changing. H.L. Mencken is famously paraphrased as saying, "No one ever went broke underestimating the intelligence of the American public." The original quote from his September 1926 "Notes on Journalism" in the *Chicago Tribune* is not as pithy,[5] but is more apt given the worldwide nature of the game industry. "No one in this world, so far as I know—and I have searched the record for years, and employed agents to help me—has ever lost money underestimating the intelligence of the great masses of the plain people." Mr. Mencken, reporting as another of your humble agents 90 years later in a medium you would never have imagined, this statement is as true as ever and the world is not better for it.

## NOTES

1. Exceptions including *Pitch Black*, the Burger King Xbox games, and *Dikembe Mutombo Saves the World in 4 ½ Weeks* exist, but are few and far between.
2. For the three most economically powerful narrative forms, books, film/TV, and games, I cannot think of a single example that consistently did all three well, by any measure. *Star Wars*, *Lord of the Rings*, and *Star Trek* might make a hobbled example if you selectively pick through the sheer volume.
3. When they bring eight figures of funding, even I can find a job for them somewhere, but keep them out of the way.
4. Kyle Orland, Steam Gauge: Do strong reviews lead to stronger sales on Steam? Ars Technica, April 23, 2014: https://arstechnica.com/gaming/2014/04/steam-gauge-do-strong-reviews-lead-to-stronger-sales-on-steam/
5. "No one in this world, so far as I know—and I have researched the records for years, and employed agents to help me—has ever lost money by underestimating the intelligence of the great masses of the plain people. Nor has anyone ever lost public office thereby." H.L. Mencken, Notes on Journalism, *The Chicago Tribune*, September 19, 1926.

# CHAPTER 3

# Intellectual Property in the Game Industry[1]

## THE IMPORTANCE OF INTELLECTUAL PROPERTY

Intellectual property (IP) is the most important branch of law for video game developers and publishers to understand. IP is a vital topic in video game development contracts, employment agreements, distribution, advertising, and every license in the game industry. As houses are made from wood and stone, video games are made almost exclusively from IP.

IP laws protect developers and their creative work. IP protects the developer from pirates and competitors who want to exploit their game work and use it without any compensation.

What does someone buy when they buy a game? In the old days before digital distribution, there were retail computer and video game stores. People would actually drive or walk down to a physical building called a video game store. They bought a box with a manual and a CD made from less than five dollars' worth of material. How, then, could people be persuaded to pay 60 or 70 dollars for a product we call a "game?" People are persuaded, even eager, because they are really buying a larger entertainment experience beyond the physical goods. This experience is legally enjoyed by consumers through a limited license to the IP. The game code, manual text, box art, title, game art, music, story, game world, middleware, and graphics are all IP.

As we venture into the next generation of game consoles and continue to see an increase in the number of gaming devices and distribution platforms, including mobile, social, and tablet, more money than ever will be invested in game development. Since its founding, the video game industry has both embraced and been driven forward by technological changes and opportunities. There is nothing to indicate that this trend will not continue to fuel the next generation of development. Game development for many large titles already meets or exceeds film budgets in terms of years in production and total budget.[2] As a result of this trend, protecting that ever-growing capital investment from competitors and pirates is becoming increasingly important. Of equal importance is harnessing the IP of a game for maximum value to recoup costs and generate profits. This can mean anything from developing a video game franchise based on the IP to exploiting the in-game IP in film, television, and merchandise, or in other ways. As simplistic as these statements are, the questions and strategies generated by them are more complex.

IP is an emotionally charged issue in the software community at large and the game development community in particular. Many people are in favor of open-source initiatives and are against software patents, patents in general, or even IP in general. These points of view are clearly influential and hotly debated at the highest public policy and legislative levels throughout the world. Still, as an educational and reference tool, this chapter serves as a guide to what the legal issues currently *are*, not how they might eventually evolve or how they *should* be.

Putting all disputes aside, everyone agrees that there is room for improvement in the IP system and that the system is evolving. In addition, the current system is complex. Competitors are sophisticated and will try to use the IP system against your company. For this reason alone, it is important to understand the current IP legal framework.

In an effort to start summarizing these concepts and as a preview of the remainder of this chapter, here is a table of examples from a game project and the type of IP law used to protect each component.

| Copyright | Trade Secret | Trademark | Patent |
|---|---|---|---|
| • Music | • Customer mailing lists | • Company name | • Inventive game-play or |
| • Code | • Pricing information | • Company logo |   game design elements |
| • Story | • Publisher contacts | • Game title | • Technical innovations |
| • Characters | • Middleware contacts | • Game subtitle |   such as elements in |
| • Art | • Developer contacts | • Identifiable |   software, networking, |
| • Box design | • In-house development |   "catch-phrases" |   or database design |
| • Website design |   tools |   associated with the | • Hardware technical |
| • Advertisements | • Deal terms |   game or company |   innovations |

## COPYRIGHT

### Introduction

Copyright is arguably the most important IP protection for most game companies. Generally speaking, copyright protects original works of authorship fixed in a tangible medium of expression, and easily qualifies as the best tool for protecting game property because of its ease of use, power, and versatility.

Similar to patents, copyright is an area of law that has its roots in the United States through the Constitution. If we go back even further, my British colleagues remind me that copyright goes back to 1709 and England's statute of Queen Anne. Sticking to the United States for now, we derive copyright law from the same section that is used to derive patent rights. Article I, Section 8, Clause 8 provides that Congress shall have the power "To promote the progress of science and the useful arts, by securing for limited times to authors and inventors the exclusive right to their respective writings and discoveries." The "writings" language focuses on how Congress derives its power to make laws for copyright.

Another critical element of the phrasing above shows that copyright is meant to protect these writings for a limited time.

In the EU, member states have similar protections for expressions fixed in a medium for a limited time, primarily under their domestic legal regimes, though it has also been provided for at the EU level (which is very roughly analogous to the "federal" level in the United States) by a range of EU legislation including the Treaty on European Union (one of the EU constitutional documents) as well as primary legislation including the Copyright Directive and the Copyright Duration Directive. As a result, while it is possible to talk about copyright law across in the EU in general terms, there are often differences between countries (especially the common law and civil law countries, such as the United Kingdom or Ireland on one side and France or Germany on the other) so this chapter can only give a general overview of EU copyright law and its comparison with U.S. law.[3]

## What Can Be Protected by Copyright?

In the United States, eight categories of works are eligible for copyright protection. These are listed in the statute 17 USC 102(a). They are literary works; musical works, including any accompanying words; dramatic works, including any accompanying music; pantomimes and choreographic works; pictorial, graphic, and sculptural works; motion pictures and other audiovisual works; sound recordings; and architectural works.[4]

Interactive entertainment is protected as either an "other audiovisual work" or, perhaps surprisingly to some, as a "literary work." Practicing attorneys often discuss which is more appropriate, but filings using either designation are common. Games are not unusual in this way as other creative endeavors also fall into more than one category. The only time this is important is for the registration of copyright. Registration under the literary work category may seem strange for a computer program, but literary works are defined in Section 101 of that statute to include works expressed in "words, numbers or other verbal or numerical symbols or indicia, regardless of the nature of the material objects such as books, periodicals, manuscripts, phonorecords, film, tapes, disks, or cards, in which they are embodied." Clearly the source code is a collection of words, numbers, and symbols, stored on some media.[5]

As far as games are concerned, copyright covers stories, characters, imagined environments and geographic locations,[6] music, graphics, and even the software source code itself. Moreover, it also protects the entire game as registered under the category of audiovisual or literary work. However, the full scope of copyright protection is not absolute and is often misunderstood to provide a wide-ranging monopoly over a video game concept or method of play. In reality, copyright protects the *expression* of ideas, not the *ideas* themselves. This leads to two consequences. First, no game ideas are protected by copyright until they are fixed into some expressive medium (like code or print or a saved art file). Second, similar ideas expressed in different ways are permitted uses that do not necessarily infringe on another's copyright.

Determining infringement in copyright requires comparing the fixed expression in the copyrighted game to the fixed expression of the accused infringer. With the rise of short development cycles in social and mobile, this comparison is more of a problem than ever, but game industry copyright cases have been illustrative of this quandary since the early 1980s. There were copyright cases involving arcade machines and Atari before Facebook and Apple.[7]

The position in the EU is essentially the same in terms of the split of copyright into categories of work, the need for works to be fixed in a medium, and the classification of interactive entertainment primarily as a literary work.

## What Rights Are Conferred by Copyright?

Another counterintuitive element of copyright is that it is not the right to do anything; instead, copyright is a negative right. It does not grant the holder the right to reproduce a work, but rather it grants the holder the right to prevent others from reproducing a work. The list of rights specifically stated in the U.S. statute (and in EU law) are the rights to make copies, make derivative works, distribute, public performance, and public display.

Copyright is also easy to invoke. Copyright comes into being as soon as an original work is fixed in a tangible medium. As soon as plans are drawn or code is written, copyright is present. In contrast, patents and trademarks have important and complex application processes with registration fees, and trade secrets require that certain steps be followed within the company, with constant vigilance to protect the secrets. Even though registration is not necessary to invoke copyright, it is still a good idea for most works because it changes damage calculations and is necessary to bring a litigation.

In the EU, generally speaking, there is no registration requirement for copyright works: copyright in a work exists as soon as the work has been fixed in a medium and there is no legal or practical requirement to register with a national regulator (this is also the practice internationally in most other countries that have signed the Berne Convention). Some countries, such as France or Spain, offer a voluntary registration system (which then provides a rebuttable presumption of ownership of the copyright work).

## Some Examples of Copyright

One key element of copyright is that the definition of art is surprisingly broad beyond the most minimal standards of original expression. From Botticelli to *Breakout*, all fixed original creations can be protected by copyright. Early game industry litigations fought over whether or not games were protectable with copyright, but eventually as games grew in complexity those issues were resolved in favor of copyright protection.

The game *Breakout* is an interesting example because it was the subject of a series of cases surrounding its originality and the minimal level of creativity necessary for copyright. Atari tried at least twice to register the game for copyright, but registration was initially rejected because of the perceived lack of originality and simplicity in the artistic display in the game. *Breakout* was merely a rectangular object moving in one plane that reflected a small ball into a multicolored wall of rectangles. The ball eliminated a portion of the wall of rectangles and rebounded toward the bottom of the screen, where the player attempted to move the lower rectangle to redirect the ball back toward the wall of rectangles. Atari had to fight a series of cases over the application rejection from 1989 to 1992, but eventually won the fight.[8] This series of cases is important, not only to game IP, but to copyright in general. The cases stand for the proposition that courts or the Register of Copyright will not judge the creativity or artistic quality in copyright. Any original fixed work in a tangible medium is protected.[9]

Copyright is also the main claim for games accused of cloning. In recent years, many cases of cloning have been filed. One example from 2012 was *Spry Fox vs. 6Waves* over cloning *Triple Town* with *Yeti Town*. This resulted in a settlement agreement where ownership of *Yeti Town* was actually transferred to Spry Fox.[10] In 2015, *Machine Zone v. Ember* was filed, alleging that the game *Empire Z* was merely a "re-skin" of *Game of War* and copied elements such as the overall plot, theme, mood, setting, pace, characters, economy, and sequence. This case was settled by the parties in early 2016. In 2016, *DaVinci Editrive v. Ziko Games* was filed. While this case involved card games versus video games, it is illustrative to the video game industry as the copyright allegations included copying of game rules, character roles, and life points, and winning requirements. Ultimately the court dismissed the infringement claims prior to trial. Finally, in a bizarre twist, in 2017 *Psychic Readers Network. Inc. v. Take-Two Interactive Software, Inc. and Rockstar Games, Inc.* was filed. This case alleged that a character in *Grand Theft Auto: Vice City* infringed a copyright in a character, Ms. Cleo, who was previously used as The Psychic Readers Network's spokesperson. Additionally, Zynga has been involved in multiple cloning cases since the start of its company. As sophistication grows and development costs for social and mobile remain relatively low, cloning is occurring more frequently. Still, this is not a new phenomenon in the game industry. In the early 1980s, Atari was involved in litigation over its *Pac-Man* IP against a Phillips game entitled *K.C. Munchkin*.[11]

## Copyright Filing Information

Although any work is copyrighted as soon as it comes into existence, you can also register the copyright for additional rights in the United States.[12] Copyright registration is absolutely necessary to litigate over copyright infringement, and an early registration usually yields a better damage calculation. As a consequence, it is prudent to register copyright even before writing a "cease and desist" letter to potential infringers (see Subsection iii: Protecting Copyright). Balancing all the factors, the registration is so cheap, easy, and necessary for real legal teeth that the cost and effort necessary for the federal registration are easily worth it.

### Process and Cost

The form required to register a copyright is only a few pages long and the cost is approximately $45. The Copyright Office has detailed instructions and information on completing the forms as well as contact information for questions. Of the forms of IP that benefit from registration, this is the easiest and cheapest.

### Length of Copyright Protection

The length of copyright is another element that makes it attractive for game developers. Copyright is long, not immortal like a trademark, but long enough to outlive creators.

At different times, copyright has varied in length, and the history of copyright contains enough different lengths for such protection to make it seem comical. Luckily for computer games, in the United States, the length of copyright for works created after 1978 can easily be remembered as 95 years after publication or 120 years after creation for corporate creations. For personal creations, it is the life of the author plus 70 years.[13] In the EU, generally it is 70 years after publication or corporate creation or, for personal creations, the life of the author plus 70 years. This means that no one can copy the original *Pac-Man* until about 2100. This also means that derivative works (which are works based on one or more pre-existing works, such as a sequel or prequel game—see the Derivative Works section below) require a license until that time expires as well. For *Pac-Man*, this means that cartoons, board games, clothing, or re-creating that yummy *Pac-Man* cereal are not allowed without the appropriate legal permissions. Around the year 2100, people can go wild and cover the planet with *Pac-Man* copies and derivative works after the original game falls into the public domain.

Consider how length affects what is possible for copyright. The length of protection is intimately tied to potential revenue generation. Game developers can use copyright to protect their ideas, build new games, and sell related products for a century. Copyright in a property can literally be developed and exploited over generations. *Mickey Mouse*, *Star Wars*, and *Superman* are excellent examples of this. These IP examples have existed for decades and have been exploited across multiple media, including games.

For a period, the game industry believed that ever-increasing technological sophistication and graphical presentation were key to high revenue-generating games. Successful social and mobile games like *Farmville* and *Angry Birds* now confirm that simple, even 2D, games can achieve eight- and nine-figure revenues.[14] These games will likely remain popular to some degree over a much longer lifecycle than originally anticipated.

*Protecting Copyright*

The most basic step in dealing with copyright infringement is to send out a "cease and desist" letter. This letter simply explains that you own the copyrighted material, that the material is registered, and that the other party is using the material without a license. The letter usually goes on to explain the penalties for infringement and demands the other party "cease and desist" from using the material. If the infringement is online, a similar letter or DMCA (in the United States) or E-Commerce Directive (in the EU) takedown notice can be sent to the other party's internet service provider (ISP). Most ISPs do not want the potential liability of hosting copyright-infringing material. This letter to the infringer and/or the ISP is often enough to stop the infringer, although a potential infringer may challenge the allegation. In any event, this process should be managed by and the letters should come from your attorney as there are strict requirements for the content of the letter and legal penalties for sending a letter which does not involve a legitimate claim.

*Penalties for Infringement*

Heavy potential punishment is a necessary part of any substantial IP protection, and copyright has it. Punishment for copyright infringement allows game developers to prevent infringing parties from selling works that include the developer's copyrighted work. In those legal jurisdictions that permit it, developers can also sue for damages and profits equal to the profits the infringing parties made from selling the illegal works. Furthermore, willful copyright infringement carries a statutory penalty of up to $150,000 per work infringed in the United States.

In a typical copyright lawsuit filed in June 2004, Midway brought a case against Sony Ericsson for violating its copyright on the game *Defender* from 1980.[15] Midway claimed that Ericsson was using the game on its mobile phones without permission. Midway requested that the court award damages and reimbursement of its legal fees, and require Sony Ericsson to turn over all mobile phones, software, and other materials in its possession related to the alleged copyright violation. The case was settled out of court and dismissed a few months later, but still serves as an excellent example of what remedies can be requested in copyright cases.

There are also potential criminal penalties that can result in prison time when people are caught violating copyright by selling or distributing games over the internet, under 17 U.S.C. § 506(a) and 18 U.S.C. § 2319. An instance of this came to light in February 2004 when Sean Michael Breen, leader of the Razor1911 warez group, received a four-year prison sentence and was ordered to pay nearly $700,000 in damages for copyright infringement. He was one of 40 people arrested in a sting operation by the U.S. Customs Service "Operation Buccaneer."[16] Another example surfaced in early 2006 when Yonatan Cohen was convicted of criminal copyright infringement in Minnesota for making a game console that included unlicensed Nintendo games. He was sentenced to five years in prison, lost hundreds of thousands of dollars in cash and property, and was deported to Israel. Worse, his punishment included the use of his own resources to pay for advertisements in game magazines, warning about the penalties for copyright violation. The advertisements had his picture in the center, a picture of his copyright-violating device, a description of his punishment, and a caption that read: "This ad was paid for by Yonatan Cohen as part of his restitution to warn other about the dangers and penalties associated with violating the copyrights laws."

In the EU, copyright infringement can carry both civil and—in serious cases—criminal penalties. For example, Nintendo has also taken legal action across the EU against unauthorized software and hardware.[17] However, in general there is no principle of statutory or punitive damages in civil copyright infringement lawsuits, so damages are typically substantially less in the EU than in the United States.

## Derivative Works

The idea of a "derivative work" is critically important in the way that copyright is used in the game industry. A derivative work is a new work derived from an existing copyrighted work. The language of the U.S. statute defines a derivative work as a work that "is based upon one or more pre-existing works, such as a translation, musical arrangement, dramatization, fictionalization, motion picture version, sound recording, art reproduction, abridgement, condensation, or any other form in which a work may be recast, transformed, or adapted."

What does it mean when you read that a company has acquired "the rights" to make a game based on a film? In the copyright sense, this means that the game company has acquired the right to make a derivative work of the film. This is how films are made from games as well. *Doom* the movie was a derivative work created from *Doom* the game. The same concept works in reverse as well. *Shrek* was first a film and then a derivative work was created, turning the copyrighted material in the film into a game. Now, it is easy to imagine that this process gets complex quickly. Consider *The Lord of the Rings*, a world described in a series of books by J. R. R. Tolkien. The entity that controls the copyright to this world has granted a copyright license to make derivative works for board games, computer games, films, and replica weapons; all of those products are derivative works that also have their own copyright. Any material in a derivative work that is not contained in the underlying work is copyrightable as a new work. Furthermore, this new material may even be licensable itself!

Continuing with *The Lord of the Rings* example, this property offers a fascinating derivative-works case study in the game industry. Starting in 2001, Electronic Arts (EA) developed games, including the first *Battle for Middle Earth* game, based on a license from the Peter Jackson films. This meant that the games from EA could only produce game content, or derivative work, that came from the Jackson films. In 2005, while creating the *Battle for Middle Earth* sequel and other *Rings* games, EA acquired a license to produce a game based on the entire world of fiction as described in the Tolkien books. This license to make derivative works based on the books opened up a great deal of new territory for creativity. Here, EA was licensing a subset of material from one derivative work and later went on to acquire a license for the entire base of material.

## The Public Domain

What happens to copyrighted works after the protection expires, and how does that affect game copyright specifically? The short answer is that formerly protected work that loses its IP protection passes into the public domain. This is a particularly exciting idea because anyone, even game developers, can use material in the public domain to create new works. As a rule of thumb, the older a work is the more likely it is to safely be in the public domain. The table below shows a greatly simplified set of rules for determining when a work passes into the public domain. Law professor Laura Gasaway has produced a much better chart, which is one of the most cited tables for determining the expiration of copyright. The Gasaway chart and another one from Cornell University are referenced in the table below.

| [a]Is the Work in the Public Domain? | |
| --- | --- |
| **Before 1923** | **Public Domain** |
| 1923 to March 1989 | Depends if the work was published with a notice of copyright registration and if the registration was renewed. |
| After March 1989 | Under copyright for 70 years after the death of author, or if a work of corporate authorship, the shorter of 95 years from publication or 120 years from creation. |

[a] For U.S. works only. More thorough charts can be found through UNC-Chapel Hill or Cornell.
*Note:* Additional information can be found at the following:
http://copyright.cornell.edu/resources/publicdomain.cfm
http://www.unc.edu/~unclng/public-d.htm

Before making any final decision, it is prudent to check with IP counsel before using works assumed to be in the public domain. Particular caution should be used for works created outside of the United States or works created in the United States between 1923 and 1989. There may also be special circumstances surrounding a particular work that limits its use in a game. A common example of these special circumstances is when public domain works have been previously used to create new works. As discussed above, these new works are derivative works. They have their own new IP protection for the new elements contained within them, but the underlying public domain works remain in the public domain.

The story of Robin Hood is an excellent example of a special public domain situation, because the story is so old it is practically a fairy tale; there may have been someone that performed similar feats in medieval England, but the myriad of stories do appear a wee bit exaggerated. It is also true that there have been countless books and movies using the Robin Hood story. There have also been several video games based on Robin Hood, his merry men, the Sheriff of Nottingham, and Maid Marian. The main point here is that the underlying story and characters are part of the public domain, but when creating new stories using this inspiration, developers should be careful not to infringe on modern works that still have copyright protection. The license-hungry game developer should be encouraged by a secondary point implicit here: there are many popular stories and characters now available for free game development, including much of the great art and literature from the 19th century and earlier.

Another important example of the public domain comes in the form of myths, history, and cultural lore. Anyone can use these as familiar settings to build games because they are so old and their authorship is collective and forgotten.

Before the trademark dispute and subsequent cancellation of the Microsoft project *Mythica*, the game was going to use a place named Muspellheim. *Dark Age of Camelot* also uses the name Muspellheim. They can both do this because Muspellheim is a place from Norse mythology which both have used as a setting for their games. That story is not under copyright protection because the author or authors of those myths have been dead for centuries. This is similar to using "Mount Olympus" or "Hell" as a setting in a game. On the other hand, using "The Death Star" or "Tatooine" for game development names would be an entirely different case because these places, as story elements, are the IP of the *Star Wars* universe. These names were created recently by an author and are protected by copyright as story elements. Even though they are such a pervasive part of our cultural consciousness and even more well known than Muspellheim, they cannot be used in games without permission because the stories they are part of are still protected by copyright. Any use of these names in new and similar stories would contribute to a finding of copyright infringement.

· Historical events are also not subject to copyright, but the stories created out of them are. An example is World War II, a fertile area for game development in the last five years. No one can copyright the specific events of that or any time period. *Battlefield 1942*, *Call of Duty*, and *Medal of Honor* can all use tanks, weapons, and uniforms that are historically accurate. Furthermore, they are not infringing each other's copyright because the games are merely representing historical facts.[18] That said, historical events also involve real people who may have proprietary rights separate from copyright. In 2014, *CMG v. Maximum Family Games* was filed, alleging that the inclusion of General Patton in the *Legends of War* game violated his right of publicity. The case settled in 2015 following the filing of a motion to dismiss by Maximum Family Games.

It is important to remember that copying a story inspired by historical facts is still copyright infringement, but merely copying the historical facts is not. For instance, a developer cannot make a game based on the movie *Saving Private Ryan* without the appropriate license. A developer can however, make a game about Pearl Harbor or other World War II events as long as she or he is creating the game around the historical event and not the movie of the same name.

## Scènes à Faire Doctrine

The scènes à faire doctrine is similar to public domain property. This doctrine recognizes that some expressions of ideas are so often used that they cannot be copyrighted by themselves. An example of this is the fairy tale beginning, "Once upon a time..." So many fairy tales begin that way that a fairy tale-based game could certainly begin that way, too.[19] Other scènes à faire doctrine examples would be the generic elements of a fantasy story such as wizards or dragons. These races and their general stereotypes are not copyrighted, but specific instances of these races that are clear characters, such as Gandalf or Drizzt, would be.

Despite scènes à faire originally being a French term, the same doctrine is not formally recognized in EU copyright law, although the requirements of originality for copyright works arguably would help arrive at a similar result if necessary.

## Fair Use

The concept of "fair use" is commonly discussed and misunderstood in copyright law. As a general notion, fair use is the idea that one party may use a portion of a copyrighted work for a limited purpose without paying the copyright holder for a license. This concept is derived in U.S. law from a U.S. statute that states four conditions must be met, as per the table below.

As one might imagine, fair use can be a muddy issue at times. It is commonly brought up by parties opposing copyright infringement, but it is not a perfect defense.

**Four Factors in Fair Use**

| | |
|---|---|
| 1. The purpose and character of use | Educational uses and uses in parody are more often protected than strict commercial copying |
| 2. The nature of the copyrighted work | Using sections of a commercial work is more likely to result in a finding of infringement. Copying creative fictional works are more likely to result in a finding of infringement than copying factual compilations |
| 3. The amount and substantiality of the portion taken | Taking a large portion from a work is more likely to result in a finding of infringement than taking a small portion |
| 4. The effect of the use on the potential market | Demonstrably weakening the market for the copyrighted work is more likely to result in a finding of infringement |

There are two common pitfalls relating to fair use to keep in mind. First, fair use is a U.S. concept. Most other countries, especially in Europe, do not contain provisions allowing copyrighted material to be used without a license,[20] except in some limited situations (such as for news reporting or legitimate educational purposes). This means that a game company hoping to incorporate some copyrighted material into a game as a "parody" or other traditionally shielded type of fair use may run into problems when selling its game in other countries.[21] A small clip intended as a humorous interlude may lead to the company in litigation or forgoing sales outside the United States.

The second issue to remember about fair use is that it is a *defense* to a claim of copyright infringement. This means that a copyright holder in the United States can certainly sue the company that included the clip for using a copyrighted work or a derivative of that work without a license. After the case is brought, the law now grants the offending company the opportunity to argue the merits of fair use. This means that a company plainly operating in the traditional boundaries of fair use is still open to litigation and therefore open to the associated costs and bad publicity associated with a copyright litigation. In short, the decision to use copyrighted material in a game under the protection of fair use poses a risk and should be weighed heavily.

## Common Questions About Copyright

### Is Mailing a Sealed Envelope Proof of Copyright?

Mailing a sealed envelope to a person with a copy of the company's newest game is not remotely the same as registering the copyright for the game. Sometimes called "the poor man's copyright," this procedure has no legal effect. At best, it may prove that the material was in a certain form on a certain date, but that evidence is open to challenge since an individual can mail an unsealed envelope to themselves. Actual copyright registration is easy and inexpensive, so there is little reason to resort to this when mailing a form and payment to the Copyright Office is nearly as easy, or (outside of the US) there is an alternative national registration system available.

### In the United States, Is a Copyright Holder Entitled to $150,000 in Damages per Instance of Infringement?

The statutory damages clause for copyright infringement is often misinterpreted. A copyright holder is entitled to *up to* $150,000 in damages per instance of copyright infringement in the United States. This is for *willful* infringement of a registered copyrighted work. Furthermore, it is not per copy of the registered work, it is per *instance* of infringement. Making 10,000 copies of a particular game or film does not multiply the damages by 10,000. The game or film is one copyrighted work and that counts as one instance of infringement. The damage calculation may end up becoming more than $150,000 through other damage-calculation mechanisms such as calculating ill-gotten profits or lost sales, but it is not the result of multiplying the number of copied units by $150,000. The damages may also add up because most games actually contain many copyright works. The number of copies does not directly multiply the damages under the willful damages statutory section. The number of works, not the number of copies, is most significant. That said, as noted previously, statutory damages for copyright infringement are not typically available for countries outside the United States.

## TRADE SECRET

### Introduction

Trade secret can be thought of as the oldest form of IP. Even 2 million years ago, *Homo habilis* could keep his competitive advantage for a new stone tool through IP protection. He could keep the use and construction of that tool a "trade secret." The mechanism then, as now, was merely to keep the idea a secret. The processes have grown more complex, but at root the idea is same.

In modern times, a trade secret is loosely defined as some information that may be used for business advantage that a company keeps secret. This is the only form of IP that is not disclosed publicly; patents, copyrights, and trademarks all rely on some form of public disclosure. Trade secrets are company business secrets. A pretty good legal definition comes from the U.S. Uniform Trade Secrets Act, which defines a Trade Secret as follows:

> "Trade secret" means information, including a formula, pattern, compilation, program device, method, technique, or process, that: (i) derives independent economic value, actual or potential, from not being generally known to, and not being readily ascertainable by proper means by, other persons who can obtain economic value from its disclosure or use, and (ii) is the subject of efforts that are reasonable under the circumstances to maintain its secrecy.

### What Can Be a Trade Secret?

Any idea can be a trade secret as long as it is an idea that confers some business advantage and can be kept secret. Trade secret rights can extend to virtually any concrete information that grants a business advantage such as formulae, data compilations, devices, process, and customer lists. The most well-known example of a trade secret is the formula for Coca-Cola. The formula is known by some people at the company, but it is not known for certain by anyone else. The secret has been held by the company for more than 100 years. Though many public descriptions exist, none have been verified.[22] Furthermore, great steps are taken to prevent anyone from discovering the secret. Other examples of trade secrets include notes on game development, business contacts, license terms, and other internal business items that are valuable to game development but not protected with the other IP tools.

Two advantages of trade secret are that they have no registration cost and can be protected quickly. Trademarks require using the mark, and patents require an application and a lengthy approval process. Both also require registration fees. While there is no registration fee for trade secrets, it would not be entirely fair to say that their protection is free. A company must make structured efforts to keep valuable business information a secret if that company wants to claim that information as a trade secret.

In the EU, trade secrets are also referred to as "confidential business information." Analogous to the United States, there is no EU level or federal law relating to their protection. For now, they are protected at a member-state level under regimes that vary from country to country but are all broadly similar to the U.S. position. The key is always to ensure that the information you wish to protect is valuable, confidential, and *kept* confidential. Further afield, there is a general obligation on most countries under an international treaty called the TRIPS Agreement to provide protection for *"undisclosed information"* (though the means of implementing that vary very widely).

## What Rights Are Conferred by Trade Secrets?

The rights given to a trade secret holder include the right to prevent others from using the trade secret unless the other party discovers the secret through legitimate research. Speaking in terms of the Uniform Trade Secrets Act, a company has the right to prevent others from "misappropriating" a trade secret. The Act describes misappropriation in this way:

> "Misappropriation" means: (i) acquisition of a trade secret of another by a person who knows or has reason to know that the trade secret was acquired by improper means; or (ii) disclosure or use of a trade secret of another without express or implied consent by a person who (A) used improper means to acquire knowledge of the trade secret; or (B) at the time of disclosure or use knew or had reason to know that his knowledge of the trade secret was (I) derived from or through a person who has utilized improper means to acquire it; (II) acquired under circumstances giving rise to a duty to maintain its secrecy or limit its use; or (III) derived from or through a person who owed a duty to the person seeking relief to maintain its secrecy or limit its use; or (C) before a material change of his position, knew or had reason to know that it was a trade secret ad that knowledge of it had been acquired by accident or mistake.

## Examples of Trade Secrets

As an example, consider mailing-list data for subscribers of an MMO as a type of trade secret. These people have subscribed to Company A's MMO for years and have each paid literally hundreds of dollars to the publisher. If an employee steals the MMO contact list, this employee can have easy access to people interested in playing an MMO and willing to pay for it in the long term. This information could be enormously valuable to a competitor.

Development tools could also be trade secrets. Consider a development tool that may intelligently populate a 3D level with environmental objects by pulling these objects from a specified directory. This software could be written in-house for one development project, but could easily be modified to work with other projects, saving programmers and level designers many hours of work by placing a "skeleton"[23] level down according to certain conditions. Now this tool is certainly also covered by copyright, but if it is never sold, published, or patented, it could also be a trade secret. To be clear, like Coca-Cola, some elements of the tool could remain trade secrets even if the tool itself were sold. An employee leaving with the code for this design tool and taking it to a competitor is stealing a trade secret.

Details about licensing and publishing agreements can also be a trade secret. In fact, license agreements and other contract secrets are one of the most common trade secrets in the game industry. Often both parties do not want deal details leaked to the public. This class of secrets covers obvious clauses such as how much is paid and when. It also covers less obvious but equally important information such as which employees are "key employees" for fulfilling a development agreement.

## Trade Secret Information
### Length of Protection
Trade secrets last as long as the owner of the information prevents it from becoming common knowledge. This, like trademark, is potentially immortal. The only limitation is the time that the information can be kept "secret" for.

### Process and Cost
Unlike patents, copyright, and trademarks, there are no formalities—such as registration—required to obtain trade secret rights.

It is often said that having a trade secret is "free." This is true to some extent. There are no registration or maintenance fees required. Yet, trade secrets require a process. They must be handled carefully, and some efforts must be made by the company to keep them secret as described later in this chapter.

### Protecting Trade Secrets
Common protections include recording trade secrets and having employees sign documents stating that they understand that certain information is a trade secret and that the information has special restrictions on dissemination. Controlled access is an important part of a trade secret. If the trade secrets are electronic files, allow only certain people to access those files, consider encryption for those files, and place special protections on modifying or copying the files.

Protection of trade secrets also includes not telling anyone the information unless that person needs to know it, but it also can include other internal security measures. Measures such as restricted access to the information internally, passwords, encryption, locked cabinets, and non-disclosure documents all help protect the company's trade secrets.

If you find that someone has leaked trade secrets, you should take specific actions. First, your company should do whatever is necessary to stop the leaked information. This may include further restricting access, changing passwords, and perhaps moving databases. This may also include sending ISP and/or webmaster notices if the trade secret information is being hosted online. The company usually also places the offender on notice that he or she is distributing a trade secret. This notice, similar to other such webmaster/ISP notices, will demand that the offender "cease and desist" from distributing the secret. Finally, if this fails to remedy the harm caused by the leak of the trade secret, litigation may be in order. Similar to copyright and other types of IP enforcement, each of these steps should be done in concert with your attorney.

## Penalties for Infringement

Virtually every country has a sanctions system for misuse of trade secrets or confidential information. For example, in the United States, the Uniform Trade Secret Act allows damages for misappropriating trade secrets. These damages can be measured in three ways. First, the damages may be measured as a loss of profit by the party that originally held the secret. Second, the damages may be measured as profit by a party that used or disclosed the misappropriated trade secret. Finally, if appropriate, the measurement could be a reasonable royalty payment for the trade secret. In addition, or as an alternative to damages, a party may be able to enjoin (or stop) the misappropriating party from using the trade secret. Legally, this is referred to as seeking an injunction against the misappropriating party.

## Trade Secret Is State Law in the United States

In the United States, copyright, federally registered trademarks, and patents are all controlled almost exclusively by federal law. Trade secret, on the other hand, is controlled by individual state law. Therefore, it can vary more than other IP laws because it can differ from state to state. Throughout this chapter, information has come from general principles contained in state law or from the Uniform Trade Secrets Act, a model that approximately 40 states have adopted or have used as a guide in creating their own law. There is no substitute for a qualified attorney familiar with state laws when it comes to trade secret matters. As a rule, most attorneys will be comfortable working with trade secret law in their home state, New York, and California.

## Common Questions about Trade Secrets

### Can Trade Secret Status Help Me Protect My IP from Reverse Engineering?

Unfortunately, trade secret cannot provide full protection from one of the biggest assaults against game IP: reverse engineering. A truly legal reverse engineering job is performed when hardware or software is inspected and ultimately re-created without misappropriating a blueprint, source code, or other related information. This process, while in no way easy, has been accomplished for some relatively secure gaming systems and software. However, trade secret can protect game developers from reverse engineering since the difficulty of reverse engineering is sometimes well beyond the realm of human capability, and is only possible if some inside information (i.e., a trade secret) is leaked to the public. Trade secret status can help protect against this leak, and potentially cut off reverse engineering attempts before they become feasible.

### At What Stage Should a Game Company Use Trade Secret Status?

The best advice for a gaming company embarking on any new project is to maintain some planned secrecy at every stage. Try to keep key in-game calculations, customer lists, community information, and key business contacts a secret. As long as proper non-disclosure measures are followed along the way, it is possible to amass quite a bit of trade secret knowledge that should prevent your game ideas from being stolen or reproduced. The major reason that game companies lose trade secrets is the cost and trust issues associated with maintaining such secrets. Quite often, a small game company may be started with a group of friends who feel that such measures would be unnecessary because of a high level of trust between the founders. Although this may be the case, it is always better to ensure the protection of valuable resources with the proper measures before there are any problems.

## TRADEMARK

### Introduction

Where trade secret focuses on keeping information about a company behind closed doors, trademark focuses on pushing information out into the public. In fact, a successful trademark is one that allows consumers to instantly recognize the company and its products when they see the mark. The Xbox, PlayStation, Apple, and Facebook logos are immediately recognizable and consumers have certain thoughts and feelings associated with those marks. That brand recognition and association with a particular company is the purpose of trademark.

Trademarks are arguably the second most important IP protection for game companies after copyright since a good trademark can set a company and its games apart from others in the minds of consumers. The Lanham Act is the primary trademark statute in the United States and also governs false advertising and trademark dilution, as well as trademark infringement. It sets out the basic rules governing trademark registration, infringement standards, and the penalties for infringement.

### What Can Be Trademarked?

The most common trademarks are a word, name, symbol, graphic, or short phrase used in business to identify a specific company's products. More exotic trademarks can be smells, sounds, or colors, but these are rarely used.[24] Trademarks come into being when they are used in business by a company to identify products or services. To identify a trademark for a game company, the company only has to use a superscript TM after the mark, like this—mark™. Of all the types of IP, only copyright is easier to invoke because it only requires the fixation of a creative work.

Simply placing the™ designation after a word puts the world on notice of "common law" trademark rights. Common law trademark rights are derived from the use of the mark in commerce. Through business use, trademarks become associated with a company and perhaps also with a particular product or service within the company. Common-law rights are also controlled by state law, and the mark is not protected throughout the United States. The mark is only protected in the area where it is in use. The position is the same in other common-law countries, such as Canada, the United Kingdom, India, or Australia, and in practice in many other countries too (in Germany, for example, a business can gain unregistered trademark rights simply by use of the mark in the course of their business).

### Examples of Trademarks

The strongest trademarks are words that have only the meaning that a company has given to them, like Xbox, Sony, Facebook, or Nintendo. The words do not mean anything to the general public outside of the company's definition of them. In other words, the more imaginary the trademark is, the stronger it is.

Microsoft has learned some lessons twice the hard way in the game context. The first time was just before the launch of the first Xbox. The Xbox trademark was in use by another software company when Microsoft started marketing the Xbox. Worse, the competing company was a publicly traded company that should have been easy to find in a standard trademark search.[25] Clearly, this is something that should have been discovered and negotiated much earlier in the launch cycle, or perhaps even another name should have been chosen. This case was eventually settled out of court and probably cost Microsoft a substantial amount of money.

The second and more recent trademark lesson for Microsoft came in 2003 with the planned MMORPG *Mythica*. One of the most popular games in that market, *Dark Age of Camelot*, is made by Mythic Entertainment. This potential trademark conflict was so obvious it did not really require a search, and could have been uncovered simply by asking just about anyone familiar with the genre. In response to the clear "Mythica"/"Mythic" conflict, Mythic initiated a case against Microsoft for trademark infringement.[26] Around the time of the case, Mythic Entertainment's CEO Mark Jacobs is famously quoted as telling a Microsoft lead designer at E3 that Mythic was going to call its next game "Microsofta." Whether causally related or not, Microsoft canceled the whole *Mythica* project after the dispute arose. Microsoft settled the suit with Mythic, agreeing not to use the term "Mythica" and to drop its U.S. applications to register "Mythica" as a trademark. As part of the settlement, Microsoft also assigned Mythic the rights to international trademark applications and registrations for "Mythica" as well as the associated domain names.

The lesson here is that trademark searches should not be considered an additional frivolous cost for a game company. Instead, these searches are an essential part of the registration process and, in the past, mistakes have and will cost game companies literally millions of dollars and potentially be involved in the failure of entire projects.

## Trademark Information

### Length of Protection

Trademarks can be immortal. If the mark is used continuously in commerce and the relevant fees are paid, the mark can exist forever. There are some marks in the United States, like Coca-Cola, Levi Strass & Co, Prudential, and Heinz, for example, which have been used for more than 100 years.

### Process and Cost in the United States

In the United States, a trademark may also be registered with the federal government for wider and stronger protection. The registration is more complex than the copyright registration process, but not as complex as the patent registration process. For this reason, it is usually done through a law firm with paralegals and attorneys that specialize in trademark registration. The process should begin with a trademark search that examines U.S. and perhaps international sources to try to discover if other companies have been using the mark, in which case the search can try to determine whether the mark is being used in a related field. After the company has the results of this search, it can decide to move forward with the federal registration process or reconsider the mark. As routine as this initial search process is, sometimes it fails in spectacular ways—even for very established companies.

After the trademark search, the federal registration process with the United States Patent and Trademark Office (USPTO) begins. This process usually takes less than a year and costs approximately 3000 dollars, including the earlier trademark search. After the mark has been federally registered, this registration and the litigations surrounding it are controlled by federal law. The registration is, at this point, good throughout the entire United States.

The fees for renewing a trademark are currently lower than patent maintenance fees. The fees can vary based on how many trademark "classes" are covered by the trademark. A class can be thought of as a class of products. At the time of writing, the cost for renewing a trademark in one class and filing the appropriate declaration of use is approximately $600.[27]

### Protecting Trademarks

All trademarks should be noted with the appropriate symbols. Use the symbol ™ to indicate whether the mark is being used in business. If the trademark registration is successful, the applicant can use the "®" symbol following the mark as an indication that the mark has been registered with the USPTO or another national trademark office.

Policing trademark is similar to policing other types of IP. One important difference is that a trademark used by unauthorized companies can actually damage the value of the trademark. If this unauthorized use becomes rampant, the mark runs the risk of "genericide," where it loses all value. This has happened in the United States to trademarks that were so often misused, they became household words, such as aspirin and thermos. Both of these were trademarks at one time, but have died a death from misuse and over-popularity.[28]

### Penalties for Infringement

The penalties for trademark infringement can be harsh and are similar to copyright infringement. These penalties can include the destruction of the infringing items if the items are considered counterfeit. An injunction, stopping the use of the infringing trademark, is also an option. Monetary damages based on loss of profits or ill-gotten gains are also possible. Similar to copyright, personal liability through the corporate shield is also possible. The specific damage calculation for each case is dependent on the circumstances surrounding the infringement.

### Picking a Good Trademark

Trademarks are divided into five categories. The categories are broken down to reflect the relative strength of the mark. Mark strength is an indicator of strength of protection. That strength of protection should also contribute to IP value. The five categories of trademark strength are fanciful, arbitrary, suggestive, descriptive, and generic (see the table below).

*Fanciful* marks are the strongest marks. They have no meaning other than the meaning a company associates with them. Examples of fanciful marks include Xbox, Bioware, NVIDIA, *Tetris*, and Eidos.

*Arbitrary* marks are also strong, but less so than fanciful marks. They are words that are not associated with the particular product until the company associates them. An example of an arbitrary mark is Apple for computers, Android for the operating system, or id for a development studio.

*Suggestive* marks can be a natural word that suggests the product it represents, but does not directly describe it. These are the weakest marks that companies can normally obtain protection for. Examples of suggestive marks are Electronic Arts for a maker of video games, PlayStation for a console game platform, *Sonic the Hedgehog* for a fast-moving hedgehog, *Space Invaders* for a game starring invaders from space, or *Centipede* for a game featuring a centipede.

*Descriptive* marks are extremely weak marks. They are essentially useless unless a company has used them so much that they have acquired something called "secondary meaning." Secondary meaning can only be acquired through extensive marketing and public exposure. Examples of descriptive marks include Vision Center for a store that specializes in glasses, or Computerland for a computer store.

*Generic* marks are things like video card, controller, or video game. The term generic is the polar opposite of trademark and a generic term can never be converted to a trademark in the United States or virtually anywhere else.

| Judging Trademark Strength | | |
|---|---|---|
| **Mark Category** | **Description** | **Example** |
| Fanciful | Words that have no meaning beyond that given by the company | Xbox |
| Arbitrary | Words previously unassociated with a type source | Apple (for computers) |
| Suggestive | Words that suggest something about the source | Electronic Arts |
| Descriptive | Words that merely describe the source | Computerland |
| Generic | Generic descriptor; cannot be a trademark | Video game |

It should be obvious that you should not name your next game and development company *Game* by Game Development Company. Those terms are too generic to become trademarks at all. Examples outside the game industry such as Exxon, Intervolve, and Kodak are great trademarks because they do not have any other meaning besides the meaning the company generates for them. When naming a new company or product, it is worth trying and create a fanciful or arbitrary mark. The increased strength legally afforded to creative marks is a fascinating example of how IP law respects and promotes creativity.

*Notable International Variation*

Although trademark law is respected in most countries, the realities of enforcing a trademark on foreign soil are different than enforcing a trademark within the United States. For example, some countries in Europe require use of the mark in commerce, whereas others give a grace period but still require use within several years. Also, the registration of a mark in the United States does not mean that the mark is enforceable in another country; it merely means that should a foreign business with a similar trademark attempt to bring its product into the United States, you could then enforce your rights.

An interesting phenomenon to take note of in the foreign market is the Community Trade Mark (CTM) that one can apply for in the EU.[29] This mark, if granted, can be used across all of the 27 Member States of the EU, and can be a cost-effective way of establishing trademark rights over a broad array of countries. However, there are complexities and alternatives to this type of trademark that are beyond the scope of this chapter. The most important alternative to discuss with your IP attorney is the use of the Madrid Protocol to obtain international protection. In short, this is an area that becomes complicated very quickly and if your company has the products and resources to consider international protection, it should make sure that it has appropriate counsel to arrange for such protection.[30]

## Common Questions about Trademarks

### Do I Have to Use a Trademark in Commerce?

Actual use is always better for bolstering trademark rights, but in the United States it is possible to establish such rights for a short time merely by establishing intent-to-use. In 1988, trademark law changed when this intent-to-use provision was added. Prior to this addition, a mark needed to be used in commerce; since 1988, it has been possible to merely apply for a federal registration with the stipulation that there is a bona fide intent to use the mark in commerce.

As discussed above, using a trademark in commerce without registration grants common-law protection for the trademark. In this way, actual use offers additional protection beyond a filing of intent-to-use. Trademark law offers some protection here, including protection against infringement called "passing off."

### Can I Let Fans Use My Trademark Without a Formal License?

This is commonly done in the game industry for both copyrighted material and trademarks. Game companies often create fan site packages that include material and conditions for using that material. The allowed uses are case specific and it is often not economically feasible to attack every website "infringer" that pops up. Game companies also recognize the advertising value in game-related communities. In short, make sure the fan sites know what uses your game company is comfortable with. Be as clear as possible about the rules and try to stress that appropriate attribution is important.

For example, a fan website kit may include appropriate legal attribution for a trademark. The notice may say something similar to "*Title* is a trademark of GameCompany" or "*Title* is a registered trademark of GameCompany." This situation becomes more complicated if there is a substantial commercial component to the website or if the website is spreading misinformation that is harmful to your game sales. In the case of a commercial component, the website may be making money using your game company's trademarks and perhaps copyrighted material. As mentioned above, the appropriate action, if any, is dependent on the individual circumstances. A negotiated license and/or a "cease and desist" letter may be in order to stop unwarranted uses.

*Can I Trademark My Game Title?*

Here, the answer is "Yes." Normally, trademarks are not meant to cover a title that will be used for one property only. Recall that trademarks are a sign of the source of a product. Films, books, and other creative products usually need some type of product extension such as merchandising or a sequel. However, despite the normal rule that applies to most other goods and services in the United States, there is a special exception for video games in the United States Trademark Office that states game titles may seek trademark protection.[31] While the United States might be favorable to trademarking a game title, a developer or publisher may still meet with significant restrictions or difficulties in obtaining similar protection in foreign jurisdictions.

## PATENTS

### Introduction

The patent system in the United States is descended from the 1623 Statute of Monopolies in England, which sought to overturn earlier royal monopoly grants but preserved inventor's rights for 14 years with grants of "letters patents" for "new manufactures."[32] More recently, in the United States, patents go all the way back to the Constitution. In Article I, § 8, clause 8 grants Congress the power to "promote the progress of science and the useful arts, by securing for limited times to authors and inventors the exclusive right to their respective writings and discoveries." Since that time, patent law has undergone and continues to undergo revision, sometimes significant.[33]

Traditionally, in the EU, patents were handled by each member country individually. Now, the EU is moving toward a unified patent system and the participating member states are currently working under the assumption that it will become effective and operational sometime in 2018.[34] In the meantime, an applicant can obtain a bundle of patents in each of several European countries at the same time under the European Patent Convention.

Although extremely important for some hardware, software, development tools, and other middleware companies, patents are not used as often in the game context. This may change as the industry matures, but for the time being, patents are not often utilized throughout the majority of the game industry. By way of example, in the United States there are approximately the same number of game industry patents each year as patents on toothbrushes. Still, each year there are large patent litigations in games. This increase has caused a substantial burden for developers, who must often take on the cost of defending these cases if the publisher and developer are named in a patent infringement complaint.

### What Can Be Patented?

In the United States, the Patent Act defines potentially patentable subject matter as any "new and useful process, machine, manufacture, or composition of matter."[35] Examples include machines, pharmaceuticals, medical equipment, video cards, or a better mousetrap. Patents do not usually protect games themselves because they do not usually meet the statutory criteria. Yet, there are a growing number of game-related patents, usually in the areas of hardware, digital distribution, networking, and inventive game-play.

The position is similar in Europe and internationally, with one vital caveat for games: it is often much harder outside of the United States to patent software inventions. For example, in the EU there is a complex prohibition on software patents under the European Patent Convention.[36] Another point to be aware of is that some countries allow applications for lesser patents known as either "utility patents," "lesser patents," or "innovation patents," which do not exist in the United States. These are essentially similar to "regular" patents but protect lesser innovations for less time (but are easier to obtain).[37]

A new case in the United States, *Alice Corp v. CLA Bank International*, is a Supreme Court case that has substantially limited what can patented. While certain game patents are still being allowed, anything that might be labeled as a software- or business-method patent has been much tougher to get through the USPTO and the courts. The case centers on the notion that an "abstract idea" implemented by a computer is not patentable. That, of course, sets up a real head-scratching legal problem in the game industry and outside of it. Most of the life-changing ideas of the past 30 years have been abstract ideas implemented on computer systems.

## What Rights Are Conferred by Patents?

A common misconception is that a patent grants the right to make an invention, but this is not true. Similar to copyright, patents grant a negative right, that is, a right that prevents others from doing something. In other words, a patent confers the right to prevent other people from making, using, selling, or importing an invention. The patent owner is under no obligation to ever actually construct the patented invention, but can prevent others from practicing the invention.

## Patent Information

Patents are perhaps the most complex form of IP protection. It is important to understand the details about this form of IP if you plan to use it in your business.

## Length of Protection

Patents have a limited lifespan and that lifespan is relatively short compared with other forms of IP. A lay person might think that a patent expiration date would be printed right on the front of a patent. Unfortunately, nothing could be further from the truth. Currently, patents that pay the required maintenance fees are valid for 20 years from the time they are filed. Before June 1995, this calculation was not so simple. These older patents are valid for either 17 years from the patent issue date or 20 years from filing—whichever is longer.[38] Just to make the calculation more complicated, it is not unusual for patents to be shortened or extended for some time through a variety of mechanisms. It is possible to *estimate* a patent term by looking at the basic date on the face of a patent, but a full review of the patent's history and related documents is necessary to find an exact expiration date.

## Process and Cost in the United States

Of all the types of IP registration, the patent process is the longest and most complicated. The process takes two to four years and involves creating all of the written material for the patent application including all relevant figures. The process also includes regular correspondence with the patent office, and complying with or writing rebuttals to patent office arguments. Although it is possible to go through this process without a patent attorney, it is strongly not recommended.

There are two main sections that make up a patent. The first section is called the specification, and is the narrative description that makes up most of the written material in a patent. This section includes the background of the invention that goes through the state of the technology leading up to the invention. There is also a detailed description of the invention with figures and examples. In theory, a person reading this section can learn everything there is to know about how to make and use this invention. Remember that a patent is a deal with the government: in exchange for sharing complete knowledge of the invention with the world, the patent holder is granted a limited monopoly on that invention.

The second main section is the patent claims. These claims are numbered sentences found at the end of a patent. There has to be at least one claim, but there is no absolute upper limit on the number of claims; however, in the United States, every patent claim over 20 costs an additional amount of money, so large numbers of claims are economically discouraged. The average patent has about 3–15 claims. The patent claims are the most important section of the patent because this is the portion that describes exactly what the patent protects. In fact, material in the specification that is not included in the claims is given away to the public. Be very careful that the patent claims adequately and completely describe your invention.

The cost of filing a patent application varies based on several factors. These factors include the complexity of the technology, the number of other patents in the field, and the amount of material that your company can provide the patent attorney. If the technology is complicated, there are many patents in the field, and you call your patent attorney with an idea written down on an index card, the cost is going to increase. A general price range for the total cost of application can be between $15,000 and $30,000. This includes the costs to file an application and to shepherd it thorough the patent office. The range also depends on the number of mailings called "Office Actions" from the patent office and the time spent preparing answers to those Office Actions.

Beware of companies that offer to "file" a patent application for $2,000 or some other very small number. There are at least two areas where these companies are hiding costs. The first is that the USPTO fees are usually not included in these costs. Second, the low estimate is usually only for "filing" the patent application. The cost of answering office actions and doing the other work necessary to get the patent is not included in that estimate. This is similar to stating that skydiving costs $200, but the parachute is extra.

The good news is that patent costs tend to be spread out over the whole period of the application. There will be costs to prepare and file the application, but paying for the Office Action work is not necessary until many months later when the patent application has been acted on by the patent office. It is also possible, but unlikely, that an application can go straight through to become an issued patent.

There are also ongoing costs for patents in addition to filing costs. In order to keep a patent enforceable during its term, maintenance fees must be paid to the USPTO.

These maintenance fees are due at 3.5, 7.5, and 11.5 years after issuance. The fees change often, and the best source of information regarding these fees is your IP attorney. If the fees are not paid, the patents will expire and it takes a substantial effort to revive them, if it is possible at all. The difficulty reviving the patent is dependent on the length of time since the fees were due and the circumstances surrounding the failure to pay the fees.[39] Make certain that your company plans for this and has someone designated to monitor that these payments are made.

Outside of the United States, you can expect a similarly long, complex, and expensive process compared with other forms of IP protection. You should also be aware that the process itself can have very important differences compared with the United States. For example, Europe traditionally uses a "first to file" approach to patents (the first applicant for the patent is the person who gets it by default, not the person who invented the patentable invention first). The United States has only recently adopted a type of "first to file" in March 2013 as its standard under the America Invents Act, so the differences are hopefully becoming smaller, but we will likely never achieve complete harmonization.[40]

### Protecting Patents

If another company is violating your patent rights, the first step in policing this type of IP is to put the other company on notice by sending them the patent and a letter about the potential infringement. Hopefully, the parties can work out some suitable licensing settlement, but this is sometimes not the case. If the parties cannot come to an agreement, litigation may be in order.

### Patent Litigation and Penalties for Infringing Patents

Generally speaking, patent litigation itself is punishment for both parties. Even the winner of the litigation often incurs substantial costs in time, money, and other resources. Patent litigation is complicated, ultra-niche litigation. It is not surprising that it is expensive, and costs often run well past $2 million in legal fees. There is also no doubt that this process will become substantially more expensive in the future.

Winning a patent litigation normally results in two remedies. First, the patent holder can win an injunction that stops the losing party from practicing the invention. Second, the infringing company may be forced to pay damages for past infringement and potentially a royalty on units sold going forward.

### U.S. Patent Pending and Provisional Patent Applications

The use of "patent pending" is only appropriate when an application or provisional application has been filed with the USPTO or another national patent office. The marking is not mandatory, but can be important when proving notice and calculating potential damage for patent infringement. Some people also argue that the notice adds value to the product in the eyes of investors and consumers and expresses a certain level of business sophistication.

In the United States, provisional patent applications are often an attractive option for small or mid-sized game companies with a patentable invention. These applications cost less than pursuing a standard patent application and preserve the priority date for the invention. These provisional applications resemble complete patent applications except that they will not be examined at the USPTO without further action on behalf of the inventor. The inventor has one year from filing a provisional application to file a standard patent application based on the provisional one. If successful, the applicant will be able to use the date of the provisional application as the date of invention. Finally, the expiration date of the patent is still counted from the date the full application is filed so that the company does not pay any time-related penalty for filing the provisional application.

It is common for an early-stage game company to be cash poor, but perhaps they have an invention or several patentable inventions that are potentially worth a great deal. This is particularly true with middleware companies. The company may fear its competition stealing the invention, but still wants to market the product and raise money. This is potentially a great position for a provisional patent application. After the company files the application, it now has three issues covered. First, the invention is on file with the USPTO and the invention priority date is set. The company can market the invention without fear of losing it due to a statutory bar or competitor copying. Second, the company has spent a fraction of the full cost of a patent application. Finally, the company can point to the pending application for both product sales and as a valuable addition to the company for capital acquisition.

## Patent Invalidity

Patent invalidity is the process of determining the viability of the claims in a patent or seeking to invalidate or cancel one or more of the claims covered by the patent. There are two circumstances when patent invalidity is particularly important in the game industry. The first instance is when a game company is trying to get a patent issued through the USPTO. The second instance is when a game company is being sued by a patent holder for infringement. In the first instance, the game company will want to show that its patent application represents a valid invention. In the second instance, the game company will try to prove the patent holder's patent does not represent a valid invention. This area of patent law is enormously complex and the ideas contained in the sections below should be considered as minimal summaries.

## Anticipation and Obviousness

There are many mechanisms that lead to patents being declared invalid. Two of the most often discussed mechanisms are called anticipation and obviousness. Anticipation is found when something in the prior art meets every element of a patent claim. Prior art is any evidence that the concept embodied in the patent is already known, for example that the concept was previously described, shown, or included in other technology. As set forth above, patent claims are the numbered paragraphs at the end of a patent document that explain what the patent "claims" it protects. Each one of the claims has subsections that are indented as individual steps, and those steps are called "elements." An easy way to think about anticipation is using this idea: that which infringes if after would anticipate if before. In other words, a patent cannot be valid if there is something found in the prior art that would have infringed the patent. This means that there must be something in the prior art that met each and every portion of the claim being invalidated.

The second common way patents are declared invalid is through obviousness. With obviousness, every patent claim portion does not have to be met by just one invention or publication. Instead, inventions and publications can be blended together with other knowledge that was present before the patent. The standard here is what a person of ordinary skill in the relevant scientific discipline would know and do with the information available to him or her. A simplified way to look at this involves three steps. First, were all of the pieces of an invention present? Second, was there is a reason to put those pieces together? Third, could a person of ordinary skill put those pieces together to make the patented invention? If these steps are all met, the patent is invalid for obviousness.

## Timing a Patent Filing

Before a recent revision of U.S. patent laws, people were allowed a year to use or sell their inventions before they had to file a patent application and there was no disadvantage for doing so. This grace period was very much out of synch with international patent laws. As of 2018, this grace period still exists, but the United States has changed from a first-to-invent to a first-to-file jurisdiction. Game developers that wish to file for a patent must be wary of using that grace period because they could lose the "race to the patent office" while they are biding their time.

As mentioned above, there are other ways for patents to be found invalid beyond those discussed in this chapter. These include keeping information from the Patent Office, affirmatively lying to the Patent Office, and a variety of technical issues. As always, the best advice beyond understanding this simple summary is to consult your patent attorney and the more specialized sections of this text.

## Reasons to File a Patent Application

People usually only consider enforcement, litigation, and licensing as the reasons to file a patent application, but there are many others. First, patents and patent applications are a symbol of sophistication for your company. Companies often demand some concrete proof of IP before agreeing to protect it in contract negotiations and licensing. Patents grant your game company that concrete proof and gravitas. Second, patents and patent applications change the valuation of your company. Investors consider these as substantial assets, especially when they are referenced in license agreements. On average, a company with patents will be valued higher than a company without patents, all other things being equal. Third, patents and patent applications can increase pricing on your products. Software and hardware that is patented or patent pending has a higher value in the marketplace because, by definition, it is not available elsewhere. Fourth, a patent application creates an intellectual moat and prior art "bomb" for people that file later. Even if your application publishes and is never approved, that publication by the USPTO alone ensures that no one can come after you and patent the same invention. Fifth, patents provide potential patent counter-claims if a patent case is every brought against your game company. When two companies with substantial patent portfolios are involved in a litigation, the defendant often has grounds for counter-claims based on its portfolio. These counter-claims raise the stakes of litigating with a game company that has patents. Lastly, patents can be used for direct enforcement and licensing, but this is a very long, complex, and expensive proposition. In fact, it is usually a last resort, resulting in about 1–2% of all patents ever involved in a litigation.[41] The items at the start of this paragraph are far more common uses for patents.

## Common Questions about Patents

### What Can Our Company Put "Patent Pending" On?

Writing "patent pending" can only be done if an actual patent application or provisional patent application has been filed with the national patent office. Putting this marking on a product that does not meet these criteria could result in liability.

While the mark of "patent pending" does not directly grant patent rights to the user, it serves to put potential future infringers on notice. Some companies hold the common misconception that they should always put patent pending on any invention. Yet, patent pending is not like trademark. This notice is does not grant the common-law rights that the symbol ™ does. Also, if the patent is not granted, it is not proper to keep this marking on the unpatented item. As a final consideration, in the United States, placing patent pending on a product when there is no patent application is a violation of 35 USC § 292. There are financial penalties for marking products incorrectly.

### Patent Agents and Patent Attorneys in the United States: What Is the Difference?

As you can see by all the information presented in this chapter, patent law is a complex legal specialty. It may not be surprising to learn that most attorneys practicing patent law have additional qualifications and specialized study. In the United Kingdom, becoming a patent attorney is a very different legal educational process from other attorneys. In the United States, law school is the same for all attorneys and all practicing attorneys are required to take a state bar to practice law, but only patent law has an additional examination necessary to be a "registered patent attorney." This exam covers patent law, and particularly the rules dealing with patent applications. The test is administered by the USPTO and may be taken by either attorneys or non-attorneys. One requirement for this exam is a college-level scientific or technical education. The exam is difficult and in some years only about 50% of people pass it. An attorney that passes this exam is considered a "patent attorney." A non-attorney that passes the exam is a "patent agent." Patent agents can aid in writing patent applications and other matters before the USPTO, but their abilities are more limited than registered patent attorneys.

## Rights of Publicity and Moral Rights

### Publicity Rights

Publicity rights, also known as rights of publicity, are sometimes considered an IP right because they are intangible property rights. Furthermore, these rights are considered in any creative endeavor that may use someone's image. Generally speaking, publicity rights are a set of rights that allow a person to control the commercial distribution of their own name, image, likeness, voice, or other identifiable representation of personality. Developers and publishers should be aware that this can include use of the distinctive voice, a nickname, a catch-phrase, or even tools of the trade for an individual.[42] This is the right that allows a celebrity to be paid to endorse a certain product and simultaneously allows that celebrity to prevent a business from faking an endorsement by that celebrity. The rights of publicity are similar to trade secret rights in that, in the United States, they are governed by state law. The state that matters is where the person currently lives. There is no federal registration process or federal law for publicity rights. These rights come about through state law statutes,[43] or some have come about merely through court cases with no statute behind them.[44] Importantly, there are state law statutes in many states responsible for the bulk of game development in the United States, including California, New York, Texas, Massachusetts, and Washington. Also, keep in mind that some states allow publicity rights to pass to a person's estate so they may be protected for a period even after death (see the table below). While some states have no post-mortem right of publicity, and most others are limited to a certain number of years, one state, Tennessee, the home of Elvis, has a perpetual right of publicity.

| States that Recognize the Right of Publicity for Deceased Persons | | | |
| --- | --- | --- | --- |
| California | Indiana | New Jersey | Tennessee |
| Connecticut | Kentucky | Ohio | Texas |
| Florida | Michigan | Oklahoma | Utah |
| Georgia | Nebraska | Pennsylvania | Virginia |
| Illinois | Nevada | South Carolina | Washington |

Publicity rights exist for several policy reasons. These include the idea that the right to one's identity is among the most fundamental human rights. It is also closely tied to the right of privacy, protecting a person from unwanted commercial exposure. Also, there is an argument that rights of publicity prevent fraud and unfair business practices that could derive from a fake endorsement.

Publicity rights are important in the game context in a few instances. First, using a person in a game or to advertise a game usually requires that person's permission. The same is true for using a person's voice or other recognizable characteristic. Failing to obtain the person's permission could result in a court granting an injunction to halt the sales of the game and/or awarding damages to the person whose image was used without consent. These damages will likely have a punitive characteristic on top of the court-derived fair market value for licensing the person's right of publicity. It is also possible that a developer or publisher could be required to remove the infringing use of the person's likeness, image, or other proprietary right. Finally, a game-maker could be left in the unenviable position of being forced to obtain a license from the aggrieved individual.

While the right of publicity can be a broad protection against unauthorized use, it is not without its limitations, including the First Amendment rights of a developer or publisher. However, to judge a video game right of publicity allegation against First Amendment protection, it is necessary to analyze the type of use. The First Amendment may allow the use of an individual's name, likeness, etc. when it is not intended solely to attract attention "to a work that is not related to the identified person" or used for "appropriating an individual's commercial value as a model rather than as part of a news or other communicative use."[45] In *Rogers v. Grimaldi*,[46] the court of appeals in New York created a test which questioned

(1) whether the product at issue is wholly unrelated to any underlying work incorporated therein, and (2) whether the use of the individual's name is merely a disguised commercial advertisement. This test sought to review whether use of a likeness in a product, like a video game, creates a misleading impression that the depiction demonstrated an endorsement. The "transformative use"[47] defense is also used to weigh right of publicity versus First Amendment protections in a video game and goes a step further than the *Rogers* test, and hinges on a determination of whether the purpose of the game merely exploits the name or likeness of a party for monetary purposes or whether the video game contributes distinctive and expressive content. While this may seem complex, in reality it comes down to whether the video game's main value is based on the creativity, skill, and reputation of the creator. If this can be demonstrated, then the transformative elements in a game should warrant it First Amendment protection.

Even with the *Rovers* test and the transformative use analysis, right of publicity suits have flourished in the video game industry for the past decade. From *Kirby v. Sega of America Inc.*[48] in 2006 to *No Doubt v. Activision Publ'g, Inc.*[49] in 2011, we have seen various musicians alleging that their rights of publicity have been infringed in games.[50] Many people in the video game industry believed that the Supreme Court's decision in *Brown v. Entertainment Merchants Association* in 2011, declaring that video games are protected by the First Amendment,[51] would end this type of claim. However, we have seen quite the opposite, specifically in the context of sports games.[52] In the *Keller v. Electronic Arts Inc.* and *Hart v. Electronic Arts, Inc.* cases, which dealt with the depiction of former NCAA college football players in games, the courts refused to find for the video game company on First Amendment grounds. The cases settled after the courts opined that neither game was sufficiently transformative to avoid a right of publicity suit.[53] We have also seen several right-of-publicity litigations brought by or on behalf of historically famous or infamous individuals, including John Dillinger,[54] Manuel Noriega,[55] and General George S. Patton[56] with varying degrees of success. Developers and publishers should also be aware that "fame" is not necessarily a requirement for bringing a right-of-publicity suit.[57]

When negotiating for a right of publicity, the most critical license terms are the territory, the term of the license, the way the likeness will be used, and whether or not the likeness will be used in advertising. Moreover, the subject of the license will likely ask for certain terms including review and approval rights over the actual in-game or advertising uses. For game industry uses in the 21st century, worldwide rights and a perpetual license are going to be preferable, but the cost to obtain these rights will reflect their broad nature. Another consideration is whether or not the game developer will require the services of the person to create voiceover or take motion-capture recordings. These fees will often be charged in addition to the mere likeness license.

Potential licensees should also be aware that in the United States most celebrities and actors are members of a guild for performing artists called SAG-AFTRA.[58] These guilds have additional requirements above and beyond contacted payments to the celebrity. Most critically, the Guild requires recurring payment for use of the celebrities and payments into the pension and health fund for the Guild.

Publicity rights in the way described above are unique to the United States. Other countries around the world have developed publicity rights that, on the whole, arise from the same fundamental policy reasons, that is, the human right to protect one's name and image coupled with the economic right to control its commercial exploitation though the implementation of those policy reasons in law varies around the world.

For example, in Commonwealth common-law countries, including the United Kingdom, Canada, and Australia, publicity rights have been created by case law,[59] drawing on the common-law rights of privacy and of passing off (or, in other words, by fusing together an individual's right not to have their person broadcast in public together with their right to avoid having their person associated with a product without authorization). However, these rights are not nearly as robust or as detailed as the U.S. system (reflecting, perhaps, these countries' reluctance to enshrine a formal or detailed publicity rights system). In other countries, including France,[60] Germany,[61] and the People's Republic of China,[62] publicity rights are part of statutory law, although, again, the degree of protection varies considerably. The moral rights doctrine (discussed further below) developed in many Francophone and European Union countries also has an impact on publicity rights to the extent that it permits a person to assert their right to be recognized as the true author of a work.

Consequently, when looking to license the likenesses or other brand usage of persons outside of the United States, it is worth bearing in mind that broadly similar legal considerations will apply—above all, the need to obtain a license from the relevant person(s). However, the exact manner of ensuring legal compliance, the costs of doing so, and the penalties for non-compliance will vary considerably from country to country.

## MORAL RIGHTS

Moral rights are a concept that originated in the civil law systems of France and Germany and spread from there, assisted in part by international treaties such as the Berne Convention.[63] Moral rights are rights granted to the authors of creative works to (1) be identified as the author of the work in certain circumstances, for example when copies are issued to the public; and (2) to object to derogatory treatment of the work or film that amounts to a distortion or mutilation or is otherwise prejudicial to the honor or reputation of the author. Moral rights are therefore rights concerned with protecting the reputation of an author. They are similar in a sense to publicity rights but are not as wide-reaching since they apply to an author's *work*, not to the author generally.

There are some important caveats regarding moral rights. The first is that they are personal to the author and cannot be assigned, transferred, or sold (although, in contracts, the owner of the moral rights will frequently try to give them as much force as possible). Second, a moral right has to be publicly *asserted* to be useable (which is why you will see, in many non-U.S. books, some wording at the very start explaining that the moral rights of the author are asserted). Third, the author can waive his or her moral rights; consequently, whenever there is an assignment (which is a written transfer of the author's rights, obligations, and benefits to another party), sale, or transfer of a copyright work, a well-drafted contract will include a waiving by the author of any corresponding moral rights. Lastly, moral rights do *not* apply to computer programs (meaning, in practice, computer code, but *not* related works such as game artwork). For all that, it is very rare for moral rights to cause issues in game development.

## IP STRATEGY 101

When looking at your bottom line, your IP is the lifeblood of your company. Here are some tips for how to best protect your IP in your day-to-day business.

### Have a Relationship With Experienced IP Counsel

At the risk of sounding repetitive, this cannot be said enough. And you should ideally find an attorney with game industry experience. This relationship is the beginning of educating the development team about IP rights surrounding the game project and building protections for those rights. This person can help developers of any size protect IP by drafting and reviewing documents and offering advice. Having this relationship ensures that the developer has taken the appropriate steps in advance of pitching the game. This relationship also ensures the best possible case-by-case advice while interacting with publishers or investors.

### Protect IP in Advance

Use trademarks properly, including using the appropriate symbol ($^{TM}$ or $^®$), when they are used in documents. Keep trade secrets, especially when pitching a game, and understand that sharing those secrets can jeopardize their protection. Publishers and other parties understand that developers cannot give away the farm—that some delicate information is proprietary is expected. Developers can always describe processes in general without going into detail. For copyright protection and date confirmation, developers should always write critical game design ideas out in detail and save concept art and early screen shots. Before pitching ideas to publishers and investors, discuss patent registration possibilities with your attorney. Finally, and most importantly, keep good records to document the earliest possible ownership, development, and use of the idea for all types of IP.

### Protecting IP When Pitching a Game to Publishers and Investors

Understand that publishers and investors want to limit their legal exposure and that many "standard" non-disclosure agreements (NDAs) are essentially one-sided documents to protect the other party and not you or your business. The development team should have its own NDA or a mutual NDA and ask if the publisher or investor would consider signing it. This negotiation can take some time and should be done before the pitch day. It is impolite and unprofessional to wait until the last minute to produce this document. Advice of IP counsel in this area is critical in drafting an NDA to protect the developer's interests and in deciphering the other party's NDA.

### The Process Is Complex, but Results Are Achievable

Since the process of protecting IP is often so complex and attorneys are a necessary part of it, why should a game developer even bother? First, a knowledgeable game developer can ask good questions when dealing with IP advisors, saving everyone time and money.

Second, a game developer familiar with IP may recognize the early warning signs of IP infringement in game development, before money is wasted on creating an infringing character, story line, or feature. In addition, much of IP protection requires planning and structure within the development company. An educated consumer of IP advice is best situated to understand that advice and implement structure within the company that protects IP. Most importantly, all the contracts and licenses surrounding games deal with IP, from the work-for-hire contracts for employees to publishing deals, royalty structures, and movie rights. Even though the developer is working with attorneys, the developer makes the final decisions and should know that the ultimate responsibility for protecting and selling the game rests on him or her. Given everything discussed in this chapter, that burden requires an understanding of this extremely important topic.

## Strategies for Small Companies and Individual Developers

Small companies and individual developers should concentrate on low-cost options to protect their IP. These companies do not usually have the staff or the resources necessary for elaborate IP strategy. Most of these companies will not even have a single employee tasked solely with developing and implementing an IP strategy.

The low-cost options for IP protection include simple copyright registration for commercially available products. The plan may also include federally registering the company's one or two most important marks to receive the ® designation or using™ to achieve common-law protection at the very least. The company's most important mark is usually the name or name/logo combination of the company. Trade secret processes are also relatively inexpensive and easy to put in place for a small company.

Small companies and individuals will probably not be as interested in international protection, but this option should be considered carefully for a company distributing their games over the internet. These companies will also be less interested in patent protection unless it is involved in the core business model, such as hardware development.

## Strategies for Large Developers and Publishers

Larger developers and publishers should implement everything in the lower-cost plan for small companies above, but should also expand IP protection to include more resource-intensive protection. This includes federally registering the trademark of all major titles released by the company. A developer or publisher may also want to file for a federal registration of the trademark to cover other categories of goods, especially if they intends to sell game-branded merchandise or otherwise enter into merchandise licensing agreements. This may also include international registration and policing of the company's most important trademarks. Additionally, as previously stated, a company may want to retain one of the third-party trademark monitoring companies to continually check for any infringing marks. Large publishers and developers should also consider filing separate copyright applications for music and other protectable components associated with game titles.[64]

An upgraded IP program may include building a patent portfolio. Some game companies pay bonuses to employees in the company that submit patentable ideas and help complete the patent process. After a company has developed and/or purchased a patent portfolio, larger companies should consider monetizing this portfolio by seeking out licensing partners. These patents can be used as friendly negotiating tools with partners to add value to negotiated transactions or they can be used offensively to force competitors into paying licensing fees or designing their product around the patented invention.

Patents, even though they are legally a purely offensive instrument, also have a certain perceived defensive value. This value comes from the fact that litigants often find companies with large patent portfolios to be "menacing." A large patent portfolio is usually indicative of the company having significant legal resources and sophistication. Of course, there is also the idea that a company with a large patent portfolio may file a counter-claim for patent infringement in any litigation against the company.

## Three Important Points

Before we conclude this chapter, let us take another look at all the different forms of IP and some of the important details (see the table below).

Even the largest game development and publishing companies can make trivial errors in IP protection that cost significant money or, worse, the rights to a whole game. These errors can sometimes be avoided with an introductory understanding of IP and a relationship with a competent, experienced attorney. Failing to take these steps is the metaphorical equivalent of leaving the city gates open and letting the Visigoths rush in.

| IP in the Game Industry | Patents | Trademark | Trade Secret | Copyright |
|---|---|---|---|---|
| Length | 20 years | Immortal | Immortal | 70–120 years |
| Cost | High | Medium | Medium | Low |
| Ease of obtaining | Tough | Medium | Medium | Easy |
| Use | Rare | Often | Often | Often |
| Registration? | Yes | Recommended | No | Recommended where available |
| Coverage | Medium | Narrow | Large | Large |

Game developers can take three steps to avoid these potentially disastrous IP pitfalls.

- First, developers should a have a basic understanding of IP protection and what it means to them, especially the areas that are most important to the creation of games. Sources of information include this chapter as well as the IGDA IP Rights White Paper. The IGDA White Paper was written by an international collection of attorneys and game developers with the goal of spreading IP information to the game development community. The White Paper is available for download free from the IGDA web site (http://www.igda.org/).

- As a second step, developers should have an attorney with broad experience in IP, especially trademark and copyright. This attorney, who may or may not be the same attorney used for other business issues, can help set up the most efficient and protective internal structures to protect IP. As discussed throughout this chapter, an attorney can also aid in negotiating the myriad of game contracts that are literally filled with IP-related language.

- Third, developers should ensure that their employees and contractors sign appropriate agreements assigning all the IP they produce to the company. These three steps are necessary to build solid legal defenses around valuable game property. It is not an understatement to say that the life and future of your game depends on it.

## NOTES

1. By S. Gregory Boyd and Jas Purewal. Gregory Boyd is partner and co-chairman of the Interactive Entertainment Department at Frankfurt, Kurnit, Klein, and Selz; Jas Purewal is partner and founder of Purewal & Partners. This IP chapter originally appeared in *Mastering the Game* by David Greenspan (2013) and was published by the World Intellectual Property Organization (WIPO). This version has been updated with new cases, dates, and discussions. The authors are grateful to Sean F. Kane for editing and updating this chapter.
2. Why Have Video Game Budgets Skyrocketed in Recent Years? *Forbes*, October 31, 2016: https://www.forbes.com/sites/quora/2016/10/31/why-have-video-game-budgets-skyrocketed-in-recent-years/#15606eaa3ea5.
3. See the WIPO study, *The Legal Status of Video Games: Comparative Analysis in National Approaches*, involving a survey of national legislation on copyright protection of video games covering the following jurisdictions: Argentina, Belgium, Brazil, Canada, China, Denmark, Egypt, Germany, India, Italy, Japan, Kenya, The Republic of Korea, Rwanda, Russia, Senegal, South Africa, Spain, Sweden, the United States, and Uruguay; and Andy Ramos, Laura Lopez, Anxo Rodriguez, Tim Meng, and Stan Abrams, "The Legal Status of Video Games: Comparative Analysis in National Approaches," World Intellectual Property Organization, July 2013.
4. Architectural works that are publicly viewable, when used as a general part of the scenery in games, do not normally require a license to be represented in a video game because of statutory exceptions. However, be wary of prominently featuring buildings (such as making them the focus of a game level), destroying buildings, using the interior of a building, or distinctive sculptural elements on the exterior of buildings, all of which may cause an issue. For example, Sony had an issue when it used the interior of Manchester Cathedral for in-game combat (http://en.wikipedia.org/wiki/Controversy_over_the_use_of_Manchester_Cathedral_in_Resistance:_Fall_of_Man).
5. The Copyright Office maintains a useful website at http://www.copyright.gov/ to help people through the process of copyright registration, and provides informational documents called Circulars. These Circulars, written in non-technical English, explain copyright registration and other topics for creative works. At the time of writing, the *Copyright Office Circular 61*, freely available on the website, gives detailed information about the copyright registration of computer and video games.
6. Examples of this include Middle Earth, Pandora from *Borderlands*, Mos Eisley from the *Star Wars* universe, Azeroth from *Warcraft*, and the post-apocalyptic world and cities in *Fallout*.
7. *Pac-Man* was the source of an early copyright infringement case against *K.C. Munchkin*. *Atari, Inc. v. North American*, 672 F.2d 607 (7th Cir. 1982).
8. *Atari Games Corp. v. Oman*, 979 F.2d 242 (D.C. Cir. 1992).
9. If you are unfamiliar with what *Breakout* looked like you can view the following link: https://upload.wikimedia.org/wikipedia/en/thumb/2/2b/Breakout2600.svg/1280px-Breakout2600.svg.png
10. Dan Pearson, Spry Fox wins ownership of Yeti Town as part of Triple Town settlement: Copyright case victory vindicates developers, gamesindustry.biz, October 15, 2012: http://www.gamesindustry.biz/articles/2012-10-15-spry-fox-wins-ownership-of-yeti-town-as-part-of-triple-town-settlement
11. *Atari, Inc. v. North American Philips Consumer Electronics Corp.*, 672 F.2d 607 (7th Cir. 1982)

12. U.S. Copyright Office, Frequently Asked Questions about Copyright: http://www.copyright.gov/help/faq/
13. This discusses what publication is, among other questions. U.S. Copyright Office, Definitions: http://www.copyright.gov/help/faq/faq-definitions.html
14. The annual revenue for *Angry Birds* in 2016 was 190.3 million Euros (or $225 million). Annual revenue generated by Rovio Entertainment from 2010 to 2017, Statista: https://www.statista.com/statistics/579828/rovio-revenue/
15. David Jenkins, Midway sue Sony Ericsson, Gamasutra, July 2, 2004: http://www.gamasutra.com/view/news/94949/Midway_Sue_Sony_Ericsson.php
16. Operation Buccaneer Wikipedia entry, last modified December 14, 2017: http://en.wikipedia.org/wiki/Operation_Buccaneer, and Tor Thorsen, Game pirate gets four years jail time, Game Spot, February 12, 2004: http://www.gamespot.com/news/game-pirate-gets-four-years-jail-time-6089247
17. See for example the UK case of *Nintendo Company Ltd &Anor v Playables Ltd &Anor* [2010] EWHC 1932 (Ch) (28 July 2010) available at http://www.bailii.org/ew/cases/EWHC/Ch/2010/1932.html
18. Having said that no copyright infringement exists, trademark infringement has still been alleged in certain circumstances. In 2012. EA sued Textron (makers of Bell Helicopters), seeking a declaratory judgment concerning its right to include Bell Helicopter trademarks in its game. The case settled in 2013 following the court's decision to not dismiss Textron's trademark claims. In May 2013, EA publicly announced that it would no longer license any weaponry for use in its games. Malathi Nayak, Video game maker drops gun makers, not their guns, Reuters Market News, May 7, 2013: http://www.reuters.com/article/2013/05/07/video games-guns-idUSL2N0CS2A220130507.
19. See the Fort Apache case discussing a Paul Newman film: *Walker v. Time Life Films, Inc.,* 784 F.2d 44 (2d Cir. 1986).
20. P. B. Hugenholtz, Martin Senftleben, Fair Use in Europe: In Search of Flexibilities, November 14, 2011 available at http://papers.ssrn.com/sol3/papers.cfm?abstract_id=1959554.
21. Although some countries, such as the United Kingdom, are enacting or proposing to enact specific copyright infringement defences for parody works.
22. With modern chemical analytic methods, discovering the composition of any food product borders on trivial, but this is a well-known example in the legal field.
23. By "skeleton" level, we mean a basic outline structure that can be added to and changed by the developers as they polish the level.
24. For a list of more exotic trademarks, see the Sound trademark Wikipedia entry, last modified May 7, 2018: this Wiki article. http://en.wikipedia.org/wiki/Sound_trademark, and the Tiffany Blue Wikipedia entry, last modified February 2, 2018: http://en.wikipedia.org/wiki/Tiffany_Blue
25. Tony Smith, Microsoft buys Xbox name off true owner, The Register, June 18, 2001: http://www.theregister.co.uk/2001/06/18/microsoft_buys_xbox_name_off/
26. Todd Bishop, Microsoft ends development of "Mythica" game, *Seattle Post-Intelligencer,* March 15, 2011: http://www.seattlepi.com/business/article/Microsoft-ends-development-of-Mythica-game-1137016.php
27. The USPTO has online forms that can be used for filing purposes. U.S. Trademark Office Online Forms: https://www.uspto.gov/trademarks-application-process/filing-online
28. There are law firms and companies that specialize in searching for infringing uses of trademarks. These companies can perform searches on a regular schedule and send your game development company reports on potential infringers. As with most types of IP, one of the early steps in policing the IP is sending a "cease and desist" letter. Later steps can include litigation over the trademark.
29. This is done by application to an EU organization called the Office for Harmonisation in the Internal Market (OHIM): http://oami.europa.eu/ows/rw/pages/index.en.do

30. World Intellectual Property Organization (WIPO) Website explaining the Madrid protocol: http://www.wipo.int/madrid/en/

31. Trademark Manual of Examining Procedure (TMEP) section 1202.08(b): What Does Not Constitute a Single Creative Work. Interestingly, coloring books allow a user to trademark titles for a single version as well.

32. History of United States patent law Wikipedia entry, last modified April 23, 2018: http://en.wikipedia.org/wiki/History_of_United_States_patent_law

33. The America Invents Act in 2011 was the first change to the patent system since 1952. See Leahy-Smith America Invents Act Wikipedia entry, last modified February 16, 2018: http://en.wikipedia.org/wiki/Leahy-Smith_America_Invents_Act

34. European Patent Office, When will unitary patents be available? September 17, 2017: HYPERLINK http://www.epo.org/law-practice/unitary/unitary-patent/start.html

35. 35 § U.S.C. 101.

36. The prohibition derives from a provision in the Convention that "programs for computers" are excluded from patentability to the extent that a patent application relates to a computer program "as such." This rather ambiguous phrase has been interpreted in different ways over time, though at the time of writing the trend seems to be toward loosening up the European hostility to software patents. For example, software patenting has been permitted on the basis that it has a technical effect on *hardware* or even that the software permitted other software to work significantly better.

37. Utility patents derive from the German concept of *Gebrauchsmuster*, or the utility model for patents. See Gebrauchsmuster Wikipedia entrey, last modified April 15, 2016: http://en.wikipedia.org/wiki/Gebrauchsmuster

38. Greg Boyd, Nintendo Entertainment System—expired patents do not mean expired protection, Gamasutra, November 11, 2005: http://www.gamasutra.com/view/feature/2457/nintendo_entertainment_system__.php

39. United States Patent and Trademark Office, 2590 Acceptance of Delayed Payment of Maintenance Fee in Expired Patent to Reinstate Patent [R-08.2017], last modified January 24, 2018: http://www.uspto.gov/web/offices/pac/mpep/s2590.html

40. Leahy-Smith America Invents Act Wikipedia entry, last modified February 16, 2018: http://en.wikipedia.org/wiki/Leahy-Smith_America_Invents_Act

41. *Brown v. Entertainment Merchants Association*, 564 U.S. 786 (2011) https://www.supremecourt.gov/opinions/10pdf/08-1448.pdf, and Gene Quinn, Patent litigation statistics: 1980–2010, IPWatchDog, March 24, 2012: and http://www.ipwatchdog.com/2011/08/02/patent-litigation-statistics-1980-2010/id=17995/

42. In 1974 a court found that tobacco company Winston's use of doctored photo infringed the rights of racecar driver Lothar Motschenbacher even though his facial features were not visible.

43. *California:* Cal Civil Code § 3344-3344.1. (Prohibits the unauthorized commercial use of name, voice, signature, photograph or likeness. Allows the rights of a deceased personality to continue for 70 years after the death of the personality.).
    *Florida:* Fla. Stat. § 540.08 (prohibits the unauthorized publication or use for commercial or advertising purposes of the name or likeness of any person which continues for 40 years after their death).*Illinois:* Ill. Rev. Stat. ch. 765 § 1075/1 *et seq.* (an individual has the right to controlling whether and how to use their identity for commercial purposes. This right continues for 50 years after death).
    *Indiana:* Ind. Code § 32-36 (prohibits the unauthorized "commercial use" of a personality's name, voice, signature, photograph, image, likeness, distinctive appearance, gestures, or mannerisms. Several exceptions are listed; for example literary works, musical compositions, fine art. This right continues for 100 years after their death).
    *Kentucky:* Ky. Rev. Stat. § 391.170 (prohibits the unauthorized commercial use of the name or likeness of a "person who is a public figure" until 50 years after their death).

*Massachusetts*: Mass. Gen. Laws Ann. ch. 214, § 3A (Prohibits the unauthorized use of name, portrait, or picture of a person for advertising or trade purposes.).

*Nebraska*: Neb. Rev. Stat. § 20-202 (Prohibits the exploitation of a natural person's name, picture, portrait, or personality for advertising or commercial purposes, as an invasion of privacy.).

*Nevada*: Nev. Rev. Stat. § 597.770-597.810 (Prohibits the unauthorized commercial use of any person's name, voice, signature, photograph or likeness during life and continuing for 50 years after death.).

*New York*: N.Y. Civil Rights Law § 50, 51 (Prohibits the unauthorized use for advertising or trade purposes, of the name, portrait, or picture of any living person.).

*Ohio*: Ohio Rev. Code Ann. § 2741.01 *et seq.* (Prohibits the unauthorized use of "any aspect of an individual's persona" for commercial purposes during life and for 60 years after death.).

*Oklahoma*: Okla. Stat. tit 12, § 1448, 1449. (Prohibits the unauthorized use of another's name, voice, signature, photograph, or likeness, in any manner, on or in products, merchandise, or goods for the purposes of advertising or selling. This right continues for 100 years after death.).

*Pennsylvania*: Pa. Cons. Stat. tit. 42, § 8316. (Prohibits the unauthorized use of name or likeness.).

*Rhode Island*: R.I. Gen. Laws § 9-1-28, 9-1-28.1(a)(2) (Prohibits unauthorized use of any person's name, portrait, or picture for advertising or trade purposes.).

*Tennessee*: Tenn. Code Ann. § 47-25-1102, -1103, -1104, -1105, -1106, -1107 (Prohibits the unauthorized use of an individual's name, photograph, or likeness in any medium for the purposes of advertising, fund raising, or solicitation of donations or purchases. The right continues for 10 years after death.).

*Texas*: Tex. Property Code Ann. § 26.001 et seq. (Prohibits the unauthorized use of a deceased individual's name, voice, signature, photograph, or likeness in any manner, including commercial and advertising uses for 50 years after death. This law does not apply to the rights of living individuals.).

*Utah*: Utah Code Ann. § 45-3-1 *et seq.* (Prohibits unauthorized commercial use of an individual's personal identity in a way that expresses or implies approval or endorsement of a product or subject matter.).

*Virginia*: Va. Code § 8.01-40. (Prohibits the unauthorized use of a person's name, portrait, or picture for advertising or trade purposes until 20 years after their death).

*Washington*: Wash. Rev. Code § 63.60.010 *et seq.* (Provides every individual or personality with a property right in the use of their name, voice, signature, photograph, or likeness. The protections for an *Individual*, that is, a natural person, continue until 10 years after their death, while the right of a *Personality*, that is, any individual whose "publicity" has commercial value, continues for 75 years after their death).

*Wisconsin*: Wis. Stat. § 895.50(2)(b). (Prohibits the unauthorized use for advertising or trade purposes of the name, portrait, or picture of any living person.).

44. The following states have common law Publicity Rights: Alabama, Arizona, Connecticut, Georgia, Hawaii, Michigan, Minnesota, Missouri, New Hampshire, New Jersey, South Carolina, and West Virginia.

45. Restatement (Third) of Unfair Competition §47, Cmt. c (1995).

46. 875 F.2d 994 (2d Cir. 1989).

47. *Comedy III Prods. Inc. v. Gary Saderup Inc.*, 25 Cal. 4th 387, 407 (2001).

48. Kierin Kirby claimed that use of her likeness and catch-phrase in a video game violated her right of publicity. The court held that Sega's decision to set the game in space and make the character a space-reporter, instead of a musician, was sufficiently transformative to avoid any liability.

49. The musical group *No Doubt* sued the publisher of *Band Hero*, alleging right-of-publicity violations arising from the use of avatars representing the band in the game. The court held that Activision's use was not transformative as the avatars were performing the same activity by which *No Doubt* achieved its fame.

50. The band *The Romantics* also sued Activision in 2008, alleging that the game *Guitar Hero* violated their rights, but the case was ultimately dismissed.

51. The Supreme Court strongly held that video games qualify for First Amendment protection and that the "basic principles of freedom of speech … do not vary" with the creation of a new and different communication medium. Specifically, the court stated that "[l]ike the protected books, plays, and movies that preceded them, video games communicate ideas—and even social messages—through many familiar literary devices (such as characters, dialogue, plot and music) and through features distinctive to the medium (such as the player's interaction with the virtual world). That suffices to confer First Amendment protection."

52. In *Brown v. Electronic Arts Inc.*, former football great Jim Brown filed a suit against EA based on unauthorized video game use of his image and player statistics. In granting EA's motion to dismiss, the court opined that EA's use was protected by the First Amendment.

53. In Hart, the court held that "[i]f a product is being sold that predominantly exploits the commercial value of an individual's identity, that product should be held to violate the right of publicity and not be protected by the First Amendment, even if there is some 'expressive' content in it that might qualify as 'speech' in other circumstances. If, on the other hand, the predominant purpose of the product is to make an expressive comment on or about a celebrity, the expressive value could be given greater weight."

54. In 2011 a court granted a motion to dismiss in *Dillinger LLC v. Electronic Arts Inc.* finding that EA's use of Dillinger's name in a game was protected by the First Amendment and that Dillinger had no right of publicity protections since he had died prior to the statute becoming effective.

55. In 2014, a court dismissed *Noriegav. Activision Blizzard* since Activision Blizzard's First Amendment rights trumped any right of publicity protections Noriega might be due. The court also found that Noriega was so infamous that it was inconceivable that his reputation could have been damaged by his inclusion in the game. Finally, the court looked at the game as a whole and considered Noriega's limited use to be sufficiently transformative.

56. As previously stated, the claims in *CMG v. Maximum Family Games*, involving the inclusion of General Patton in the game *Legends of War: Patton*, were settled in 2014 following the filing of a motion to dismiss.

57. In 2005, *Topheavy Studios v. Doe* was filed, which involved the publishing of a video game that contained images of an underage plaintiff exposing her breasts that had been taken at a trivia contest on South Padre Island. The case resulted in a temporary restraining order being issued barring the further production of copies of the game.

58. SAG and AFTRA were two independent guilds for more than 60 years. They merged in 2012 to create the combined guild, which essentially represents every American actor or celebrity of prominence. http://www.sagaftra.org/

59. See, for example, *Re Pacific Dunlop Limited v. Paul Hogan and Ors* [1989] FCA 185 in Australia (the "Crocodile Dundee" case) or *Robyn Rihanna Fenty v. Arcadia* [2013] EWHC 2310 (Ch) (the "Rihanna t-shirts" case) in the United Kingdom.

60. See Article 9 of the French Civil Code and Article 226-1 of the French Criminal Code, which together enshrine the right to "respect of private life" and impose penalties on persons infringing it.

61. In Germany, the doctrine of publicity rights is known as the "Allgemeines Persönlichkeitsrecht" and is derived from the German constitution, the German Civil Code and court decisions.

62. See Article 99 of the General Principles of Civil Law of the People's Republic of China

63. Berne Convention Wikipedia entry, last modified May 5, 2018: https://en.wikipedia.org/wiki/Berne_Convention.

64. Larger projects often have more protectable IP and large developers have the resources to spread the protection around. More registrations often result in more potential claims if there is a theft down the road. So, a large developer with multiple filings can litigate several registrations and several different types of IP in one case and has more granular coverage if just one element is taken (such as just taking the music from a game).

# CHAPTER 4

# Negotiating Key Game Agreements

## WHAT DOES IT REALLY MEAN TO "NEGOTIATE"?

Whenever one person talks to another about a deal, there are a lot of moving parts. How experienced are both people in buying or selling this item or service? How clever are the parties involved? How well do the parties understand the rules and strategies of negotiation? Last and most important, how much does each party want to do the deal?

The first three questions are fairly self-explanatory. Experienced, bright people who know negotiation strategies are pretty obviously going to perform better than people who do not have those tools. The fourth element above—"how much does each party want the deal"—is more complicated. To begin to unpack that question, negotiation studies have created a term called BATNA.

BATNA stands for Best Alternative to Negotiated Agreement. Consider buying apples at the local farmers' market. You can walk up and down the lanes, looking at the apples in the different stands. You can judge the quality of the apples and then compare the prices. If you think a stand is too expensive, you do not have to buy from it. If one stand is very cheap, but the apples are rotten, you do not have to buy from it either. You have a lot of choices at the farmers' market. When you are at one apple stand, your BATNA is to walk to the next stand.

Contrast that experience with hiring a superstar CEO or landing a big publishing agreement. There are not that many superstar CEOs out there. There are not that many publishers interested in each game (for most developers). You have to be more careful with those negotiations than you are at the farmers market. Your BATNA is worse if the deal falls through. Put another way, supply and demand alters negotiation power.

## STRATEGY AND PLANNING: WALKING AWAY

Know your goals going into any negotiation. Do we have to get at least 3 million dollars for the development of this mobile game? Do we prefer to pay the CEO less than $250,000 as a base salary and not give up more than 3% of equity in the company? All other things being equal, the party that knows what they want going into a negotiation will do better than one that does not know what they want.

One goal that should always be considered is the "walk-away" point. If the CEO asks for more than a $250,000 base, we will have to move to the next candidate. If we cannot get at least 3 million dollars, we cannot develop the game to our standards. If the film company will not indemnify us for the movie IP, it is too risky to make the game because we may get into litigation. You should write down the "walk-away" point prior to going into the negotiation because it is so easy to get caught up in the discussion and fall in love with the deal. After the agreement is signed, it is very difficult to back out.

## EMOTIONAL POSITIONING

Is it best to be compromising or aggressive? Anyone that answers this question with one answer or the other is wrong. Anyone that has just one style is going to fail in negotiation at least half of the time. The different postures are just tools. Sometimes you need a hammer and other times you need a saw. One cannot be substituted for the other. Normally, it is best to start out nice and compromising and only move to an aggressive position if forced to do so. Compromisers respond well to other compromisers, as do some aggressive people, as long as they are still perceiving progress toward their goals. Aggression is useful when another aggressive negotiator refuses to respond to a compromising posture, or when you need to force a final position from a compromiser. Aggression can also be useful when the other side is obviously in the wrong and is offering an off-market position: *surely, Disney, you are not saying that we have to continue working if you are not paying us.*

Remember, you can always go from nice to aggressive, but it is very difficult to go the other way. People remember when someone is aggressive, especially if it includes a personal affront. People take insults personally. But true insults are rare. The more common problem is implying something that people take personally. The most common example is a party stating or implying they know more about an industry or have more experience in a negotiation subject. Something as simple as saying that a definition/section/price term is standard in the game industry really says that the person speaking knows a basic piece of industry knowledge and the other side does not. This pushes on the other side's insecurities and may create a personal affront. Normally, it is not even a true statement. Retreating to a "standard" argument is a refuge for the ignorant and weak in this author's experience. Very few things are standard. When they are, every person in the negotiation knows it and it does not need to be said. Saying something is standard is an aggressive negotiation tactic designed to establish an experiential superiority and shame the other side into accepting the deal. The right answer to that tactic is to say that, *"even if it is standard, it will not work in this deal because..."* That rejoinder does not admit that the position is standard while simultaneously showing that you will not fall for that tactic.

## DIAGNOSING A PROBLEM

When people do not agree or appear not to agree, your first thought should be to ask "why?" "Why?" is the key to diagnosing a problem and figuring a way through it. The next step is to ask more questions. A good second question is "can you tell me more about that?"

Often people will literally explain the way through a problem just by answering those two questions. Do you really disagree on ownership of the final product or do you really just disagree on control of the distribution of the product? Do you really disagree on price, or is it perhaps just the upfront development pricing, and can the difference be made up in the royalty?

This distinction is key because a perceived disagreement can often be resolved through questioning and subsequent drafting. Compare this with an actual disagreement—which can only be resolved by one company giving ground to the other.

## GOOD VERSUS BAD BUSINESS DEVELOPMENT

After you ask "why?" and "can you tell me more?", you will learn whether the issue can be addressed in the drafting or whether it is an actual difference of opinion. This is a core distinction when working with attorneys. Attorneys can make suggestions and help you to ask questions. They can help you sort out something that needs to be discussed more from items where there is real disagreement. They can also draft language when you agree on the details of how you want something to work in practice. They can negotiate on behalf of the company, if they are empowered to do so. All negotiations are easier if everyone agrees about when a deal is ready to go to contract. The majority of deals that do not close were not ready to go to contract. The parties do not really agree on fundamental issues and drafting starts too soon. How do we avoid that outcome? Make certain that the key elements of the deal are worked out prior to moving to contract writing. If you fully negotiate the elements summarized below, you dramatically increase the chances of a successful negotiation.

Conversely, failing to work through the items below prior to documenting the deal is a failure of business development. We want to avoid what would qualify as bad business development. When I see this, I often refer to it as used-car business development, because that is the skill displayed. It looks like this: we have some idea on price and some idea on what we are buying, and then we are told "now go paper this." That is a hand grenade of molten shit, not a real deal. And yet, this problem is much more common than it should be. We avoid it by working through the seven core items below:

## INTELLECTUAL PROPERTY, TERM, TERMINATION, INDEMNITY, PRICE, PAYMENT, NET REVENUE

These items are important in almost every deal in the game industry. Licenses, publisher agreements, and even employment agreements can touch these items.

- *Price*: What is the price for this deal and how is it paid? Is it spread out, up front, or on the back-end? Does it require invoicing prior to the payment or is the payment just made?

- *Term and termination*: How long does the deal run for? Can it be extended? How can it be terminated? Is the termination for breach alone or can it be for convenience as well? In the event of termination, what is paid out and when?

- *Ownership*: Who is going to own what is made under the agreement? Does it make a difference how it is developed? Is there a license back? If there is a game, who will make sequels?

- *Indemnity*: Indemnity is about who covers any third-party damages related to an agreement. What if there is a privacy or other regulatory violation? Or an infringement of third-party intellectual property? Who pays? Indemnity is like children at a party. If your child breaks something, you pay for it. If someone else's kid breaks something, they pay for it. In deals, the question is: Whose kids are whose? Who covers what in a transaction?

## Show Me the Money

They say that possession is nine-tenths of the law. Whenever possible, on either side of an agreement, try to be the person that receives the money directly. Historically, in the publisher–developer context, the publisher always received the money from distributors. Modern distribution through platforms like iTunes and Steam has changed this. Now, it is possible for games to be distributed through the developer's account. In those cases, the publisher receives the royalty split from the developer.

In theory, this should not matter, but in practice it matters a great deal. The party that receives the money first controls how deductions are made and has the initial view of critical sales data.

In a dispute between the parties, the first thing that happens is all payments are suspended and are usually held in escrow. Holding the money is key in a dispute. Refunds outside of a litigation are rare, so people tend to hold on to revenue until a settlement is reached. Payments are the lifeblood of both companies, but especially to the developer. The company that is holding game revenue is in a much more powerful negotiating position.

After you have done dozens of agreements of a particular type, there is an inclination to omit initial negotiations and skip to the end. You have a pretty good idea of how it is going to work out and you might want to just draft the agreement to that point and hold it there. This is a mistake. A colleague once told me that you "have to dance the dance." Rationally, this does not make the most sense. But there is something about going through the process that people find satisfying. There is an educational element for both parties: issues are fully explored, and people get comfortable working together. As a result, pushing for a consensus draft right away usually results in failure and the party that proposes it often loses more ground than they should. The other party still wants to "dance the dance" and press for more concessions.

## Deal Pace and Process

Two commonly discussed terms around the pace of a negotiation are deal fatigue and deal momentum. Depending on corporate needs and the size of a transaction, a deal may take a few days to several months. During that time, be aware of both of these concepts. They are psychological, not legal, but they have huge effects.

Deal fatigue is when one side appears to lose interest in the deal and may actually lose interest in the deal—not because it has suddenly become a bad deal—but because they are tired of negotiating it. Deal fatigue manifests itself in two ways. First, in some cases, people cancel the deal or genuinely lose interest in it. They say the opposing party is "too difficult to work with" as a reason to stop negotiating. This is not helpful to the negotiation. Deal fatigue can also take the form of people giving up points they should not have, or drafting quickly (and sloppily) just to tick an issue off the box.

Deal momentum is the idea that frequent drafts, emails, meetings, and calls keep everyone focused on and interested in the deal. The party that benefits most from keeping up deal momentum is the party that needs to get the deal done. Does the developer need money to make payroll? Does the publisher have to close the deal prior to the end of its fiscal year to get money off the books? But be careful: pushing deal momentum can result in rushing through items that should not be rushed through. You have to balance the benefits of keeping the ball rolling against the risk of a drafting or tactical mistake.

Both deal fatigue and deal momentum are real and substantial factors in a negotiation. They are difficult to control, but the first step in using them to your advantage is to recognize them and recognize the effects they have on the negotiation. Know that very sophisticated negotiators manage deal momentum and deal fatigue to increase leverage and generate other advantages for their side.

## Preparing for a Meeting or Call

### When Do You Have a Call or an In-Person Meeting?

One common business development failing is to ask for a call too early, on the theory that going straight to a phone call (or an in-person meeting) will avoid some negotiating hurdles. Asking for a call or meeting too early is done in the name of keeping up deal momentum, but in practice it can slow things down substantially. Remember: you have to dance the dance. There are psychological and actual structural/process-oriented reasons for doing the first couple of rounds on paper. Many of the common issues presented in a first draft of a document are not actual misunderstandings, they are just drafting issues that are easily solved by exchanging a draft or two. Simple items like honing representations and warranties or setting up invoicing terms do not require a meeting of any type. Those items are best sorted out by exchanging a draft or two. While this takes time and is frustrating to people that do not understand the optimal process, doing a couple of initial rounds on paper usually ends up being the fastest way. When people see a mark-up and have a chance to think about something, they do not have to take an immediate position or dig into any particular view. If people start round one in person or on the phone, then they become wedded to ideas that do not deserve that kind of attention, and that removes the attention from larger issues.

After a few drafts are exchanged, the real issues will surface. These are items that need to be discussed, explained, and negotiated. If a call or meeting is called too early, then people spend hours talking about less important things like "What kind of invoicing software do you use, and where is your corporate form registered?" It is a tremendous waste of time and always points toward incompetent business development and process management.

If people really want to hurry, they exchange two drafts over two to three days and then have a focused meeting on the last remaining items.

## When to Have a Call and When Not to Have a Call

The perfect time to have a call is right after the basics have been sorted out in initial drafts. Ninety-five percent of deals for day-to-day operational items are closed without ever having to talk to the other side. Calls or meetings are important when there are larger, more difficult issues that need sorting out. Those issues require the higher bandwidth communication that a meeting provides.

In some cases, you may choose not to have a meeting or a call. This usually arises after drafts have been exchanged and there have been one or more meetings/calls. Then, there are usually just one or two issues left. In some cases, those issues are so black and white that there is no reason to discuss them. Consider the negotiating power of telling the other side that you do not want to have a call on a particular issue. If done deliberately, it conveys a seriousness about the issue that no other technique provides. The language below is a firm but polite way of using the "no call" strategy.

> *I do not want to waste your time and I do not want to give you the wrong impression that there is any daylight on this issue. We are not negotiating this point, we are expressing a requirement for the transaction. [Alternatively: We are not negotiating this point, we are explaining it.]*

If used properly and carefully, this technique is a powerful way of getting your final negotiation points quickly and in a form that you want them (often without changes). Of course, beware of over-using the "no call" strategy or using it too soon. Do not violate the basic rule—you have to dance the dance. You may think that using the "no call" strategy can work to get all of your points right at the beginning or you use it as a Hail Mary when you are experiencing deal fatigue. This tactic can really only be used at the very end on one or two final points and only when you absolutely need them to be a certain way. Also, it works best when the point is simple. If you completely need to have X dollars to move forward or need the royalty rate to be set at Y percent, or you refuse to have a "catch-all" term in the net revenue deduction—those are places this tactic works best.

## Honesty

Nothing is less productive in a negotiation than dishonesty—which can often take the form of bluffing or outright lying. You will eventually get caught, and the consequences will be high. You are building credibility over the course of a negotiation, and over the course of your career. And it's very difficult to recover lost credibility. The only forgivable way to substantially change course or alter your negotiating position occurs when your superiors give you certain marching orders to start with (*"do not accept less than 20 million"*) but then change their minds. But in any situation other than that, you should definitely never lie and never be seen to "bluff" or substantially change your position.

## Issues List

After doing a mark-up of a draft, and prior to a meeting, one side may say to the other, "There are a lot of comments in this document, can you send us a list of your major issues?" Sometimes this is framed as "to narrow the issues for a call" or because the other party is "so busy and has never seen a mark-up this heavy on their document." This is a basic trap that you can use to your advantage on an unknowing counter-party. But you should not fall for it. First, notice that if you force the other side to do at least one return draft and dance the dance, you cannot fall into this trap. This request shows that the requesting party is either (a) lazy and does not want to adequately review the document or (b) sophisticated and trying to see if you will fall for their ploy. The problem, of course, is that the party that provides a list of their "major issues" essentially concedes all of the other points in the document. They are saying that A–G are important to us and H–Z are less important. So, not only has the party providing the list revealed their priorities, they have also discarded items that they may have traded on, and the other side will not take any of those other points seriously. So, beware of this common trap.

## Negotiating Against Yourself

Providing an issues list is a way of negotiating against yourself. The other side has not offered anything. And yet, here you are—giving things away. Beware of other types of negotiating against yourself. Another common tactic in this area occurs when your opponent says, "you are going to have to do better than that." By saying that, they are offering no counter-proposal; they are just baldly requesting that you improve your position in their favor. Always force a counter-proposal whenever you can.

## During a Call or Meeting

During a call or meeting, consider the following tactics to get ahead, and be prepared if anyone tries to use them on you:

### Appeal to a Higher Authority or White Knight

In some cases, you may want to table an idea or not make a decision on a certain point. Perhaps you do not have the authority to concede or approve a certain point. In those situations, you might say, "I will need to take that back to my team," or "I need to check with [Insert senior colleague] on that." That is commonly said in negotiations and people may not think anything when they hear it, but they should. It is an appeal to a higher authority. It is a temporizing measure that allows you to pause discussions on an issue. It is also a hint that a certain issue may be sensitive. It is a layered authority approach, allowing the first negotiators to take a hard line on a certain point and then back away from that line toward the end of the negotiation when the "higher authority" or "white knight" comes in to break the impasse.

Be careful to not use this maneuver too often. If you always have to check with someone else, then the other side may get the impression that you are not empowered to negotiate the deal. The layered authority maneuver also provides a second bite at the apple.

If you want to reopen an issue, you can say that the deal cannot be finalized "until the (CFO/CEO) signs off on it." People may use that as a way to go through the agreement, build goodwill and come back at the end for a final push on a few issues. They will come back and say, "I'm sorry but the (CFO/CEO) will not sign off on this unless we (get the payment terms down/change the price/improve the indemnity)" etc.

## Silence

People have an intense desire to fill silences. There are two main uses for silence. The first is more information. On the phone or in person in a meeting, you can often get people to give you more information by just not saying anything. It sets up an interesting power dynamic where they feel they have to fill the space. The second use of silence is in closing a point when you have explained your position and it appears that talking more would only hurt your side. There is a great scene in the 1984 classic Pulitzer Prize-winning play Glengarry Glen Ross, by David Mamet.[1] In that scene, one of the salesmen describes selling some land to a couple at their home. He sits at the kitchen table and has them prepared to sign. He holds the pen out, sitting in silence, knowing that the next one to say anything loses.

## Locking in an Admission

Walls are not built with single stones. In negotiations, you often have to lead someone down a path to get where you need to go. It is critical to see the path and all of the emotional, financial, and logical steps to get to the desired goal. Consider when someone says that, if they could have more time, they could have built the game for less money. A potential employee might say they do not mind assigning all the IP to the company as long as you exclude their side project. A publisher may say they are not going to indemnify a developer because they are not providing materials. You might ask,—"But if you were providing materials, you would indemnify for those, wouldn't you?" These are valuable admissions. In those cases, where the intermediate step is necessary to get to a larger goal, I usually repeat that back to them in the meeting. I get them to say "yes" in front of other people. When necessary, I remind them of the admission. Lastly, I often include it in some way in the documentation so they cannot go back on it later.

## Anchoring

A concept similar to locking in an admission is the behavioral advertising concept of anchoring. Anchoring is using one number at the start of the discussion with the knowledge that people are psychologically predisposed to work around that number. Biologically, we have a bizarre and powerful susceptibility to build a negotiation around the first numbers we hear. We have extensively studied that people will start a discussion on everything from the potential salary of a computer programmer to guessing the number of countries in the UN, based around literally random numbers they hear before the negotiation. Whenever possible, be the person that frames the negotiation with your numbers.[2]

### This is Standard

Saying something is standard is an interesting negotiation technique. Very few things are standard. What you are really communicating is that you believe you know more than the person you are negotiating against and they should take your word for it. Consider how this makes the other person feel. If you have enormous leverage or an enormous experience gap over the person you are negotiating with, this may work. However, using the same line on someone more experienced than you will undermine your authority. They will know that you either (a) actually think incorrectly that this is standard or (b) tried to use a simplistic negotiation trick on them. How often does saying that something is standard or "corporate policy" actually work? It depends on how close to immovable something is, how much it is actually an industry standard, and the leverage differential between the parties. Saying that a price, net revenue definition, or an indemnity is standard is going to be very hard to sell. Saying Apple's developer terms or Steam's platform terms are standard is going to be easier to sell. Keep in mind that, for enough money and with enough leverage, even standard documents and clauses with industry titans can change. Do not take this as the final answer if something is important to you.

Now that we have reviewed a number of general strategies and concepts, consider how those might play out in one of the most important agreements in game development: the publisher agreement.

## KEY POINTS IN THE PUBLISHER AGREEMENT

### Price and Performance

How much does it take to make the game? Pricing is usually related to a calculation of development hours plus normal additional costs. How many hours of production, art, coding, and administration are going to be required to build the game? Plus, there are fixed costs for office space, legal, accounting, and insurance, and there are always unexpected issues to account for. Perhaps, if a developer is very good, the developer can pad the pricing with some expected profit margin prior to a royalty collection.

How do you measure success? This is difficult, but prior to launch it is even more difficult to measure quality than it is to measure it post-launch. During development prior to launch, there will be a Game Design Document (GDD), which is essentially a specification for the creation of the game. Ideally, it will contain as much detail as possible on what will be in the final game: how many levels, how many playable characters, and what those levels and characters will be able to do. This is only the beginning, but imagine thinking about something simple like how many trees are in the game or what the concept art looks like. How do you judge that beyond a certain production quality? Even more complex, how about overall game design decisions or story decisions? These may be generally described in a GDD, but judgment on the final product is usually made by the publisher.

After the game is launched, the measurements can be more quantitative. What is the Metacritic score 30 days after launch? How many copies have been downloaded? What are the sales? How many monthly or daily active users do we have? What is the revenue for virtual property or DLC ?

## Using Scales for Upside or Downside Protection

After the development budget, there is often a royalty associated with a game. How much should a person pay for a license or a game, or for anything for that matter? That depends on what each person thinks the benefit will be. If you think a film license combined with your game will earn 2 million dollars, it may be worth 1 million to buy it. What if it only earns half a million dollars ? When two people disagree on the value of something, one way to move past that is to use a sliding compensation scale. The issue is time and the unknowns in the future. If both people had a perfect crystal ball, they may be able to agree on a royalty rate. Using a scale, the parties essentially model the future. This accounts for different potential outcomes.

These scales normally come in two forms. First, a milestone schedule with flat dollar figures, that may read like the following table:

| Sales Figures | Royalty |
|---|---|
| 1 million dollars | $200,000 |
| 2 million dollars | $400,000 |
| 3 million dollars | $600,000 |

Second, it could be an escalating or de-escalating percentage instead, if the parties are more comfortable with that description. Note that this could still be stated as a dollar figure, if the parties prefer. Consider this example. The party receiving the royalty (perhaps a developer or a licensor) wants some downside protection. They want to make sure that even if there are low revenue figures, they still get a certain return. In the table below, at a million dollars, the payment is $200,000 at 1 million, $360,000 at 2 million, and $510,000 at 3 million.

| Sales Figures | Royalty (%) |
|---|---|
| 1 million dollars | 20 |
| 2 million dollars | 18 |
| 3 million dollars | 17 |

In other situations, the percentage could increase as revenue goes up. This might make sense in a situation where a publisher wants to be certain to recover relatively larger amounts at lower revenue numbers, but where the developer argues, if the game is a mega-hit, that it was mainly due to superior design and execution.

One common pricing problem is the difficulty agreeing on performance measures. Objective measures are more important than ever when you disagree on potential outcomes. Varying objective endpoints as shown in the tables above allow the parties to disagree on how the world may turn out, but agree on what the result should be in varying circumstances.

## Downside Protections

What do we do if the game performs worse than expected? No one likes to consider those options, but failed games are definitely more common than hit games. So, if things do not go well or a project is canceled, what are some normal consequences?

### Termination

Terminating the agreement is a normal consequence of failed development. The question is what happens after termination, and what is fair? First, there are normally two types of termination. The first is termination for breach. In this case, one party is not fulfilling its duties under the agreement. Most commonly for each side, the publisher is not making payments or making the proper payments, or the developer is not delivering acceptable game builds (or live game performance). The second termination type is for convenience. This is another way of saying that the project is canceled, but that this is not attributable to the failure of any particular party.

Termination for breach is complex because all breaches are different. Normally, the parties exchange their version of the facts via letters and work out a settlement. That could include the reversion of rights to one party and likely some type of payment. It is hard to go beyond that description because these situations are unique.

Termination for convenience is where no party is at fault. In almost every case, this comes from the publisher's side. Publishers are often given the right in a publisher agreement to terminate if their resource allocation plans or corporate strategy change. Developers are almost never given the option to terminate an agreement for convenience.

The examples below are deliberately open-ended to raise questions about termination. The "right" answer varies based on each situation and on the leverage of the parties involved. Reading through these and making sure they are covered in any agreement (one way or the other) will save some pain during termination.

If the game has launched, there should be a wind-down period. This allows players to disengage with the game and maximizes the revenue from the title. Retail units are sold off during this period and the live game is usually run with a skeleton team. Also consider prior sold DLC and other player purchases. Giving enough notice for the wind down is necessary to avoid a regulatory action. A state attorney general or the FTC could take an interest in a game that sold virtual goods right up to the day it was turned off.

Is there a license reversion? If the game is canceled for convenience, it makes sense to pull the license back to the licensor so that they can make another game. However, if the license is terminated for developer breach, perhaps the publisher gets a second chance to make the game with another party. And what about the sequel to the game?

Perhaps the agreement is terminated in the live game phase. Perhaps there is a developer bankruptcy. In that case, consider how one might divide revenue from the sale of assets of the game. In some cases, the publisher purchases the game or purchases the developer to prevent bankruptcy, essentially assigning all rights to the publisher.

## Net Revenue Definition[3]

The net revenue definition is the most hotly debated term in almost any negotiation, but it does not have to be. Consider the following net revenue definition from a game development agreement:

"Net Revenue" shall mean all monies paid to and received by Publisher from the Game sold by Publisher, its subsidiaries and affiliates, less deductions for the following (to the extent applicable): (1) state, federal, and international taxes on sale, lease or license, such as sales, use, excise, value-added and other taxes, (2) costs of insurance, packaging, custom duties, shipping and similar charges not born by customers, including foreign exchange rates (3) all royalty and/or license fees payable to third parties, including but not limited to platform and channel operators, distributors and those third party licensors holding rights to assets embodied in the Game; (4) price protection, reasonable reserves, costs of goods sold, credits, chargebacks, credits, free goods and promotional codes and merchandise, and additional reasonable, unaffiliated third party expenses as may be specified by Publisher, all of which shall be actual and verifiable.

So, to summarize: (1) is essentially just taxes; (2) is more taxes, packaging, and currency risk; (3) is the real core of net revenue—the actual money paid out to the platforms and licensors; and (4) is a catch-all pit, especially the last element: "additional reasonable unaffiliated third party expenses as may be specified by the Publisher."

As you can see, this is a very publisher-friendly definition. Essentially every conceivable cost is taken out of net revenue. This is an actual fully negotiated clause where the publisher had significantly more leverage than the developer. One item that is not deducted is the cost of marketing and advertising. That was a win for the developer. However, take a look at (4). The end of that is dangerous. It was modified from its original form, which was very developer un-friendly. The last clause after the comma, "all of which shall be actual and verifiable" is the modification, which was some help for the developer. Still, if it is at all possible for the developer, the entire subsection (4) should be removed.

Traditionally, publishers (or investors) received the money first from retailers when the games had been placed on the retailer shelves. Publishers were paid out of the first dollars and then publishers liked to make as many deductions as possible to make the net revenue number as small as possible.

Any ambiguity in the net revenue definition will always harm the developer. If the publisher states that net revenue includes the deduction of "other costs" at the reasonable discretion of the publisher, be assured that they will use that.

One argument for developers is to specify that the publisher must be very experienced in the distribution of games. Of course, the publisher has to agree. As a result, the publisher should know what types of third-party costs are involved in the distribution of games. Publishers should also have other developers that they have provided royalty reports for. Developers should consider asking publishers for a few redacted reports from other similar games. Ask for sample calculations based on these real reports and include them as exhibits to the agreement.

## Hiring and New Company Investment

I am commonly asked about creating a "joint venture" or helping a company buy part of a project or part of another company. These are corporate transactions. They will usually be complex, with substantial legal fees and certain tax consequences. In some cases, this may be exactly what the clients are intending, but in many cases it is not really their intention. They do not actually have to own stock in something or options in a corporate sense, they just need the effects of ownership, like control and a revenue share. In this short section, I will propose some alternatives to corporate ownership that are useful and simple. These can be used between two different companies or individuals. They are commonly used in an employment context as well as a development context.

Start with this question: Do we really need corporate ownership? Do we want this to be a stock transaction? Do we want to deal with the tax consequences of ownership? Do we want to deal with corporate formalities like forming an entity, doing accounting for it, paying yearly taxes for it? Do we want to deal with voting and annual meetings and other corporate formalities? In the case of large companies getting together and putting millions of dollars into a project, the answers to the questions above are usually "yes." Large corporations work well with other corporations doing actual corporate work. The associated cost and annual filings are not a large issue for a company. However, in many cases, actual corporate work is not necessary.

If all the parties want is to assign ownership, assign control, pay back an investment, or divide up revenue, a simple IP agreement is usually enough. Imagine working with a senior consultant or investing in a game studio. In that case, even if the amount of money is in the millions of dollars, an IP agreement could be all you need. In that case, the parties can assign ownership to one party or to both parties. They can decide where and how the project will be launched, including distribution and sequel development. They can work out the investment amounts, payment schedule, recoupment, and a royalty distribution. All of that can be done in several pages over the course of a few days to weeks. It is usually less than one-third the time and cost involved in working up corporate documents.

On a related note, consider a consultant or founder who insists on "owning" part of the company. The "simple" way to achieve this is to grant that person equity or options in a corporate sense. This is what everyone thinks of first, but it may not be best for everyone. Those shares come with a tax burden. They come with ownership rights and voting in the company. They also usually do not go away. If the person leaves after working on the project for three months, they usually still own those shares.

Instead, consider simulating equity using something called synthetic equity, or less popularly, phantom equity.[4] The idea here is to give all the upside of equity without the downside. This is a contract right that acts just like equity if there is a sale. But, there are no voting rights and no tax burden. Also, if the person leaves or is fired, you can sunset the synthetic equity over a period. If the person works four months, leaves, and then the company is sold five years later, you can set it up so that you do not owe the person anything. The point is not to take advantage of the person. The point is that synthetic equity allows the parties to create a custom solution that is fair based on the deal. It is a contract right that is not tied to how equity and options work. It is flexible and should always be considered as an option for hiring new people and motivating executives.

## Some Final Words

The second half of this chapter is devoted to re-publishing an essay originally written for the Vilnius Games Conference in 2016. Please forgive that some of the material in the essay repeats and expands on the material above. In everything from independent contractor agreements to game publisher agreements, far too much value is given to "owning the code." Do not find yourself on the wrong side of this ubiquitous illusion.

## CODE OWNERSHIP IS A TRAP

### The Wise Ones Propagate the Myth

One of the third whiskey pieces of advice I hear "sophisticated" game developers giving young people at conferences is to make sure you "own your code" when you finally get a development deal. Ownership of the code is entirely unimportant and it will often be used as a weapon against developers to trade much more valuable rights. Think of it as simple misdirection, the modestly elevated progeny of a "your shoe is untied" type of distraction. When a publisher has you looking away, they might pick your pocket.

First off, we should admit that developers have less leverage in negotiations than funders. A funder can be an outside investor, traditional publisher, or newer publishing platform that may provide development funds. For the purposes of this short essay, I will refer to all of those as "publishers" and also for this short essay, the leverage difference is always in mind. I am not proposing developers ask for things they would never receive. Developers may be able to receive some or all of items discussed here or else it would not be worth writing about. Most importantly, for this article, developers should stop focusing on what is unimportant or simplistic and keep their eye on what really matters around ownership.

Second, a very brief note on how copyright functions. Copyright is the main protection for game code. One person can "own" the copyright in the code and other rights or sub rights relating to ownership can be licensed out to other parties. In the law and in this article, the person that owns the rights and is licensing them out is referred to as "the Licensor" and the person receiving the rights is referred to as "the Licensee."

### The True Nature of Ownership

As noted above, legally, ownership in code is controlled through copyright. In law school copyright is referred to a bundle of sticks. How many sticks are in the bundle? There are an infinite number of sticks in the bundle. This is one of the truly wonderful and meaningful areas of the law where mathematics, philosophy, and psychology land hard in reality to actually affect every game development deal. Just like in the real world, you do not have to be aware of the speed of sound, earth's gravitational constant, or behavioral economics. You can be entirely ignorant of those and yet they still affect your everyday life. The process works automatically and with a cold efficiency wholly indifferent to your awareness of the rules. The same is true for copyright in game development and its bundle of sticks. With focus and attention you can build something or get ignorantly bludgeoned to death with that bundle of sticks.

What are the sticks? The sticks are all the different ways ownership can be divided. In this little article we will just talk about three of the most important ones. After you know about these, you can start to imagine other sticks in the bundle—and what you can do with them.

## Ownership—Control—Cash Flow

### Copyright Ownership

When people think about ownership, the "trap" part is one of the sticks, but not the whole bundle. Plain vanilla copyright ownership in the code is important, but not by itself, and it is not the most important stick in the bundle. The development agreement should include who owns the copyright in the code itself. Preferably, this should be just one party to the agreement. Co-ownership gets messy because in the United States that means that each party can fully and separately exploit the code without accounting or revenue to the other party. Keep in mind, just because a party may not "own" the code means very little. For instance, you can be a mere licensee of the code and still (1) have a copy of the code; (2) re-use the code; or (3) make improvements or derivative works (sequels) using the code; or even (4) re-sell, publish, or sublicense the code. All of the things above are little "sticks" in the bundle of copyright that can be licensed out. So, of the three items discussed in this article, ownership, control, and cash flow—ownership alone is the least important. I would give the publisher copyright ownership of the code every time if the developer gets the correct license rights including the items above and some of the other elements of control and cash flow discussed below.

### Control

One of the key sticks in the bundle of ownership is control and even that has many elements. For the purposes of this article, we can consider three control elements: credit, translation, and sequels.

Who gets credit for making the game and creating the idea? And how is that credit displayed to the world? Many developers have learned the hard way that a publisher can have a larger, longer, and more prominent splash screen on a game opening. Furthermore, one of the people at the publisher could be anointed with a "Director" or "Creative Director" or even "Co-Creator" title. This has to be set out right from the start of the agreement, or the world will never know the truth about who made your game. Furthermore, titles are not empty appellations. If someone at the publisher becomes the director of your game, you may lose power and final authority over creative decisions. How credit is related to control might not be obvious. But the reality of this relationship is important.

Consider translations and localizations of the game. Who controls that, who selects the people to do it, who pays for it, and what audit rights does the developer have? Localization is often ignored but critical to a game's success. Besides being expensive and complicated, these studios doing the work are your ambassadors to that part of the world. Their translations, feel for the game, and other subtle cultural changes are the difference between success and failure for a title. This is a key element of control and not a decision to make on cost alone.

Sequels are the most clearly felt pain for developers who fall into the simplistic trap of code ownership. One of the fundamental rights of telling your own story is having control over how and if to continue that story. Many developers have thoughtlessly given that up. Where possible, make certain the developer has control over how sequels are told. The developer should have creative direction. The developer should have a first right of refusal on developing the sequel. If the developer wants a sequel, but chooses to not develop it themselves, for economic or other reasons, they should have approval over who continues the story. Perhaps they also maintain certain creative input or veto power over story elements. All of this can only be negotiated in advance in a good development deal. But note that without a prior explicit agreement, the publisher will usually acquire these rights by default.

### Cash Flow

The flow of money is also more important than code ownership. Understanding cash flow requires understanding what goes into it and how exactly it is calculated. First, there is the royalty. This is often stated as 10% or 20% or (X) % of certain dollars to the developer (or publisher). But that is only the start of the story. If you get 20%, then ask, 20% of what and how is it calculated? Is it gross dollars—not likely. OK, then it is some form of net dollars. Now listen very carefully. Really. I'm not kidding.

*There is no standard definition of net revenue!*

Now read that last sentence again.

There may be a publisher's "way of doing things." Those are always designed to benefit the publisher. There may also be some things that the accounting department adds or subtracts that are difficult to change. None of that matters when you are staring at your opportunity to negotiate a new, fairer definition. If there is something that goes on "automatically," then we will account for it here. How much is automatically deducted? Two percent? OK then, the developer will just take 2% more of net.

If there is ever some discretionary wiggle room in a net revenue calculation, do not accept a publisher argument that "it is not in our interest to take advantage of you here." When a developer sees that, then the appropriate response is to say "any deductions not explicitly in the definition of Net Revenue must receive prior approval from the developer." If it is reasonable, the developer will approve it. If not, then perhaps it should come out of the publisher's portion. Net revenue in the game industry is not a dumping ground of Hollywood Accounting where publishers should be encouraged or allowed to toss in every cost. We owe it to each other as professionals in the game space to anticipate costs and agree on what should be a deduction. There are so many cases where games have the opportunity to rebuild on the mistakes of traditional media. Net revenue is one of those places, but it takes a daily vigilance. The lazy, thoughtless status quo move the ball toward traditional media's dumping ground of Hollywood Accounting (which truthfully is not good for either party).

Keep in mind that if a publisher gets 80% and the developer gets 20%, then 80% is fair payment for the publisher doing "their job" and any deduction from net revenue is tacitly an agreement that this was at least partly a "developer job." Net revenue affects developers disproportionately. They are usually much more cash flow constrained than publishers. Though it is not mathematically or economically entirely accurate, it is instructive to consider that a developer is taking out a loan against future revenue to pay for any net revenue deduction. Whenever a developer gets stuck in a net revenue negotiation, the right question to ask is always: Which party fairly has responsibility for this cost? What does the publisher 80% pay for? Maybe advertising and marketing should be included as a publisher internal cost, not a net revenue deduction. If the developer is paying for "everything," in the net revenue definition that means the 80% publisher split is meant to be internal publisher operating costs plus profit. Is that fair and does it mean the percentages should be moved to account for it?

Keep in mind that if a developer cannot get the net revenue "wins" it needs, then it should feel empowered to revisit the split to account for any inequity. Conceding internal accounting process issues in the net revenue definition is fine, but do not leave the fundamental fairness issue unaddressed. Account for it by changing the royalty split.

Now is the time to ask questions and probe deeply. This is the honeymoon period. It is the nicest a publisher will ever be to a developer. Ask so many questions and get them to lay out so much of the important things on paper that they won't have wiggle room later. This is the entire point of the contract process. Assume there are large and important elements missing from the contract and make certain those are written out and explicitly addressed. Here it is important to say that developers should not chase unicorns or invent specters either. Your attorney will help you understand what the differences are between real and imagined risks.

How publishers treat you now is a sign of what is to come. Are they totally honest now? Do they treat you like you are smart now? Are they forthcoming on internal processes? Do they seem internally organized and able to speak with one voice? Most publishers are risk-averse and disorganized entities that act a bit like super-organisms. Everyone is doing the best they can with the information they have. Everyone that talks to a developer will overstate their authority a bit. It isn't malicious. It is human nature. Still, we have to get it in writing or it won't matter. Ask good questions. Ask them questions repeatedly. Get the publisher to commit by putting it into the contract. For instance, if they assure you that you will be involved and have final approval over advertising spend, then put it in the contract. If it is not in the contract, it is not real.

Put in a sample calculation. If we are all friendly and the omniscient publisher does this all the time then we won't have any problem just putting it all right down here. There is no real reason a publisher cannot put in a sample royalty calculation based on real numbers with real deductions and talk through various scenarios with the developer. Insist on it.

Consider this sample calculation. Net revenue equals gross dollars minus—what? Maybe platform fees, license fees, discretionary costs not listed? These definitions can go on for five or six lines of text in a real contract. Know what every one of them means and insist on seeing their effect in a sample calculation.

What about advertising? What about internal costs? What about other "soft costs" or costs at their "discretion"?

Keep in mind that net revenue means one thing in practice. What is the developer paying for? It is the developer's account. The publisher is loaning you money against future revenue. Still, if advertising or marketing is deducted, that means that the developer is paying for advertising or at least sharing in those costs. Do you have control over the creative, over the spend amount, over the placement? If you don't, is it fair for you to pay for it?

Invoicing and quarterly reports are another place developers can lose money. Today, the standard is real-time same-account access to numbers. In the past, publishers were able to generate reports on sales and give developers the reports. That made sense because we were dealing with a lot of retail partners worldwide. The standards were set in a pre-internet, pre-social media era. Technology was not as advanced as it is now. Today, we have multiple tracked log-in access and real-time reporting to everything that matters. That is the standard. Put in the agreement that this is how the developer will receive reporting and how the developer will be paid.

Auditing is important. Even if you never use it, you want to have the right to use it. Make sure you list exactly what you can audit. If you have the right to audit something you often don't have to audit it. In a low-level dispute, you can write an email and say, our publisher agreement says we can audit X. So, why don't you just give X to us? So, think about everything you might want access to in the agreement, especially if you are not able to get real-time account access to all revenue streams.

Consider who gets paid first. This was not a choice at the start of the game industry or even in the first 10 years of this century. Players used to pay retailers and publishers first every time. Now, a developer can insist on having the primary platform accounts for Steam, Apple, and Android etc. in their full control. Clearly, with the larger platforms like Xbox and PlayStation, the publishers and the platforms will get paid first. But remember that the large publishers are not a developer's only option. The best possible way to calculate royalties and net revenue is to calculate it yourself. There are few things in life more satisfying than writing out a check to your publisher in this context. There are many developers that send publishers money every quarter now—but only if they were thoughtful enough to ask for it in their development agreement.

## Now You Know and They Cannot Fool You

In most development agreements publishers allow developers to "own" their code. The developers are very pleased with themselves and go to sleep each night feeling they won their negotiation. In truth, they often give away all or substantially all of everything discussed here including crediting, sequel control, and, worst of all, real monetary participation. When I was a much younger attorney, developers fell into the drafts described here all too frequently. Maybe we have a chance to do a little better in the coming years.

A final word. You should always seek the advice of your own attorney. Every situation is different. Also, understand that I wrote this to help you, knowing full well that one day you (a developer) will likely use it against me when I am on the publisher side. That does not mean you will win. Whitman and I have anticipated this:

Do I contradict myself? Very well then, I contradict myself. I am large and contain multitudes.[5]

I wish the intractable hell on all of you—of having the publisher and developer literally yelling at you on a conference call, quoting things you have written as evidence for their position. *Then, in the same moment, you will truly live and wish you hadn't.* Further, I assure you all of your good deeds will be properly punished.

Knowing the rules of the game elevates the discussion and this is my intent. It is immoral and largely no fun to beat up on the ignorant. Economic realities and the myriad contextual elements of the deal will dictate who prevails on any individual point. It is my hope that sharing these strategies will let all the parties go into these agreements with their eyes open. It is one thing to "fool" an ignorant developer. I would rather not have that as a standard in the industry going forward. I would rather have it that each side knows we are talking about an infinite bundle of sticks, and considers and accepts positions deliberately, with an understanding of the consequences.

## CONCLUSION

Negotiating in any of these contexts can be complicated. Listening to your adversary and partners is key as well as balancing the larger picture, with the details to get the job done well. It is a worthy lifelong pursuit, but we should not lose track of why we are negotiating and what we are spending our time on.

It is about the art at the end of the day. We have to feed ourselves and our children, but we cannot forget that it is (or should be) about the art. No matter where we sit at the table, we all choose to be here. After we have enough money for rice, beans, and shelter, the way we spend our days is mainly a story we tell ourselves and other people. I hope there was more to that choice than just making money because there are easier ways to do it than making games. The biggest key to negotiating is to be honest with each other. Commit to doing what we say we are going to do. Show that commitment by writing it out in the contract. The contract is not "the paperwork," it is the very foundation of *the work*. Literally every choice in the contract comes down to building the game. Take it seriously. For each choice, ask: Is this going to make the game better? Is this better than not having the game made or having it made on a shoestring budget? Are these the people you want to work with? Is this game going to be more of your or less of vision because of the choices you make? Is it something you can feel good about, including how you treated the people involved? Is this a day well spent or a compromise?

## NOTES

1. Made into a 1992 film starring Al Pacino, Jack Lemmon, Alec Baldwin, Alan Arkin, Ed Harris, and Kevin Spacey.
2. A very digestible book covering anchoring and other behavioral economics concepts is *Predictably Irrational* by Dan Ariely, published by HarperCollins in 2008.
3. There is an additional discussion on Net Revenue in the Code Ownership section at the end of this chapter.
4. These both refer to the same thing, but the phrase "phantom equity" fell out of fashion because it sounds fake, or as if you are trying to take advantage of someone.
5. I doubt Walt Whitman ever thought that he might be abused in this way.

# CHAPTER 5

# Game Industry Contracts

Y OU WILL LIKELY ENCOUNTER a variety of agreements (also known as contracts or "deals") over the course of developing and releasing a video game. If you don't handle agreements regularly, then they may all seem fairly similar. That surface-level similarity is not lessened by the fact that most agreements have at least a few parts in common. There's usually a section (often toward the beginning) that generally describes what the agreement is about. Then, elsewhere in the agreement, there are sections that include the few details you probably care most about, for example, who's doing what, how much is being paid, when things are due, etc. (quick hint: if these "important parts" involve a lot of complex details, timelines, or technical specifications, they are usually included in a separate schedule or appendix at the end of the document). Beyond those parts, it appears that there are a bunch of other paragraphs that don't have much to do with "the deal" and that some people say just don't matter. You may have heard those other paragraphs referred to as "boilerplate" or "legalese," typically by someone that doesn't know as much about agreements as they think they do.

Rather than painstakingly dissecting all of the sections of one agreement that you might encounter while developing a video game, this chapter casts a slightly wider net and will discuss a few agreements that might cross your desk. In addition to discussing the purpose of each of those agreements, we will pull out and analyze some of the unique parts of each agreement that it would be worthwhile for you to know more about. At the end of this chapter you will also find a rundown of some of those other "boilerplate" provisions that you will find in many different agreements to give you some idea of what they all mean and why they are included in agreements despite some people thinking that they don't matter.

## DEVELOPMENT AGREEMENT

The development agreement (also referred to as the development and publishing agreement or the "devpub" agreement) is one of the most important agreements that a game developer may ever enter into concerning their game. If a developer is developing the game for release by a third-party publisher, then their development agreement with that publisher will control most aspects of the developer's relationship with the publisher, including all obligations and payments exchanged between the two companies concerning the game as well as the ultimate ownership of the game and any underlying intellectual property in the game. The development agreement is a complex document, and you or your company are strongly encouraged to work with an attorney to review and negotiate the document on your behalf. An in-depth review of an entire development agreement could take a quarter of the length of this book, so here we will focus on unpacking just a few of the more important terms that you might find in a development agreement.

## NET REVENUE

"Net Revenue" shall mean the revenue actually received by Publisher in accordance with United States Generally Accepted Accounting Principles ("GAAP") from sales and licenses of the Game less any (a) sales, use, excise or other taxes or duties which Publisher is required to withhold or which are imposed upon Publisher with respect to sales and licenses of the Game, (b) normal and customary rebates, cash and trade discounts, and credits for returns and allowances, (c) actual returns, refunds, chargebacks, and unused prepaid balances, and (d) fees, royalties, commissions, and other amounts paid to third-party salespeople, sales agents, and distributors based on sales or licenses of the Game. Net revenue is calculated on a worldwide basis unless otherwise stated.

The definition of net revenue can be the most important financial term of a development agreement because it sets the size of the pot from which the developer's royalty percentage is calculated. The definition will usually include a list of items which the publisher would like to exclude from the total revenue amount used for calculating the developer's royalty. A developer should closely scrutinize each of these items to make sure they are not overly general or broad because each of them will become an amount that is deducted from the gross revenue the publisher receives from sales and licenses of the game before the royalty received by the developer is calculated. Net revenue definitions can vary significantly and deductions can range from the obvious (e.g., taxes) to the more obscure (e.g., commissions to third-party salespeople). A developer should always ask for an explanation of any term included in a net revenue definition that they do not completely understand as all of those terms can have an immediate impact on the developer's bottom line and innocuous, general terms can end up costing the developer significant sums of money.

For reference, the definition of net revenue is often included in an early section of the agreement, commonly referred to as the "definitions." That section also typically includes the definitions of most of the other capitalized terms included throughout the agreement.

## DEVELOPMENT

Developer shall be solely responsible for designing and developing the game, which shall include, without limitation, all programming, story and game design, key art, graphics, animation, voiceover, music, sound effects, documentation, testing, bug correction, platform conversions, and localization for all non-final builds (first playable, alpha, QA testing build, beta), the final gold masters of the game, and all downloadable content for the game. Developer shall use its best efforts to design and develop the game in accordance with the development schedule and technical specifications below. In furtherance of this project, Developer agrees to appropriately staff such development efforts and to maintain adequate supervision to ensure the development is carried out in a professional, efficient, timely, and competent manner in accordance with the development schedule below. Developer agrees to work exclusively on the game developed under this agreement and no other game for a period beginning on the start date and ending on the date that publisher approves the final milestone described in the milestone schedule. However, beginning six months before the due date of the final milestone described in the milestone schedule, Developer may begin negotiations with third parties for the development of other games.

This section intends to make clear that the developer is 100% responsible for developing the game, and not just for developing the game according to their own plans and timelines, but according to the schedules and specifications that the developer and publisher have agreed upon. This section also includes an obligation on the developer to properly staff and supervise the development project, which prevents the publisher from claiming that they don't have enough people or that their staff were not doing as directed during development. It should be highlighted that this section includes a period of exclusivity for the developer, and the developer should take very seriously any term which prevents them from taking on other work or working on other internal projects. Publishers may insist on this kind of exclusivity to ensure that they have a developer's full attention for the majority of the development period, and to ensure that their payments are not going toward other projects. This exclusivity period essentially means that the developer must be able to keep their studio operating on only the budget of this project for that period.

## KEY PERSONNEL

Developer agrees to maintain development and ancillary staff in accordance with the staffing plan included below which both Parties agree is appropriate to meet the development schedule and cost constraints of this agreement. The "Key Personnel" set forth on the staffing plan shall be part of the full-time development team for the game during the development period, and developer will use all commercially reasonable efforts to retain such Key Personnel for the entire development period. Developer shall not reassign any Key Personnel to any other project without the prior written consent of Publisher. Developer may only replace such Key Personnel with personnel of equal or greater experience and skills as determined in good faith by Publisher. Developer shall provide Publisher with no less than fourteen (14) days' prior written notice of any proposed replacement of Key Personnel and Publisher shall have the right to approve or reject any such replacement(s) in its sole discretion. All development work related to the game shall be performed either by employees or independent contractors of Developer, all of whom shall have entered into binding and confidential agreements with Developer which (a) assign all of such individual's right, title, and interest in and to the game (and any parts of or contributions thereto) to Developer; (b) waive such individual's moral rights to the extent allowed by law; and (c) ensure the confidentiality of the game to at least the same degree as does this agreement. Developer agrees to update and provide Publisher a full and correct version of the staffing plan included below on at least a quarterly basis.

More often than not, a publisher will only work with a developer when they have faith in that developer's lead people. In order to turn that faith into a transaction for the development of a game, the publisher will typically want assurances that those trusted people will actually be working on the game at all times. This translates to the developer agreeing that certain named people, typically set out in a schedule or appendix, will be committed full-time to the game in specific key roles and lead positions for the entire development period for the game. Where the exclusivity period discussed in the "Development" section above is intended to guarantee the undivided attention of the developer, the "Key Personnel" provision is intended to guarantee the undivided attention of the persons within the developer whom the publisher feels are the most important to the game's development. Before signing a development agreement with key personnel provisions, a developer should have a frank discussion of this obligation with all persons to be named as key personnel in the agreement to ensure that they can fully commit to the project for the entire development period.

## MILESTONES

Developer shall complete the various milestone requirements set forth in the milestone schedule below, and time is of the essence with respect to the deadline for the requirements under each such milestone. Publisher shall determine in its reasonable discretion and with the reasonable assistance of Developer, whether or not Developer has satisfied the requirements of a milestone. Publisher shall notify Developer within fourteen (14) days after the due date of such milestone as to whether the Developer met the deadline. In the event of a dispute as to whether the requirements of a milestone have been completed by the milestone's deadline, Developer shall be given fourteen (14) additional days after being notified by Publisher of the non-completion in order to cure the non-compliance by completing the requirements of the milestone. After such fourteen (14) day cure period, Publisher shall again assess whether Developer has completed the requirements of the milestone. If Developer fails to complete the requirements of the milestone before the end of such cure period, there shall be no further cure period. Milestones must be completed sequentially and to complete all of the requirements of a milestone all work related to all previous milestones must be complete (regardless of whether all of the requirements of the previous milestones were completed by the respective deadline for each). In the event that, for whatever reason, Developer fails to complete all of the requirements of a milestone before the deadline for such milestone, then Developer shall be deemed to be in material breach of this Agreement. Publisher shall have the right to review and approve annual and quarterly budgets of the Developer.

## DEVELOPMENT COSTS

Publisher shall pay to Developer monies for Developer's reasonable costs and expenses for the development of the game, incrementally upon Developer's completion and Publisher's approval of the milestones set forth on the milestone schedule.

As I'm sure you know, large game development projects are typically divided into milestones for the purposes of ensuring that the publisher regularly receives deliverables for review and approval, upon which the publisher pays the developer a portion of the total budget for the game. As the developer completes milestones by certain dates, the publisher is provided with verifiable evidence that development of the game is progressing as it should toward an agreed-upon completion date. The milestone schedule should set out targets that must be met or completed with each milestone, for example, completion of certain game-play or interface elements, or a certain number of completed levels or zones. While a developer should definitely review the milestone schedule to ensure the feasibility of meeting the timelines and due dates it sets, the developer should also pay close attention to the process that the agreement sets for the approval of milestones. The publisher holds the purse strings so it is in the developer's interest to have as much detail as possible in the agreement regarding how and when milestones will be approved, according to what measures, and what the procedure is when milestones are rejected. The approval of milestones will ultimately dictate when the developer receives payments from the publisher so the value of fully understanding the milestone approval process cannot be overestimated.

## PUBLISHER RESPONSIBILITY

As between the Parties, Publisher shall have responsibility for and control of the marketing, production, and distribution of the game in all markets throughout the world. Publisher shall make a reasonable effort to market, produce, and distribute the game following its completion and acceptance by Publisher; provided, however, that Publisher shall have the ability to cease marketing, production, or distribution activities related to the game at any time and for any reason thereafter without liability to Developer. Publisher will, using its commercially reasonable judgement, determine which countries and markets in which to offer the game. Publisher shall be responsible for all operation and support related to the game, including the operation and maintenance of all servers for the game and the staffing and administration of end user support for the game. Publisher may fulfill its operation and support obligations however it deems fit, within commercially reasonable limits.

This section is the publisher analog to the developer responsibilities set out in the Development section discussed above. The difference in the forcefulness of the obligations between the two sections illustrates the difference in position between the two parties. The developer is essentially being hired to develop a game according to certain strict parameters and terms of exclusivity, and the publisher is only agreeing to receive the game from the developer and subsequently market, distribute, and support the game according to its own discretion within commercially reasonable limits. This is the arrangement that a publisher will almost always prefer, and developers would be wise to remember that no matter how much work they put into developing a game in an arrangement such as this, the publisher will ultimately control marketing and support for the game, which can have an enormous impact on the game's ultimate success or failure.

## EXPENSES AND MARKETING COMMITMENT

Unless otherwise agreed to by the Parties, Publisher shall bear all costs and expenses related to the marketing, production, and distribution of the game. Publisher shall spend at least $X million on marketing and promotion of the game worldwide (which includes at least $X million in marketing and promotion of the game in North America) prior to the date that is one year after the commercial launch of the game in North America. Publisher shall also bear all costs related to the creation and hosting of an official website and social media pages (e.g., Facebook, Twitter, Instagram, etc.) associated with the game, and the creation, maintenance, and moderation of online forums for the purposes of community development.

This section states that it is the publisher's responsibility to cover costs related to the game's production and distribution, but perhaps more importantly, it sets the amount of money that the publisher must put into marketing the game. While some good games can occasionally find an audience without significant marketing support, those are the exceptions to the general rule that even the best games can require a great deal of marketing and promotion to be successful in a crowded field. By setting a minimum marketing budget that a publisher must commit to a game (which can include both a worldwide amount and amounts for specific regions as seen here), a developer can begin to determine what kind of launch the game will receive from the publisher. With some research and discussion with colleagues, a developer may also be able to compare this budget with the marketing budgets and minimum marketing commitments of other recent titles to determine if it is acceptable for the game being developed.

## DEVELOPER APPROVAL

Developer shall have a right to approve or reject marketing materials for the game, including packaging, promotional materials, and advertising content. Developer's trademark shall appear on the front of all packaging and promotional materials alongside Publisher's in approximately equal size and conspicuousness, and separately on the game's opening splash screens. Developer will also have the right to include a complete credit list in the game's on-screen credits and in the game manual (if any).

The areas in which a publisher will give a developer control following the completion of a game are limited, so terms like this one, which require that all marketing materials must be approved by the developer, are a unique benefit that gives the developer some ongoing input on the positioning and appearance of the game to the public. That being said, equal placement on packaging and splash screens and inclusion in an on-screen credit list are fairly standard, so it is important to read these provisions with a critical eye to determine when standard terms are being characterized as significant benefits or concessions.

## MAINTENANCE AND BUG FIXING

In the event that Publisher or an end user discovers a bug or other flaw that impairs the functionality of the game, Publisher may at its option notify Developer of such bug or flaw. In such case, Developer shall use its best efforts to provide a software patch that corrects the identified bug or flaw at issue and provide Publisher with a detailed description of such patch. Publisher will thereafter make a reasonable effort to make such patch available to all end users. In the event Developer fails to provide an adequate software patch for such bug or flaw in a timely manner, Publisher shall have the right to perform or have performed by another the necessary software patch development, game modifications, or other updates itself and to recoup the reasonable cost of such modifications from royalty payments to Developer. Developer shall provide a copy of the present state of the source code of the game to Publisher at the end of each quarter within ten (10) days of the end of the quarter.

This agreement places the responsibility for bug-fixing on the developer, which is fairly typical and should be expected for most development projects. It's also worth noting that if the developer refuses to fix bugs and other issues, the publisher can outsource the work to a third party and deduct those costs from future payments to the developer. Outsourcing bug fixes can be more expensive and less efficient than having the work done by the game's developer, in addition to creating more work for the publisher. When considering what resources to commit to ongoing maintenance and bug fixing, a developer should consider the potential negative impact that not doing the work themselves may have on their royalties, the players' experience with the game, and the developer's relationship with the publisher.

## ROYALTY

Subject to the terms and conditions of this Agreement, Publisher shall pay or cause to be paid to Developer on a quarterly basis the royalties set forth on Exhibit B for such quarter. Publisher shall provide to Developer a Royalty Report substantially in the form set forth on Exhibit C within thirty (30) days of the end of each Publisher financial quarter during the term of this agreement. Upon receipt of a royalty report, Developer shall promptly provide Publisher with an invoice for the payment of royalties based on such report. The initial royalty payment shall be made to developer within sixty (60) days of receipt by Publisher of the initial invoice from Developer. All subsequent royalty payments shall be made to Developer within thirty (30) days of receipt by Publisher of an invoice from Developer. Publisher makes no warranty or representation as to the actual amount of revenue the Developer will derive hereunder. The royalties set forth in Exhibit B are gross royalties, and Publisher shall withhold the appropriate amount from such gross payments as required pursuant to the provisions below concerning withholding taxes.

You don't need me to tell you that the section of an agreement concerning royalties is important, but it is worthwhile for us to go over a few things you should look for when reviewing terms concerning royalties. At a minimum, royalty terms should include clear language indicating how the amount of royalties will be calculated (or reference the location of such terms elsewhere in the agreement), how often royalties will be paid (e.g., quarterly, monthly, biannually), and the procedures and schedules for how and when those payments will actually be made for each period (e.g., royalty reports, invoicing requirements, timelines).

It is common for a single agreement to have several royalty rates that depend on a number of factors related to the games being sold. Such factors may include the platform of the game (PC vs. console), location of the sales (domestic vs. international), whether the sales are through a sublicensed third-party publisher (often used in foreign territories where the publisher doesn't operate), whether the sales are of physical or digital copies of the game, and how many copies of the game have been sold (potentially with an escalating royalty percentage for sales above a certain threshold). The section of the agreement that sets out royalty percentages should spell out the percentage the developer will receive for all possible transactions involving the game, including sales of virtual property, in-game advertising, and any other expected or potential revenue streams.

On the subject of spelling out details, the developer will also benefit from royalty reports having as much detail as possible. Good royalty reports should at least include the calculations and totals for each stream of revenue from which the developer is going to receive a royalty. It is wise to have a form royalty report included as an exhibit to the agreement so that you can review the information and the level of detail it will include before signing. However, please note that it is fairly common practice for publishers to use the same form royalty reports for all of their developers so there may not be much room for negotiation as to what the royalty report will include.

You should pay close attention to whether the development budget or any other expenses concerning the game (e.g., promotional costs) are recoupable from the developer's royalty. If these amounts are recoupable, then the publisher must be repaid in full for those amounts out of the developer's royalty before the developer begins receiving royalty payments on sales of the game. If the game is not successful and its development costs are recoupable, then it is entirely possible that the developer will not receive any royalties from sales of the game because the developer's royalty percentage never finished paying back the recoupable development budget for the game. A developer that wants to ensure some cash flow from royalties starting from a game's release might try to negotiate a phased or split recoupment. Under such an arrangement, the developer's royalties are split according to a percentage agreed upon by the publisher with part going toward recoupment of the game's development budget and part going directly to the developer.

## OBJECTION

Developer shall give Publisher specific notice of any objection to a royalty report within twenty-four (24) months following the date that Publisher first sent such royalty report to Developer, or such royalty report will become conclusively binding and Developer waives any other right to object thereto. In the event an audit reveals an undisputed underpayment by Publisher, Publisher shall immediately remit payment to Developer in the amount of such underpayment. In addition, unless Developer commences a legal or other remedial action within twenty-four (24) months following the date Publisher first sent a royalty report to the Developer, Developer waives its right to undertake any legal or remedial action in connection with such statement.

## DEVELOPER AUDIT RIGHTS

Developer has the right to audit Publisher's calculations of royalties and net revenue on business days, within normal hours of operation with ten (10) days' notice. Developer shall be responsible for the cost of such an audit except when discrepancy of more than five percent (5%) is found in favor of Developer, in which case Publisher will be responsible for the cost of such audit. In the event that Publisher disagrees with the results of an audit, Publisher may initiate an independent review of the audit performed by a mutually agreeable third-party accounting consultant at Publisher's cost. This final review shall be the final binding calculation for the royalties and net revenue being reviewed. Developer may exercise this audit right no more than once per year and the result will be final and binding on both Parties. The results of an audit for one year may not be recalculated in subsequent years.

Terms concerning objection to royalty reports and developer audits typically provide the only practical recourse for a developer if they have an issue with the royalties they are receiving from a publisher. Note that the developer is only allowed to audit the publisher's accounting of royalties once per year. It may be worth negotiating the right to audit more often if it is expected that most of the revenue from sales of a game will be made within a short time of its release. Developers should be familiar with these terms and consult them as soon as a concern is raised that there may be an issue with the royalties being received, because these terms may include limitations on when the developer can take advantage of each option.

## WITHHOLDING TAXES

Any withholding or other taxes that Publisher is required by law to withhold and actually withholds and pays on behalf of Developer with respect to the royalties to Developer under this Agreement shall be deducted from gross payments and remitted to the taxing authority; provided, however, that for taxes so deducted, Publisher shall furnish Developer with documentation of the taxes paid on its behalf which are reasonably required by Developer in seeking corresponding reductions available (in the form of income deductions or tax credits), if any, in the determination of Developer's U.S. income taxes. The Parties shall use commercially reasonable efforts to minimize withholding and other taxes.

Without going into great detail, the provisions concerning taxes and withholdings can be at least as important as any other financial terms of an agreement. The tax provisions can also be highly varied so a developer would be well served by showing the proposed language concerning taxes to their accountant or another tax professional for their input concerning the results of the tax treatment proposed in the agreement language. To prevent surprises later on, it would also be a good idea for the developer to discuss with their accountant what the tax impact would be for the developer and publisher, according to the terms of the agreement, for different levels of sales of the game and any other products contemplated by the agreement.

## GAME OWNERSHIP

Except for the express licenses granted or as otherwise set forth in this Agreement, Publisher shall have and retain all right, title, interest, Intellectual Property Rights and other rights, in and to (a) the Game (including all Game Content), (b) any and all sequels and any other derivative works or other works based in any way upon the Game or Intellectual Property in the Game, (c) any and all trademarks, service marks, domain names, trade names, and other designations that are associated with the Game (except for Developer's trade name), and (d) all databases associated with the Game and all data contained in such databases and its arrangement.

### SOURCE CODE, DEVELOPMENT TOOLS, AND ENGINE OWNERSHIP

Notwithstanding the terms above concerning ownership of the Game ("Game Ownership"), except for the express licenses granted in this Agreement, Developer shall have and retain all right, title, interest, Intellectual Property Rights and other rights, in and to the Source Code and the Development Tools and Engine.

The combination of terms above concerning ownership of the game, development tools, and other materials and rights essentially ensures that the publisher is the owner of the game, all intellectual property relating to the game, and all potential sequels and other products based on the game, in all practical and commercial respects. On the flipside, the developer retains ownership of the source code of the game, which is fairly self-explanatory, the development tools, which typically refers to the software the developer used to create the game, and the engine, which is the software on which the game operates. While ownership of the game's source code but not the game itself does not provide the developer much benefit beyond a sense of pride, retaining ownership of the development tools and engine can have significant benefits. Specifically, by retaining ownership of the development tools and engine, the publisher can use that software for future games. If the game engine is good enough, then the publisher could even do as Epic Games has done with the Unreal Engine and generate additional revenue by licensing the engine out to other publishers for their own games.

### SOURCE CODE LICENSE

As to the Source Code, and as to any other Intellectual Property Rights that Developer may own in and to the Game, Developer hereby grants to Publisher an exclusive, worldwide, irrevocable, perpetual, sub-licensable, royalty-free, and fully paid up license under all of Developer's Intellectual Property Rights to make, have made, use, import, reproduce, have reproduced, distribute, have distributed, make derivative works of, perform, and display the game.

### DEVELOPMENT TOOLS AND ENGINE LICENSE

Developer hereby grants to Publisher a non-exclusive, worldwide, irrevocable, perpetual, sublicensable, royalty-free, fully paid up license under all of Developer's Intellectual Property Rights to make, have made, use, sell, offer to sell, import, reproduce, have reproduced, make derivative works of, distribute, have distributed, perform, display, disclose, use in commerce, market, promote, and otherwise dispose of the Engine and Development Tools in connection with the Game. Developer will provide the Development Tools and Engine, to Publisher both in Source Code and Object Code form on or before the Acceptance Date and once per quarter thereafter for the duration of the Agreement; and Publisher may make a reasonable number of archival copies of the Development Tools and Engine for purposes of backup and recovery.

These provisions essentially provide the publisher with sufficient rights in the software that the developer retains ownership of to allow the publisher to protect its investment and to safely commercially exploit the game. The exclusive license of the game's source code to the publisher ensures that, even though the developer continues to own the source code, they cannot use it in any way, thus protecting the publisher's ownership rights in the game. The license of rights concerning the development tools and engine prevent the publisher from infringing on the rights that the developer retained in that software when the publisher reproduces and distributes the game. Note that while the source code license is exclusive, preventing anyone other than the publisher from using or reproducing the game's source code, even its owner the developer, the license concerning the development tools and engine is non-exclusive, which allows the developer to reuse those materials and potentially even license them to third parties as previously discussed.

## GAME LICENSE TO DEVELOPER

Publisher hereby grants to Developer a non-exclusive, royalty-free, fully paid up license for the term of this Agreement under all of Publisher's Intellectual Property Rights to modify, make, have made, use, import, reproduce, have reproduced, and make derivative works of the Game solely for Developer's internal use in performing its obligations set forth in this Agreement, and then only for the benefit of Publisher.

In case the previous sections did not make sufficiently clear the degree to which the publisher controls the game, this provision should do the trick. This is a license back to the developer of the game that the developer created, just so the developer can perform its obligations under this agreement without violating the rights in the game that the publisher now owns. Essentially, the publisher has such complete ownership over the game that they now have to expressly give the developer a limited permission to even have the game so that the developer can work on it, without which the developer could, technically, be subject to a lawsuit for infringing on the publisher's rights in the game.

## SEQUELS, EXPANSIONS, AND PORTS

At Publisher's discretion, Publisher may decide to create sequels, expansion packs, or platform translations ("ports") of the game not described in this Agreement. In the event that Publisher decides to create any such sequel, expansion pack, or translate the game to a different platform (including, without limitation, consoles and mobile devices), Publisher shall send written notice of the same to Developer. Developer shall then have the right of first negotiation with Publisher to the development of such sequel, expansion pack, or platform translation. If Developer agrees to develop such sequel, expansion pack, or platform translation, Developer shall develop such sequel, expansion pack, or platform translation on terms to be negotiated later in good faith. Publisher may develop the sequel, expansion pack, or platform translation itself or contract with a third party for the development of such sequel, expansion pack, or platform translation if (a) Developer does not respond to such request within thirty (30) days of the date the written notice is received by Developer; (b) Developer declines the invitation to negotiate to develop such sequel, expansion pack, or platform translation; or (c) the Parties are unable to negotiate an agreement with respect to the development of such sequel, expansion pack, or platform translation after making a good faith effort not to exceed thirty (30) days following Developers' agreement to develop such sequel, expansion pack, or platform translation, and in any event if the Parties are unable to negotiate an agreement with respect to such sequel, expansion pack, or platform translation within sixty (60) days of the date the written notice is received by Developer.

The ownership provision we previously discussed provides the publisher with the exclusive right to create sequels or platform ports of the game. This provision requires the publisher to first negotiate with the developer for the development of such sequels, expansions, or ports before developing such projects themselves or hiring a third party to develop them. It should be noted that this provision releases the publisher of its obligation to negotiate with the developer for the project if an agreement cannot be negotiated within a certain period, even if the developer still wants the project.

## PURCHASE OPTION

Developer hereby grants to Publisher an exclusive, irrevocable right, to purchase Developer at any time during the period beginning on the Effective Date and ending X calendar year(s) thereafter (the "Option Period") for $X Million, whether through merger, stock exchange, or sale of all or substantially all of its assets (the "Option"), on customary terms (including, without limitation, customary representations, warranties, covenants, conditions, and indemnification provisions, which shall include a holdback of at least 20% of the purchase price as security for Developer's indemnification obligations for a period of one year); the Parties shall negotiate in good faith to execute a definitive agreement with respect to the Option exercise on such customary terms. To the extent reasonably practicable, Publisher shall structure the transaction so it will qualify as a "tax free" reorganization.

## NO SOLICITATION

From the execution of this Agreement until the expiration of the Option Period, Developer and the officers, directors, employees, and other agents of Developer will not, directly or indirectly, (i) take any action to solicit, initiate, or encourage any purchase of Developer (whether through merger, stock exchange, or sale of all or substantially all of its assets) by any person or party other than Publisher, or (ii) engage in negotiations with, or disclose, any non-public information relating to Developer to, or afford access to the properties, books, or records of Developer, to any person or party who has advised Developer that it may be considering making, or has made, an investment or purchase proposal.

The purchase option and solicitation provisions combine to effectively take the developer off the market for potential acquisition by a competing publisher or other company for a period beginning at the execution of this agreement and ending at some negotiated point thereafter. This section also locks in a potential purchase price for the developer before the development and release of the game, which is good for the publisher because a successful game could otherwise drive up the price of acquiring the developer. Publishers will almost always try to include these provisions in publishing agreements because they preserve for the publisher the possibility of acquiring a developer with at least one successful game without paying the premium that would accrue on the open market for such experience and reputation.

## MIDDLEWARE LICENSE

Over the course of creating a game, it is fairly common for a developer to decide that it is easier, better, and/or more cost-effective to license some underlying software of the game from a third party instead of creating that software from scratch. While this may seem strange initially, it is essentially the developer relying on experts in the field of the software they need, graphics experts for graphics software or sound experts for sound software, the same way game companies and movie studios regularly rely on musicians when they need music for their game or movie. Software elements that developers license from other companies to use in their games are commonly referred to as "middleware" and can include everything from the smallest audio codecs up to entire engines for rendering graphics and physics. For a developer to use middleware created by another company, that company will usually require that the developer enter into a license agreement dictating the terms of that use. The following is a review of some of the important terms that a developer might encounter in such a middleware license.

### LICENSED SOFTWARE

Pursuant to this Agreement, Middleware, Inc. ("Licensor") grants to Developer, LLC ("Licensee") a limited, worldwide, non-exclusive, non-assignable, non-transferable, non-sublicensable license to integrate the Middleware Software Kit (the "Middleware") into five (5) Licensee products (each a "Product," collectively the "Products") currently including, but not limited to, the titles set forth on Exhibit A attached hereto. Licensee may distribute the Middleware only as integrated into a Product.

This is the basic license permitting the developer to include the middleware in their game. The license is non-exclusive because the middleware creator (licensor) wants to still be able to license the middleware to other companies. The license is also non-assignable, non-transferable, and non-sublicensable, terms that the middleware creator may have included to ensure that the party they are contracting with actually uses the middleware and doesn't try to pass through its license to any other company, which would be harder for the middleware creator to track and control.

### LICENSE FEE

As consideration for the five (5) licenses granted hereunder, Licensee agrees to pay Licensor the License Fee of $X ("Middleware License Fee"). Licensor shall submit to Licensee an invoice for the applicable License Fee and Licensee shall pay the applicable License Fee within thirty (30) days of receipt of the invoice.

While this is a fairly standard fee provision, this license covers multiple products so the developer may be receiving some type of reduced rate for purchasing multiple licenses. The next provision tells us more about why the developer might be purchasing multiple licenses at one time.

## SEQUELS

A sequel is not included within the license for an initial Product and qualifies as an additional Product requiring an additional license.

## LOCALIZATIONS

Localizations for different languages or regions are included within the license for a Product so long as no additional support or updates for the Middleware are required for the development of such localizations. If additional support or updates for the Middleware are required for the development of a localization then the localization qualifies as an additional Product requiring an additional license.

## PRODUCT ADD-ONS

Product add-ons ("Product Add-Ons"), which include, without limitation, expansion packs and downloadable content packs, if at any time sold separately from the Product or bundled with the Product to be sold at an increased price, qualify as additional Products requiring additional licenses. For Product Add-Ons, one (1) Product license can be used to license each of the following, to be listed on Exhibit A annexed hereto:

- 3 Product Add-Ons with a retail sale price between $0.00 and $4.99; or
- 2 Product Add-ons with a retail sale price between $5.00 and $14.99; or
- 1 Product Add-on with a retail sale price over $15.00.

The above language clarifies that game sequels count as additional products, but regional versions of a product do not. Downloadable content (DLC) may also qualify as an additional product if it is sold separately or sold with the game at a higher price, but several DLC packs may be lumped together under one "product" depending on the prices at which they are sold. Some middleware agreements may also count as separate products versions of the game for different platforms, such that releasing a game for PC and the current Xbox and PlayStation consoles could count as three licensed products instead of one. Taking all of these factors into consideration, it's entirely possible that the developer is using all five of the licenses under this agreement for what most people would consider to be a single game with a small amount of post-release DLC.

## EXCLUDED PRODUCTS

Licensee shall not distribute the Middleware in any form other than as integrated into a Product. This license does not permit Licensee to integrate the Middleware into any continued revenue products (such as, but not limited to, free-to-play, subscription based, or pay-per-play products), any software product that will be sold or licensed to compete with the Middleware or Licensor's other products, or any non-game products, such as, but not limited to, operating systems and software bundles. In the event of any breach or threatened breach of the restrictions of this section by Licensee, Licensor may suffer irreparable harm, remedies at law may not adequately protect and compensate Licensor, and Licensor shall be entitled to commence a court action to obtain injunctive and other equitable relief and in such action shall be entitled to all remedies in law or equity. Additionally, this Agreement shall be imme-diately void and the offending product(s) shall be deemed infringing until Licensee remedies this breach by removing all offending products and materials concerning such products from public view (including, if necessary, recalling and destroying all offending product(s)), and, if applicable, purchasing the appropriate license(s) from Licensor for such products at Licensor's then-current prices.

The middleware creator is only licensing the middleware for use in distinct games and downloadable content for those games, which it can be anticipated have a lifecycle that includes the majority of sales within a certain period after release with tapering sales afterward. For continued revenue products like subscription-based online games, the middleware creator likely has a different licensing structure that involves ongoing fees instead of a flat upfront fee. As season passes and ongoing DLC plans become the norm instead of the exception, these distinctions can become murky and require significant forethought and discussion in the negotiation of these agreements. This provision also serves a completely different purpose of prohibiting the developer from including the middleware in any product other than a game, specifically calling out products intended to bundle and resell the middleware or that could otherwise compete with the middleware. The penalties set out for violating the provisions of this section are high, including a potential lawsuit and complete removal of the developer's game from the market, so a developer should ensure that the product they have planned does not run afoul of these terms before signing this license and using this middleware.

## THIRD-PARTY SOFTWARE

If Licensee uses any third-party software (including free or open source software), whether or not in conjunction with the Middleware, in a Product (or in the development thereof), Licensee shall ensure that its use does not (i) create, or purport to create, additional obliga-tions of Licensor or Licensee with respect to the Middleware; (ii) grant, or purport to grant, to any third party any rights to the Middleware or any other Licensor product or intellectual property; or (iii) cause the Middleware to be subject to any licensing terms or obligations that would require it or any derivative works thereof to be disclosed or distributed, whether or not in source code form, to be licensed for the purpose of making derivatives works, or to be redistributed free of charge.

The point of this provision is to prevent the developer from using the middleware in any product that also includes software that, due to the terms of its license, subject the entire project to certain requirements that the middleware creator would not agree to. The main concern here is that the developer may include open source software in their project, and some open source licenses require, if the open source software is integrated into a project, that the underlying code of the entire project (which could include the middleware) must be made available to the public for free. Beyond the open source software issue, the middleware creator is attempting to prevent the developer from taking any action that would subject the middleware or the middleware creator to any terms or obligations that they have not had chance to review and agree to and that could be detrimental to their products and business.

### INTELLECTUAL PROPERTY RIGHTS AND OWNERSHIP

Licensee acknowledges that the Middleware is proprietary to Licensor and that Licensor owns all right, title, and interest in and to the intellectual property therein. To the extent that Licensee modifies the Middleware, Licensee hereby assigns and agrees to assign to Licensor all right, title and interest (including any intellectual property rights) in and to such derivative works of or improvements to the Middleware. Except for the licenses expressly granted herein, Licensee acquires no right, title or interest in or to the Middleware, or modifications thereof, and Licensor reserves all rights not expressly granted. Except as otherwise set forth herein, all right, title and interest in and to the Products and all intellectual property rights relating thereto (specifically excluding the Middleware and all modifications thereof) shall be owned by Licensee.

When software is integrated into a larger project, particularly if the software must be significantly modified or tailored by the company licensing it in order to work for the larger project, there can sometimes be questions about who owns the integrated software or the modifications to the integrated software. Being integrated into another project and being customized to operate optimally within that project is a main purpose of middleware, so clearing up any confusion regarding ownership resulting from such integration and customization is extremely important. The provision above is included to make clear, in no uncertain terms, that the middleware and any modifications to the middleware are owned entirely by the middleware creator, and that the developer gains no ownership interest in the middleware as a result of using it or integrating it into their game.

### LIMITATIONS ON USE

Licensee shall limit the use of and access to the Middleware to those of its employees and third-party contractors whose use of or access to the Middleware is necessary for exercise of the licenses granted herein, provided that (i) such use and access is exclusively for Licensee in connection with work on the Products, (ii) Licensee shall ensure such employees and third-party contractors' compliance with the applicable obligations hereunder, (iii) Licensee shall be liable for any breach by such employees and third-party contractors in connection with this Agreement, and (iv) no access to the Middleware shall be permitted to an employee or third-party contractor unless it has first signed an appropriate confidentiality agreement provided by Licensee which includes that all embodiments of the Middleware will be returned to Licensee upon completion or other termination of such development. Licensee will maintain the Middleware at Licensee's address listed above, and will not remove the Middleware from such site to any other location without Licensor's prior written approval.

Game development can be a large-scale enterprise involving many people and sometimes multiple projects at different locations at one time. With the above language, the middleware creator is trying to ensure that the middleware does not leave the developer's office, that only people working on products included in the middleware license have access to the middleware, that those people will comply with all of the obligations under this agreement, and that developer understands that it will be held liable if any of those people violate the terms of this agreement.

## COPYRIGHT, CREDITS, AND LOGOS

For each Product, the credit "Uses Middleware Tech, Copyright (C) 1990–20__ by Middleware, Inc." must appear somewhere in the Licensee's documentation, and the Middleware, Inc. logo (as provided by Licensor) must appear somewhere on the outside of the Product's packaging. Licensee will pay a "no credit fee" in the amount of $X for any Product on which it does not include the above credit line and logo. Licensee must supply Licensor with ten (10) free copies of each Product in each format in which it is released. Licensee agrees it has no rights to the Middleware, Inc. name and logo and all use of the same shall inure to the benefit of Licensor. Licensee shall promptly make available to Licensor at its request any promotional, advertising, and/or marketing materials disseminated by Licensee which mention the Middleware or mention or use the Middleware, Inc. name or logo.

## LICENSEE NAME AND LOGO

Licensee grants to Licensor a non-exclusive and non-transferable right to use Licensee's name and logo and each Product's name, logo, and box cover (i) to identify Licensee as a developer using the Middleware and each Product as a product that integrates the Middleware; and (ii) to advertise, promote, and publicize use of the Middleware to develop products of a type similar to such Product after the commercial release date of the applicable Product and subject to Licensee's prior written approval of such use (including the text accompanying Licensee's property) in each instance. To the extent that each Product's name or box cover includes images or content licensed by Licensee from a third party, Licensee shall use commercially reasonable efforts to obtain approval from such third party for Licensor's use of such images or content as contemplated hereunder. Licensor agrees that it has no other rights to Licensee's name and logo, each Product's name or box cover, and that all use thereof shall inure to the benefit of Licensee.

Middleware is a business-to-business sector and the best advertising that a middleware creator can get is having their name and logo on the box and in the credits of a successful game. For this reason, many middleware license agreements include terms requiring that developers include these credits and logos on their game's packaging and in other locations or pay significant penalties. Middleware creators often also want to include names and images of the games that include their middleware and the developers of those games in their own promotional materials so middleware agreements may also include those permissions. Lastly, middleware companies will typically want copies of the games that integrate their software; the number of copies can vary and is usually open to negotiations, but the concept is common to licenses of various kinds.

## UPDATES

Licensor will provide Licensee with updates to the Middleware for one (1) year per Product (the "Free Update Period"), with each Product's Free Update Period commencing on the date that the Middleware is first integrated into the Product. Middleware updates after the Free Update Period will be available at Licensee's expense, provided that the cost for such update shall be the lowest price that such update is made available by Licensor to any developer at that time.

**SUPPORT**

Licensor will provide to Licensee reasonable technical support during the Free Update Period. Additional technical support for any Product after the Free Update Period may be secured by Licensee at least thirty (30) days prior to the end of the Free Update Period for the Product by payment to Licensor of an annual renewal fee of $X. Cost and availability of renewals that are not purchased at least thirty (30) days prior to the end of the Free Update Period will be at Licensor's discretion. Licensor will not, under any circumstances, provide technical support to anyone other than Licensee and its third-party contractors.

Game development can take a long time, often longer than the people doing the development expected at the beginning of developing the game. Integrating middleware, even very good middleware, can also take time plus a significant amount of handholding from the middleware creator in order for the integration to be as effective as possible for the final game. With that in mind, it can be important for a developer to have a clear understanding of how long they will be receiving updates and support from a middleware company and the potential cost of extending that support to correctly budget time and resources for integration of that middleware into their game. The above provision is intended to provide that understanding, but is likely open for negotiation if a developer believes that its needs will be significantly different from what this language describes.

**TERM AND TERMINATION**

This Agreement shall be effective as of its Effective Date and shall remain in effect, unless terminated pursuant to the terms of this Agreement. The licenses granted hereunder shall terminate upon Licensee ceasing to distribute the Products.

This agreement will continue for as long as the product that includes the middleware is on the market, which is good because if the license ended before that time, the game would be infringing on the middleware creator's rights and could result in a lawsuit. While this agreement has been drafted to avoid such issues, it is a good reminder to always be sure that any license to include something in your product, whether its middleware, a song, or anything else, will continue for the entire commercial life of that product. Digital distribution and backward compatibility mean that many games will continue to be available and generating some revenue for their developer many years after they are initially released. No one likes having to pull a game from an online storefront or devote engineering time to patching a game that is several years old just because the license has expired for some small part of it.

**TERMINATION BY LICENSOR**

Licensor may terminate this Agreement effective upon delivery of notice of termination to Licensee, if Licensee (a) makes an unauthorized assignment of this Agreement in violation of the terms of this Agreement and fails to cure or remedy the effects of such assignment within thirty (30) days after receiving written notice thereof from Licensor; (b) makes any unauthorized use or disclosure of Licensor's Confidential Information or makes any unauthorized use of the Middleware and fails to cure or remedy the effects of such breach within thirty (30) days after receiving written notice thereof from Licensor; or (c) fails to timely pay to Licensor the Middleware License Fee, and does not correct such failure within ten (10) days after written notice of such failure is delivered to Licensee.

## BANKRUPTCY

Either Party may terminate this Agreement upon written notice to the other Party if any one of the following events occurs: (i) the other Party files a voluntary petition in bankruptcy or otherwise seeks protection under any law for the protection of debtors; (ii) a proceeding is instituted against the other Party under any applicable bankruptcy and/or insolvency legislation where such proceeding is not dismissed within ninety (90) days; (iii) the other Party is adjudicated bankrupt; (iv) a court assumes jurisdiction of the assets of the other Party under a federal reorganization act or equivalent legislation of a foreign jurisdiction; (v) a trustee or receiver is appointed by a court for all or a substantial portion of the assets of the other Party; (vi) the other Party becomes insolvent, ceases or suspends business; or (vii) the other Party makes an assignment of the majority of its assets for the benefit of its creditors.

## EFFECT OF TERMINATION

Subject to the limitations set forth below, upon termination of this Agreement, the rights and licenses respecting the Middleware granted pursuant to this Agreement, as the case may be, will terminate and, except as otherwise provided herein, Licensee shall promptly cease use of the Middleware, and return to Licensor or (at Licensor's option) destroy all electronic and physical copies of the Middleware. Notwithstanding the foregoing, if the Middleware License Fee has been paid in full with respect to any Product the development of which has been completed as of the effective termination date, then Licensee's rights hereunder with respect to such Product shall remain in effect until Licensee ceases to distribute or have distributed such Product.

As with any licensor, a middleware creator will want the right to terminate the license if certain events occur, which typically include, at a minimum, the developer misusing the middleware or attempting to allow a third party to use it, or failing to pay the fee to license the middleware that is set forth in the agreement. This license also provides for either party to terminate the agreement if the other takes any action or is the subject of any action that is typical of a company entering into bankruptcy. While provisions allowing for termination in the result of a bankruptcy are not always enforceable, they are very common because companies often agree that they are less likely to get the full benefits of their bargain if the other side of the agreement loses some control over their company due to bankruptcy proceedings. The above terms also indicate that the developer must stop using the middleware if the license is terminated, with the caveat that the developer can continue to use the middleware in products that were completed before the termination so long as developer has already paid the entire license fee for those products under the agreement.

## END-USER LICENSE AGREEMENT

The end-user license agreement (EULA) and terms of service (TOS) are often the only agreements that you will enter into with your game's users and they are fairly different from the agreements you will enter into with any other party. While you will have almost unilateral control over what these documents require or prohibit, you may also have more people pushing the limits or outright violating the terms of these documents than any other agreement with your company. If you would like to use a EULA and TOS as effectively as possible to protect your game and your business, it helps to know what the terms of each mean.

As a threshold matter, while there are some provisions that can appear in either document, the EULA and TOS serve two different functions. At a very high level, the EULA is the license under which a user is granted permission to play your game, and the TOS are the terms concerning how they are allowed to play your game and interact with other users of the game, as both are part of a shared service. To provide some context, a game without any ongoing connection to its publisher or other users might have a strong EULA with very little need for a TOS, while an online service that has interactions between users but no significant downloadable component might rely almost entirely on a TOS with only a very minimal EULA. If that all sounds like gibberish, then a deeper dive into both documents should help.

The EULA is the document that gives the user permission to access and play a game. Much like any other license, the EULA's terms are largely devoted to protection and use of the content being licensed, in this case the software that makes up the game. That being said, a EULA's terms often reference the service on which the game operates, typically because the game and service are so intertwined that one cannot function without the other. This is also why the EULA and TOS often include similar or overlapping terms. This "belt and suspenders" approach to legal protections may seem unnecessary or duplicative, but few people opt for less protection when the thing being protected is software in which they have invested millions of dollars and that they rely upon in order to make a living. With those stakes in mind, let's see what those protections look like.

If you agree to this end user license agreement (the "License"), you may install the game software (the "Game") on your computer for purposes of playing the Game in conjunction with the Game service provided by Publisher (the "Service"). Subject to your agreement to and continuing compliance with all terms and conditions of this License and the Terms of Service, Publisher hereby grants, and you hereby accept, a limited, non-exclusive, non-transferable, revocable, and royalty-free license, to install the Game on your computer and use the game in conjunction with the Service. Any and all uses of the Game are subject to this License which you must accept before you can play the Game.

The Game and Service are provided for your individual, non-commercial, entertainment purposes only and may not be used for any other purpose or in any other way. Any use, reproduction, modification, or distribution of the Game not expressly authorized by the terms of this License is expressly prohibited. You may not sell, copy, exchange, transfer, loan, translate, reverse engineer, decompile, derive source code from, lease, grant a security inter-est in, transfer, publish, assign, or otherwise distribute the Game, Service, any other Publisher intellectual property, or anything you copy or derive from the Game, Service or any other Publisher intellectual property, in whole or in part, unless you have been expressly autho-rized to do so by the Publisher in a signed writing.

BY INSTALLING, COPYING OR OTHERWISE USING THE GAME, YOU ACKNOWLEDGE THAT YOU HAVE READ, UNDERSTAND, AND AGREE TO BE BOUND BY ALL TERMS OF THIS LICENSE AND THE "TERMS OF SERVICE" (FOUND AT PUBLISHER.COM/TERMSOFSERVICE) WHICH ARE INCORPORATED HEREIN BY REFERENCE. IF YOU DO NOT AGREE TO ALL TERMS OF THIS LICENSE, THEN YOU ARE NOT PERMITTED TO INSTALL, COPY OR USE THE GAME. BY CLICKING "ACCEPT" OR INSTALLING OR OTHERWISE USING THE GAME, YOU ACKNOWLEDGE THAT YOU HAVE READ AND UNDERSTAND AND AGREE TO BE BOUND BY ALL TERMS AND CONDITIONS OF THIS LICENSE.

The license grant included in a EULA can appear strange at first glance but much of that has to do with the context that the EULA exists in. EULAs often use "you" to refer to the end user because the document is not tailored to an individual user; some also use "we" to refer to the game publisher. In light of the less formal language, the tone of a EULA can appear very forceful. That force makes more sense when one thinks of the EULA as a trans-action that a publisher must enter into with a person that they can't speak directly with but must entrust with a very valuable piece of property.

Looking at the actual language of this fairly typical EULA opening, what is generally said is that the publisher gives the user permission to install and play the game, in exchange for compliance with all terms of this EULA. It's worth noting that this permission is depen-dent upon the user's compliance with all terms of the TOS, which is mentioned and made a part of the EULA by its reference in the third paragraph. The opening also expressly spells out that the user may only use the game for entertainment purposes and prohibits the user from doing a number of things with the game that the publisher would prefer not to happen, including copying or reverse engineering the game. Perhaps most importantly, the EULA states that the user agrees to comply with all terms of the EULA by clicking "Accept" or by using the game, which is a proxy form of agreement that is dictated by the circumstances and serves as a stand-in for the signature and exchanged copies that would exist for a normal contract.

## TECH REQUIREMENTS

You acknowledge and agree that your use of the Game and Service require certain equip-ment, software, and internet connectivity and that you are solely and entirely responsible for attaining and paying all costs and fees associated with attaining, maintaining, servicing, repair, or correction of such equipment, software, and connectivity necessary for you to access and/or use the Game or the Service. You also acknowledge and agree that the equip-ment, software, and internet connectivity required to use the Game and/or the Service may change over time as the Game and Service evolve and in the sole discretion of the Publisher, that any such changes might change the equipment, software, and/or connectivity necessary to use the Game and Service, and that in such event you, and not Publisher, are responsible for purchasing any necessary additional or different equipment, software, and connectivity in order to use the Game and Service.

As sometimes is the case with the terms of agreements, this provision is included to make clear what most people would have assumed without being told. Specifically, it expressly states that it is the user's responsibility to have and maintain any hardware, software, and internet access needed to play the game. This provision is intended to prevent or respond to any claim from a user that the publisher is responsible for providing anything more than the game itself and the service on which the game operates.

## ADDITIONAL LICENSE LIMITATIONS

The limited license granted above is subject to the additional limitations set forth below. Any use of the Game or Service in violation of the license limitations set forth below is an unauthorized use outside of the license granted herein and will be regarded as an infringement of Publisher's rights in copyright and other intellectual property in the Game. Under the License you agree that you will not, under any circumstances:

A. Sell, lease, rent, loan, sublicense or otherwise transfer the Game, or grant a security interest in or transfer reproductions of the Game, to other parties in any way not expressly authorized herein;

B. Copy, photocopy, reproduce, translate, reverse engineer, derive source code from, decompile, or modify, disassemble, or create derivative works based upon, in whole or in part, the Game, except that you may (i) make one (1) copy of the Game and any accompanying documentation for personal archival purposes only; and (ii) use image and video capture software to capture the output of the Software as audio, video and/or still image files solely for personal, non-commercial use pursuant to the Terms of Use and applicable Publisher policies;

C. Modify or cause to be modified any files that are a part of the Game or the Service in any way not expressly authorized by Publisher;

D. Violate any applicable law, rule or regulation in connection with your use of the Game or the Service;

E. Disrupt or assist in the disruption of any computer used to support the Game or Service or any other player's Game experience (which may also be a violation of criminal and civil laws);

F. Use (or allow any other person or entity to use) the Game or any of its parts, including without limitation the Service, for any commercial purpose not expressly set forth herein, including but not limited to, (a) collecting, generating, or advancing accounts or in-game resources, items, or currency in exchange for payment or for sale outside of the game, (b) playing the game in exchange for payment now or in the future, or (c) use of the Game at a cyber café, gaming center, or any other location-based site that has not been expressly approved for such use by Publisher in writing;

G. Use any third-party program that interacts with or modifies the Game or the experience of playing the Game in any way, including but not limited to, mods, hacks, cheats, scripts, bots, trainers, or any automation program that interacts with the Game in any way, or any third-party program that intercepts, mines, or otherwise collects information from or through the Game or the Service, redirects any communication between the Game and Publisher, or reads areas of memory used by the Game to store information about the Game; or

H. Host, provide, develop, facilitate, create, or maintain any unauthorized connection or matchmaking services for the Game, including but not limited to connection to any unauthorized server that emulates or attempts to emulate the Service, for any purpose (e.g., play over the internet or local network play), intercept, emulate, or redirect communications or communications protocols used by or directed to or from Publisher, or connect to the Service using programs or tools that have not been provided or expressly approved by Publisher.

This section provides an extensive list of what users are not allowed to do with the game, essentially a much more detailed version of the list of prohibited acts that is included in the EULA's opening. The list includes obviously prohibited behaviors, such as copying or modifying the game, as well as more rare and technical offenses, such as interfering with systems on which the game operates or using third-party software to automate the game or mine data from the service. These prohibitions are written expansively because the possible actions that users might take with respect to a game that would be problematic for the that game's publisher are innumerable and always changing. While some people will argue that including these prohibitions in a EULA is not an effective way of preventing end users from doing these things, only a very badly written license would omit language describing what uses of the licensed material are prohibited.

## OWNERSHIP

Publisher owns or has licensed all rights and title in and to the Game and the Service, and all data and content included therein, including without limitation, accounts, titles, computer code, themes, objects, currencies, artifacts, characters, character names, character likenesses, character inventories and profile information, locations, location names, stories, storylines, dialogue, catch phrases, concepts, artwork, graphics, structural and landscape designs, animations, sounds, musical recordings and compositions, audiovisual effects, storylines, character likenesses, methods of operation, moral rights, applets, chat transcripts, recordings and broadcasts of games, and any related documentation (collectively, "Game Content"). The Game Content is protected by the copyright and other laws of the United States, and by intellectual property protections of other jurisdictions, treaties, conventions and laws.

The Game Content includes materials licensed from third parties which may seek to enforce their rights in the event that you violate the terms of this License. Publisher and its licensors reserve all rights in and in connection with the Game, the Service, and the Game Content, including without limitation, the exclusive right to create derivative works therefrom. You agree that you will not create any work of authorship based on the Game or Game Content and that you will never use any of Publisher's trademarks, service marks, trade names, logos, domain names, taglines, or trade dress for any purposes, except as expressly permitted by Publisher in a signed writing. Any reproduction, redistribution, or modification of the Game, Service or any Game Content, or use of the Game or Service not in accordance with this Agreement, is expressly prohibited and may result in severe civil and/or criminal penalties.

> You acknowledge and agree that you have no ownership, property, monetary or other interest in the Game or any feature or content of the Game, including without limitation, the Game Content, your account, and any in-game characters, objects or currency, and you acknowledge and agree that all rights in and to all features and content of the Game are and shall forever be solely and exclusively owned by and inure to the benefit of Publisher.

This section sets out the terms concerning the ownership of the game and its contents by its publisher, and to a lesser extent the ownership of any licensed material included in the game by the third-party licensors of such content. The above language makes clear that as the owner of the game and its contents, the publisher is the only party that has the right to create other creative works based on the game. The publisher may rely on this language if it ever needs to stop a user from creating or marketing artwork or merchandise based on the game. The end of these provisions also includes important clauses requiring that the user acknowledge and agree that they do not own the game or any of its parts, including their character and any in-game objects or currency. These express terms provide significant support to the publisher being fully within its rights if it decides to change or remove any aspect of the game, including aspects of the user's character or objects in their in-game inventory.

## CONSENT TO MONITORING

While the Game is running the software of the Game may monitor your computer's random-access memory (RAM) and or CPU processes for any programs running concurrently with the game that are prohibited by this License. If the Game detects any program or software that is prohibited by this License (a) the Game may communicate that information to Publisher with or without your knowledge, which may include without limitation your name and information about your account and the hardware and performance of your computer, the time and date, your internet protocol (IP) address, and details about the prohibited program or software, and (b) the Game may exercise any rights of Publisher under this agreement, including without limitation termination of your access to the Game and/or Service, with or without notice to you. While the Game is running the Game may also communicate to Publisher certain information about your computer hardware, internet protocol (IP) address, and operating systems, for purposes including improvement of the Game and/or Service and monitoring compliance and enforcing the provisions of this License. Publisher may monitor, record, review, modify or disclose your voice or text communications without notice to you and you hereby consent to such monitoring, recording, review, modification and disclosure. Additionally, you acknowledge that Publisher is under no obligation to monitor your electronic communications, and you engage in those communications at your own risk. Publisher may, with or without notice to you, disclose your internet protocol (IP) address, personal information, chat logs, and other information about you and your activities, in response to a request by law enforcement, a court order or other legal process, or if Publisher believes that doing so may protect your safety or the safety of others.

It is not out of the ordinary for publishers to include processes in their online games that monitor user systems while the game is being played to ensure that there are no programs running that assist the user in cheating at the game. Sub-section G under Additional License Limitations above prohibits such programs, and this provision notifies the user that the game will automatically monitor the user's compliance with that prohibition and may lock the player out and notify the publisher if it finds that the user has violated the provision. Publishers operating online games also regularly collect other information and content from users as described above in order to protect users and to continue to improve the game. By disclosing in the EULA that such monitoring and recording may be taking place and expressly requiring that the user consent thereto, the publisher protects itself from claims from users that the publisher is secretly collecting user information without permission. This provision also informs users that such information may be shared with law enforcement or as a part of other legal processes.

### UPDATES

Publisher may deploy or provide patches, updates and modifications to the Game that must be installed for you to continue to play the Game. Publisher may update the Game remotely including without limitation the copy of the Game on your computer, without your knowledge, and you hereby grant Publisher your consent to deploy, download, install, and apply such patches, updates and modifications to the copy of the Game on your computer each time you launch the Game, or automatically in the background, with or without additional notification to you.

### CHANGES TO THE GAME AND SERVICE

You also agree that Publisher may change, modify, suspend, delay, limit, "nerf," discontinue, or restrict any aspect of the Game or Service, or your access to the Game or Service, including without limitation, any features or content of the Game or Service, and any hours of availability, content, data, software or equipment needed to access the Game or the Service, at any time without notice or liability to you. You acknowledge and agree that you have no interest, ownership, monetary or otherwise, in any feature or content of the Game or Service, and that all risk arising out of your use of the Game and/or Service remains with you, the end user.

### TERMINATION OF THE GAME AND SERVICE

The Game is an online game that must be played over the Internet through the Service provided by Publisher. You understand and agree that the Service and support and access to the Service are provided by Publisher at its discretion and may be terminated or otherwise discontinued by Publisher at any time, for any reason or no reason, in its sole and absolute discretion.

Publishers update games. Sometimes users love those updates and sometimes users hate them. Sometimes an update pleases some users and is despised by others. Regardless of how users feel, in order to ensure that a game continues to improve and runs smoothly for all users, publishers regularly have to update the game. Because some users may be resistant to updating a game, publishers include terms in their EULA like those excerpted above, which inform and require users to consent to their copy of the game being automatically updated without additional notice to them.

Along similar lines, game publishers also typically include language in their EULAs indicating that they can change any content in the game at their own discretion at any time. While this right flows naturally from the publisher's ownership of the game and service expressed elsewhere in the EULA, it may be phrased as a term that the user is expressly agreeing to so that there can be no question later as to whether the user consents to the publisher making such changes. As seen above, the publisher's right to change game content is often coupled with a reiteration of the fact that the user does not own and has no other interest in the game content. A EULA will often also notify and require the user's agreement to the publisher shutting down the game and service at any time and for any reason, which can be a useful clause for the publisher to point to should they ever decide to shut down the game.

## CHANGES TO THE LICENSE

Publisher reserves the right, at its sole and absolute discretion, to revise (e.g., update, change, modify, add to, supplement, or delete) any of the terms and conditions of this License from time to time as the Game and the law evolve, in order to create a new version of the License. Material changes to this License will not be applied retroactively. You will be given an opportunity to review and accept the revised License which will supersede and replace the current License and will be effective upon your acceptance. If you accept the revised License and your account remains in good standing, then you will be able to continue playing the Game subject to the terms of the revised License. If you decline to accept the revised License, any revisions to the License are unacceptable to you, or you cannot comply with any term of the revised License, then you will no longer be permitted to play the Game and Publisher reserves the right to terminate this License. Your continued use of the Game following any revision to the License constitutes your complete and irrevocable acceptance of all License revisions. If the Game requires an Update at the time you launch the Game, then you will have the opportunity to review and accept or reject the current version of the License at that time. You can review the current version of this License by clicking on the "EULA" link located at the bottom of Publisher.com.

## TERMINATION OF LICENSE

This License is effective until terminated. You may terminate the License Agreement at any time and for any reason by notifying Publisher that you intend to terminate the agreement. Publisher may terminate this License at any time for any reason or no reason, effective upon notice to you, termination or deletion of your account, or Publisher's decision to permanently discontinue offering and/or supporting the Game and/or Service. Upon termination, all licenses granted to you in this License shall immediately terminate and you must immediately and permanently remove the Game from your computer and destroy all copies of the Game in your possession.

While EULAs are not updated as often as the games they apply to, they still require regular refreshing and edits to account for changes in the applicable law and in the gaming landscape. The provision above informs users that such updates will occur, the process by which they will be notified of updates, and, similar to the EULA's opening, indicates that agreement to the updated EULA is a prerequisite to the user continuing to play the game.

The EULA being a license, it also provides instructions for how either the publisher or the user may terminate it. The clause concerning the publisher's termination of the EULA provides for various ways that the publisher might want to terminate the license, including the most common one: termination of the user's account. By stating that termination of the user's account expressly terminates the EULA and therefore the user's permission to use the game, the EULA empowers publisher employees to correctly end a game's license to a user without requiring more formal action.

## TERMS OF SERVICE

A game's TOS (sometimes referred to as the Terms of Use or Terms and Conditions) is essentially a set of rules governing a player's use of the service on which the game operates. While you may come across a few similar provisions in both a game's EULA and TOS (recall the "belt and suspenders" explanation at the beginning of the EULA discussion), a well-drafted TOS will focus more on the service of a game than on its software. As a function of the TOS focussing on the service, publishers will often find that they rely more on the TOS than the EULA when addressing issues involving user behaviors and interactions that are facilitated by the service.

> These terms of service (the "TOS") set forth the rules and conditions by which Publisher offers you access to the service provided by Publisher (the "Service") which operates in conjunction with software of the game (the "Game"), and any other of Publisher's apps, websites, games, or services that link to this Agreement. While using these products and services Publisher may require you to provide personal info which Publisher may retain and use according to the terms of Publisher's Privacy Policy. Please read the terms of this Agreement carefully. Your use of the Game and Service is subject to acceptance of this TOS and the Game's End User License Agreement and Publisher's Privacy Policy (which are each incorporated into this TOS by reference) prior to playing the Game. By clicking the "Accept" button below, or by using the Service, you agree to all terms and conditions of this TOS and that this TOS is enforceable like any written contract signed by you.

The opening of a TOS should plainly state that it provides the rules that will apply to each user's access to the service on which the game operates. A TOS may also serve double or triple duty by applying to use of the publisher's websites and other services in addition to the game service. A game's TOS will typically include an express reference to the publisher's privacy policy and incorporation of its terms. The TOS must indicate how it is entered into and is binding upon the parties, which this TOS accomplishes by informing the user that by clicking "Accept" or using the service, the user agrees to all provisions of the TOS as if it were a signed written contract.

> ### CODE OF CONDUCT
>
> While using the Game or Service, you agree to comply with all applicable laws, rules and regulations of the jurisdiction in which you reside and the following additional rules that govern your use of the Game and Service (the "Code of Conduct"). The Code of Conduct is

maintained and enforced solely and exclusively by Publisher. Publisher reserves the right, in its sole and exclusive discretion, to modify the Code of Conduct at any time, to determine what actions or conduct violate this Code of Conduct, and to take disciplinary measures for any such violation as it sees fit, up to and including termination and deletion of your Account. It is your responsibility to know, understand, and abide by the current Code of Conduct. The following are examples of actions which warrant and may result in disciplinary measures:

A. Impersonation of any person, business or entity, including without limitation, a Publisher employee, or communicating in any way which gives the appearance or impression that the communication originates from Publisher, an employee of Publisher, or the Game or Service.

B. Selecting a character name that indicates an association with Publisher, contains personally identifying information, infringes on the rights of a third party, or is offensive, defamatory, vulgar, obscene, sexually explicit, racially or ethnically insensitive, or otherwise objectionable. This restriction cannot be circumvented by misspelling, alternative spelling, or use of numbers or symbols. Publisher may, without notification to you, modify any name which, in Publisher's sole and exclusive judgment, violates this provision, and may take further disciplinary measures, including Account termination, for repeated violations.

C. Posting or communicating any person's personal information in the Game or on websites or forums related to the Game, except that a user may communicate their own personal information in a private message directed to another individual user.

D. Harassing, threatening, stalking, embarrassing, causing discomfort or distress, or providing or directing unwanted attention to any user of the Game.

E. Sending repeated, unsolicited, or unwelcome messages, or repeatedly posting similar messages in a chat or public area, including, without limitation, advertisements to sell goods or services.

F. Posting, communicating, or otherwise transmitting any content or language which, in the sole and exclusive discretion of Publisher, is offensive, including, without limitation, content or language that is unlawful, harmful, threatening, abusive, harassing, defamatory, vulgar, obscene, hateful, sexually explicit, racially or ethnically insensitive, or otherwise objectionable. This restriction cannot be circumvented by misspelling, alternative spelling, or use of numbers or symbols.

G. Taking or participating in any action with a disruptive effect or otherwise acting in a manner that negatively affects other users, whether for personal or commercial purposes, including, without limitation, posting commercial solicitations and/or advertisements for goods and services, repeatedly posting content of a similar nature, or intentionally causing a chat screen to scroll faster than other users are able to read.

H. Transmitting or facilitating the transmission of a virus, trojan horse, bot, worm, time bomb, cancelbot corrupted data, keystroke logger, or other code or computer programming routine which can alter, damage, detrimentally interfere with, or intercept, mine, scrape or expropriate any data or personal information from, any system.

I. Removing, altering, or concealing any copyright, trademark, patent or other proprietary rights notices of Publisher or transmitting content that violates or infringes upon the rights of others, including without limitation, any patent, trademark, trade secret, copyright, publicity, personal or other rights.

J. Using or exploiting errors in design, features which have not been documented, or "program bugs" (as determined by Publisher in its sole and exclusive discretion) to gain access to a part of the Game or Service that is not otherwise available, or to obtain a competitive advantage over other players.

K. Taking or participating in any action that, in the sole and exclusive discretion of Publisher, may result in another user being "scammed" or defrauded out of any in-game item.

L. Accessing or attempting to access areas of the Game, Service, or Game servers which are not available to the public.

M. Exiting, logging out, or otherwise disconnecting from the Game during live game-play. Publisher's automated processes may track these actions and issue temporary bans to users who frequently exit during live game-play. The length of the temporary ban will increase over time if a user continues to exit during live game-play.

N. Playing on another user's account for any purpose, including to complete certain in-game content, attain any in-game item, or raise that account's status or rank.

O. Any other conduct or action which is prohibited by the EULA, this TOS, or which Publisher, in its sole and exclusive discretion, determines is contrary or harmful to the spirit of the Game, regardless of whether such conduct or action is expressly listed here.

A game's code of conduct is arguably the most important and heavily relied-upon provision of its TOS. A code of conduct is often arranged as a list of prohibited activities that could harm the publisher's operation of the game or other user's enjoyment of the game. The code should also identify the publisher as the sole determiner of whether a user has violated the code, and indicate that such violations may result in termination of the user's account and/or access to the game service. By expressly prohibiting certain problematic behaviors in the TOS, the publisher puts users on notice of what actions may get them banned from the game and will give the publisher an easy reference to direct former users to if they ask for an explanation of their ban. While publishers should cast a wide net in drafting the list of prohibited activities, bad actors are constantly finding new ways to exploit online games and harass others, which is why publishers should also include a catch-all provision that prohibits any other conduct that the publisher decides is harmful to the game (see O. above).

**USER-GENERATED CONTENT**

You are responsible for all communications, images, sounds, and other materials and info that you record, communicate, upload, or transmit through the Service ("User-Generated Content" or "UGC"). You grant Publisher, from the time of recording, communication, upload, or transmission of the UGC, a worldwide, perpetual, irrevocable, sublicensable, transferable, assignable, non-exclusive and royalty-free right and license to use, reproduce, distribute, adapt, modify, translate, create derivative works of, publicly perform, publicly display, digitally perform, make, have made, sell, offer for sale and import the UGC, including, all copyrights, trademarks, trade secrets, patents, and all intellectual and other rights related thereto, in any media now known or hereafter developed, for any purpose whatsoever, commercial or otherwise, including, distributing or selling the UGC to others, without any compensation to you. You waive any moral rights you may have in the UGC to the maximum extent permitted by applicable law. You represent, warrant, and agree that the UGC and its use for any purposes will not violate any third-party rights, will not be subject to any obligation of confidentiality, attribution, or otherwise, and that Publisher will not be liable to you or any third party for any use or disclosure of the UGC.

Users playing online games undertake any number of widely varying activities, most of which will be important or entertaining to them but of little value to anyone else. However, there are exceptions in which users create content that generates positive attention and engagement for the game. A publisher may want to use that content to market and promote the game but it could be legally risky to reuse content generated in part by users without an agreement permitting the publisher to do so. The TOS provision excerpted above addresses that issue by granting the publisher a free and perpetual license to use any such user-generated content for essentially any purpose, including to promote the game or even just to package and sell it.

## NO OWNERSHIP OF YOUR ACCOUNT

The account which you use to access and use the Game and Service, including without limitation your username, password, character, and all attributes, information, and virtual good and currency of or concerning that character (collectively, an "Account"), are solely the property of Publisher. Publisher does not recognize the purchase, sale or transfer of any Account and you may not purchase, sell, transfer or trade any Account, or offer to do so, and any such attempt shall be null and void. You acknowledge and agree that you shall have no ownership or other property interest in any Account and that all rights in and to all Accounts are and shall forever be owned by and inure to the benefit of Publisher. You cannot share an Account with anyone or allow any other person to access your account, or offer to do so for any purpose. You are entirely responsible for maintaining the confidentiality of your username and password and should notify Publisher immediately if you become aware of any loss, theft or other disclosure thereof.

## ACCOUNT SUSPENSION OR DELETION

Publisher may, in its sole discretion, suspend, terminate, modify, or delete your account at any time for any or no reason, with or without notice to you. For purposes of explanation and not limitation, if an account is suspended, terminated or deleted it is the result of a violation of this TOS or the End User License Agreement, Publisher no longer offering the Service in your region, or if doing so is in the best interests of other players or the rights of a third party (in Publisher's sole discretion). Publisher may use automated systems and tools to assist in decisions concerning suspension, termination, modification, and deletion of accounts.

A TOS should make clear that user accounts are owned by the publisher and not by the end user and that the publisher may terminate accounts at any time. By including such language in the TOS, the publisher provides express terms that it can reference to counter user claims that they can transfer their accounts to other users, or that the publisher has taken their property by banning them or terminating their account. While this may not seem like a significant point to include, it is important to remember that users invest significant time and effort to participate and advance in online games, which can cause them to incorrectly compare the game account that they use and advance with real-world objects over which they exercise similar control and likely own. Having a term in the TOS that clearly addresses this confusion in the publisher's favor will be greatly appreciated and often referenced by any publisher employees tasked with responding to user complaints.

## NO OWNERSHIP OF IN-GAME GOODS OR CURRENCY

Publisher owns or has licensed all rights and title in and to all content that appears in the Game and you agree that you have no right or title in or to any such content, which includes in-game ("virtual") goods and currency, and other objects and attributes appearing or originating in the Game or associated with an Account (collectively, "Virtual Items"). While playing the game, you may collect, unlock, or otherwise gain access to Virtual Items but you have no ownership or other property interest in such Virtual Items. Regardless of how you acquired access to any Virtual Items (e.g., crafting, discovery, collection, in-game barter, transacting with Publisher) you gain only a qualified right to access those Virtual Items in the Game while they remain associated with your Account. Publisher does not recognize any purported purchase, sale, transfer, or trade of Virtual Items completed outside of the Game. You may not purchase, sell, transfer or trade any Virtual Items outside of the Game, or offer to do so, for real-world money or any other object or activity of value outside of the Game, and any such attempt shall be null and void. Publisher does not provide or guarantee, and expressly disclaims, any value in real-world money or otherwise, attributed to Virtual Items or any data residing on servers which Publisher operates or controls, including any Virtual Items attributed to or associated with your Account. You further acknowledge and agree that you have no claim, right, title, ownership, or other proprietary interest in any Virtual Items that you collect, unlock, or otherwise gain access to, regardless of any consideration offered or paid in exchange for them. Virtual Items have no monetary value and cannot be redeemed for real-world money. Refunds for transactions with Publisher involving Virtual Items may only be obtained as expressly described in Publisher's current content refund policy. Publisher has the right to delete, alter, nerf, move, remove, or transfer any and all Game content, including without limitation, Virtual Items, at any time and for any reason or no reason, with or without notice to you, and with no liability of any kind to you. Furthermore, Publisher shall not be liable under any circumstances for the destruction, deletion, modification, impairment, hacking, or any other damage or loss of any kind caused to any Virtual Items, including without limitation, the deletion of Virtual Items upon the termination or expiration of your Account.

Along the same lines as the publisher's ownership of accounts, the TOS for any online game that includes acquisition of abilities, objects, currency, or similar content should expressly indicate that all of those things are owned by the publisher and not by the user. In-game items can resemble real-world items more so than user accounts do—they are often accessed through in-game activities or purchased using in-game currency much like actual objects are attained in the real world, and, depending on the game, in-game currency may actually be purchasable with real-world currency. These factors all contribute to strong impressions among users that they own in-game items or content, which should be clearly and definitively rejected by a game's TOS. By clarifying in the TOS that all in-game items and content are publisher property, the publisher counters any claim by users that they lose such property or its value when the publisher, in its sole discretion, changes or deletes any in-game items or content. For additional clarity, the TOS can expressly state that the publisher will not be liable to users for any change or deletion of in-game items or content as the publisher has done in the language above.

### CLAIMS OF COPYRIGHT INFRINGEMENT (DMCA)

If you are a content owner and believe that content posted on Publisher.com or elsewhere on the Service infringes upon your rights in copyright, then you can submit a notice to Publisher's copyright agent (contact information below) pursuant to the Digital Millennium Copyright Act (17 U.S.C. § 512(c)) which contains (a) an electronic or physical signature of a person authorized to act on behalf of the copyright owner; (b) a description of the copyrighted work which you claim has been infringed; (c) the URL or other location information identifying the material you claim is infringing upon rights in the copyrighted work; (d) your address, telephone number, and email address; (e) a statement by you that you have a good faith belief that the disputed use is not authorized by the copyright owner, its agent, or the law; and (f) a statement by you, made under penalty of perjury, that the above information in your notice is accurate and that you are the copyright owner or are authorized to act on the copyright owner's behalf. Notices should be sent by mail to Publisher's Copyright Agent at: Publisher, Inc. 350 5th Ave, New York, NY 10118, ATTN: Copyright Agent; or by email at: copyright@publisher.com. This email address is intended solely for the receipt of DMCA notices and is not for general inquiries. Attachments cannot be accepted at this email address and any notification submitted to this email address with an attachment will not be received or processed. Please note, DMCA notices are legal notices and Publisher may provide copies of such notices to any participants in the dispute or to third parties at its discretion or as required by law. Publisher's Privacy Policy does not apply to or protect information provided in such DMCA notices.

Through various methods and means, users occasionally use game services and functionality to infringe on the copyrights of third parties. Streaming protected movies or songs using game communication tools and the recreation of protected characters from movies or books as in-game characters are just two examples, but the possibilities are really endless. Publishers that wish to avoid being held liable for such infringements by the owners of the infringed works should include a provision like the one above in their TOS. At a very high level, the Digital Millennium Copyright Act (DMCA) provides a notice and takedown procedure for responding to claims of copyright infringement, which, if followed by a game publisher, can reduce the likelihood that the publisher will be held liable for copyright infringements by its users. The notice described in the language excerpted above is the first step in the DMCA's notice and takedown procedure and the publisher employee that receives those notices should follow the procedure set out in the DMCA for the removal of infringing content from the game service.

YOU HEREBY ACKNOWLEDGE AND AGREE THAT YOU HAVE READ AND UNDERSTAND THE FOREGOING TERMS OF USE AND THAT BY CLICKING THE "ACCEPT" BUTTON OR USING THE SERVICE YOU ACKNOWLEDGE AND AGREE TO BE BOUND BY THE TERMS AND CONDITIONS OF THIS TERMS OF USE AGREEMENT.

While there is a statement of user agreement in the TOS opening, and many terms throughout the TOS include their own statements of the user's acknowledgment and agreement, there is an accepted practice of reiterating in all capitals at the end of a TOS that the user has read, understands, and agrees to be bound by all terms of the TOS. Once again, belt and suspenders never hurt anyone.

## BOILERPLATE

Many people disregard the general provisions toward the end of an agreement, even occasionally referring to them as superfluous and not worth reading. While it is true that these terms typically cover concepts that are not deal-specific and may apply in a wide variety of contracts, that doesn't mean they don't matter or can't have unique significance for one or another agreement that your company will encounter. Knowing what those provisions mean and how they might need to be edited or negotiated for a given transaction can assist you in reducing risk and preventing surprises down the road.

### CONFIDENTIAL INFORMATION

As used herein, the term "Confidential Information" means any information, regardless of form, which is proprietary or maintained in confidence by a Party, including, without limitation, the existence and terms of this Agreement, any information, technical data, content or know-how relating to discoveries, ideas, inventions, concepts, software, equipment, designs, drawings, specifications, techniques, processes, models, data, source code, object code, documentation, diagrams, flow charts, research, development, business plans or opportunities, business strategies, future projects or products, projects or products under consideration, procedures, and information related to finances, marketing plans, sales, costs, prices, or employees, which is disclosed by a Party or on its behalf whether before, on or after the date hereof, directly or indirectly, in writing, orally or by drawings or inspection of equipment or software, to the other Party or any of its employees or agents.

### NONDISCLOSURE

The Parties understand that the obligations of this section create a relationship of confidence and trust between the Parties with regard to Confidential Information disclosed by one Party to the other Party under this Agreement. Each Party agrees to maintain the confidential status of the Confidential Information, and not to use any such Confidential Information for any purpose other than the purpose for which it was originally disclosed and in the performance of this Agreement. Neither Party shall release, disseminate, distribute, publish or otherwise disclose any Confidential of the other Party to any third party or to the public, in any manner whatsoever, without the other Party's prior written consent and approval (except as provided in this Agreement). In no event may a disclosing Party's Confidential Information be used by the other Party to compete with the disclosing Party. During and after the Term of this Agreement, each Party shall protect the Confidential Information of the other Party from disclosure or misuse using the same degree of care with which it protects its own Confidential Information of like importance, but in no event less than a reasonable degree of care. Each Party agrees to permit access to the Confidential Information only to its employees or contractors which have agreed in writing to terms of confidentiality which protect the Confidential Information from disclosure that are at least as strict as the protections set forth in this Agreement. Each party agrees to promptly notify the other Party upon learning of any unauthorized use or disclosure of the other Party's Confidential Information, and shall provide reasonable assistance to the other Party to remedy and mitigate the negative effects of such unauthorized use or disclosure. All Confidential Information shall remain the sole and exclusive property of the disclosing Party.

## EXCEPTIONS

This requirement of confidentiality shall not apply to any information that is (a) in the public domain through no wrongful act of a Party; (b) rightfully received by a Party from a third party who is not bound by a restriction of nondisclosure; (c) already in a Party's possession without restriction as to disclosure; or (d) required to be disclosed by operation of law or by order of a court or administrative body of competent jurisdiction, (provided that prior to such disclosure, the disclosing Party shall first receive notice thereof from the other Party and have the opportunity to contest such order or requirement of disclosure or seek an appropriate protective order).

Terms concerning confidentiality generally include three parts, a definition indicating what qualifies as "confidential information," protection and non-disclosure clauses stating what the parties must do to protect the confidential information and prevent its disclosure, and exceptions that describe circumstances surrounding certain information that justify not requiring the parties to keep that information confidential even if the information would have otherwise qualified as confidential information under the provided definition. Regarding the definition of confidential information, these provisions often include a non-exclusive list, and you should make sure that the list at least includes any information or materials that you absolutely want protected, potentially calling them out by name if there is any confusion. You also want to look at any qualifications on information for it to be considered confidential. The provision above only requires that the information be "proprietary or maintained in confidence by a Party," but some agreements try to restrict confidential information to only materials that are expressly labeled or described as confidential when disclosed, which can be much more difficult to do correctly on an ongoing basis. Looking at the non-disclosure requirements, you want to make sure that your company can fulfill them all and that you feel they are sufficient to protect your information that the other company receives. For example, do the terms require that the company have non-disclosure agreements in place with its employees and contractors? Does your company have such agreements? Is there any limitation on where confidential information may be stored or what teams may access it? Lastly, look at the exceptions and determine whether any present a unique concern with respect to the information that might be shared under this transaction. Is there any avenue by which the other party receives information about you or your business from a third party? Might this relationship involve exchanging information that you have unique concerns about being shared with regulatory authorities? If any of these questions raise concerns for you, then it may be worth negotiating and editing some of the confidentiality terms of this agreement to address your issues.

## TERM

This Agreement shall be effective as of the Effective Date and, subject to the provisions set forth herein, shall remain in effect until terminated pursuant to the terms of this Agreement (the "Term").

## TERMINATION

Publisher has the right, in its sole discretion, to cancel this Agreement for any or no reason at its convenience with thirty (30) days' notice to the Company ("Termination for Convenience"). Publisher may terminate this Agreement effective upon delivery of notice of termination to Company, if Company (a) makes an unauthorized assignment of this Agreement in violation of the terms of this Agreement and fails to cure or remedy the effects of such assignment within thirty (30) days after receiving written notice thereof from Publisher; or (b) makes any unauthorized use or disclosure of Publisher's Confidential Information or makes any unauthorized use of the Publisher's intellectual property and fails to cure or remedy the effects of such breach within thirty (30) days after receiving written notice thereof from Publisher. Either Party may terminate this Agreement upon written notice to the other Party of a material breach of this Agreement if such breach has not been cured within thirty (30) days after receiving written notice thereof. Either Party may terminate this Agreement upon written notice to the other Party if any one of the following events occurs: (i) the other Party files a voluntary petition in bankruptcy or otherwise seeks protection under any law for the protection of debtors; (ii) a proceeding is instituted against the other Party under any applicable bankruptcy and/or insolvency legislation where such proceeding is not dismissed within ninety (90) days; (iii) the other Party is adjudicated bankrupt; (iv) a court assumes jurisdiction of the assets of the other Party under a federal reorganization act or equivalent legislation of a foreign jurisdiction; (v) a trustee or receiver is appointed by a court for all or a substantial portion of the assets of the other Party; (vi) the other Party becomes insolvent, ceases or suspends business; or (vii) the other Party makes an assignment of the majority of its assets for the benefit of its creditors.

## EFFECT OF TERMINATION

Subject to the limitations set forth below, upon termination of this Agreement, the rights and licenses granted pursuant to this Agreement will terminate and, except as otherwise provided herein, Company shall promptly cease all use of the Publisher's intellectual property, and return to Publisher or (at Publisher's option) destroy all electronic and physical copies of the Publisher's intellectual property in Company's possession. If Termination for Convenience occurs before the completion and approval of all services and deliverables contemplated by this Agreement, then Publisher shall pay Company in full for all services and deliverables completed and approved by Publisher in writing before such termination and make reasonable partial payment for services and deliverables which Company can demonstrate were in the process of completion at the time of such termination, after which Publisher shall have no further liability to Company with the exception of terms which the Agreement expressly states survive termination.

## SURVIVAL

Upon termination or expiration of the Agreement all rights and obligations of the Parties toward each other shall cease except for Sections 1 (Definitions) 5 (Ownership), 6 (Representations), 7 (Indemnification and Limitation on liability), 9 (Confidentiality), 10 (Other Terms), which shall survive any termination and/or expiration of this Agreement.

An agreement should expressly state when it will start and when it may end, and you will typically find that information in term and termination provisions. If the agreement starts on the "effective date," it is referring to a specific date that is typically defined at the start or end of the agreement. In the above example, either party can terminate if the other enters bankruptcy or materially breaches the agreement, but only the publisher has a right to terminate for convenience (i.e., an unrestricted right to terminate at any time, usually upon a certain amount of notice). It is fairly common for the termination options to favor the party that prepared an agreement so it can be worthwhile to review them to ensure that, at a minimum, your company has the same termination options as the other party, or to require an explanation if they do not.

It is worth noting that these terms do not define what constitutes a "material breach" that would warrant terminating the agreement. If you are concerned that the other party might try to walk away from an agreement due to an insignificant issue, or if the transaction is just very important to the ongoing business of your company, then you may want to limit terminations for breach to material breaches and include language that expressly states the few circumstances that the parties agree would qualify as material breach.

Termination provisions should also indicate how the responsibilities and liabilities of each party are wound down or ended upon or following termination. These responsibilities could include the disposal or return of intellectual property, physical property, or confidential information; the sell-off of previously manufactured goods; and/or the payment of amounts owed as royalties or for completed or in-process deliverables. The areas of the agreement that can be impacted by termination can concern anything the parties did under the agreement or agreed to in the agreement so it may be worthwhile to give the entire transaction a quick review before finalizing the termination provisions.

Lastly, termination provisions are often followed by a survival provision that indicates the clauses of the agreement that will remain in effect after the termination of the agreement. These provisions can include any terms that the parties agree should persist after the end of the relationship, so if there is anything about the transaction or the relationship that you want to continue, you should make sure it is included here. Common surviving terms include sections that concern the ownership of property of the parties before the transaction or created under the agreement, protections on confidential information, and terms that could be relevant to future legal claims concerning the transaction or relationship (e.g., representations, warranties, indemnifications, limitations on liability).

## REPRESENTATIONS AND WARRANTIES

Each Party represents and warrants that: (a) it has the necessary corporate power to enter into this Agreement and to carry out its obligations hereunder; (b) the execution, delivery and performance of this Agreement have been duly authorized by all necessary corporate action; (c) this Agreement has been duly executed and delivered and is a valid, binding and enforceable obligation against it in accordance with its terms; (d) no consent of any person or entity not a Party to this Agreement is required or necessary to carry out its obligations under this Agreement; and (e) the making of this Agreement does not violate any agreements, rights or obligations existing between it and any other person or entity. In addition, each Party warrants that it shall complete its obligations under this Agreement in a prompt, diligent and professional manner in accordance with all applicable rules, laws and regulations.

Representations and warranties are, in a general sense, one party conveying to the other a guarantee of the truth of a statement. The mutual representations and warranties excerpted above are fairly straightforward and primarily serve the purpose of each party conveying and guaranteeing to the other that the party has correctly entered into the agreement and that the party can and will perform its obligations under the agreement. These representations and warranties are a good basic example set that any company entering into an agreement should be able to make. If there are additional, more specific guarantees or facts that you or your company are relying upon when entering into the agreement, you should consider discussing with the other party whether they will represent and provide a warranty concerning those points.

### ADDITIONAL WARRANTIES

Company warrants that the Deliverables, as delivered by Company: (a) shall be original; (b) have not been previously published in any form and are not in the public domain; (c) shall be delivered free and clear of any liens, charges, encumbrances or restrictions, including those of Company, and/or its employees, suppliers and independent contractors; (d) shall not violate or infringe upon any right of privacy or publicity, any intellectual property right, or any other right of any person, corporation, partnership or other entity; (e) shall not contain any libelous, defamatory, obscene or unlawful material, (f) shall not contain any viruses, worms, Trojan horses, time bombs, or other software routines or malware that may negatively impact the operation of products or services including the Deliverables or any of Publisher's or any third party's products or services or damage, interfere with, intercept, expropriate or disclose to unauthorized third parties any system data or personal information; (g) shall not contain any hidden or undisclosed feature(s) (e.g. "Easter Eggs") not expressly disclosed to Publisher in writing, or any hidden or undisclosed features that contain infringing, offensive, or inappropriate content or which could adversely affect Publisher, its licensors, or the ability to publish, distribute, or sell products or services which include the Deliverables; and (h) shall not contain any software that is distributed under any licensing or distribution model that purports to require as a condition of use, modification, and/or distribution of such software, or that software incorporated into, derived from, or distributed with such software (x) be disclosed or distributed in source code form; (y) be licensed for the purpose of making derivative works; or (z) be redistributable at no or minimal charge.

The additional warranties excerpted above might be referred to as "content creation" warranties. As opposed to being mutual, these warranties are typically provided only by the entity that is creating or providing content or material (e.g., a video game) to another party that will turn around and publish or otherwise disseminate that content or material. With this context in mind, it becomes clear that warranties (a) through (e) are essentially guarantees that the content being created and provided is not controlled by a third party, and that publishing it will not be illegal or result in the publisher being sued for certain claims (e.g., violation of privacy rights, intellectual property infringement, defamation). Warranties (f) and (g) are guarantees that the content does not include any dangerous software or hidden content, and warranty (h) guarantees that the content does not include any software that would generally be referred to as "open source" because the obligations on many types of open-source software can be problematic for commercial products.

## MUTUAL INDEMNIFICATION

Each Party hereby agrees to and shall indemnify, defend and hold harmless the other Party, and its respective affiliates, directors, shareholders, officers, agents and employees from and against any and all suits, actions, damages, costs, losses, expenses (including reasonable attorneys' fees) and other liabilities arising from or in connection with the first Party's breach or alleged breach of this Agreement or any of its representations, warranties or obligations set forth herein. For the avoidance of doubt, Company shall indemnify Publisher and its respective affiliates, directors, shareholders, officers, agents and employees with respect to any third-party intellectual property infringement claims related to the Deliverables.

## INDEMNIFICATION OBLIGATIONS

The indemnification obligations of an indemnifying Party ("Indemnifying Party") under this Section are subject to the requirements that (a) the indemnified Party ("Indemnified Party") notify the Indemnifying Party in writing within a reasonable time after the Indemnified Party is notified of a claim, (b) the Indemnifying Party have sole control of the defense of the claim (except that, if an Indemnified Party elects to do so, it may participate in the defense at its own expense) and all related monetary settlement negotiations (it being agreed that any terms, including any monetary and/or licensing terms, of any settlement of a claim that directly affects the Indemnified Party shall require the prior written approval of the Indemnified Party), and (c) the Indemnified Party provides the Indemnifying Party with assistance, information and authority necessary for the Indemnifying Party to perform its obligations under this section; provided always that the Indemnified Party shall not be required to admit liability under any circumstances. Reasonable out-of-pocket expenses incurred by an Indemnified Party in providing such assistance shall be reimbursed by the Indemnifying Party promptly upon receipt of an account of such expenses.

Indemnification is essentially one party insuring the other for financial losses incurred as a result of something that the first party did wrong, typically a breach of the agreement, an inaccurate representation, or the failure of a warranty. An indemnification clause is usually relied upon when one party is sued by a third party because of a breach or failure by the other party to the agreement. In such a case, the indemnifying party (i.e., the party that breached or failed) would have to cover the costs of the lawsuit and any settlement or judgment thereof, and reimburse the other party for any losses resulting from the failure or breach. As you can imagine, indemnification is extremely costly for the party that breached or failed, which is why the agreement puts strict obligations on how they must be notified of an indemnification obligation and gives them control in defending the claim.

## GOVERNING LAW

The validity, interpretation and performance of this Agreement shall be controlled by and construed under the laws of the State of New York applicable to contracts made and fully performed in New York, without regard to the conflict of laws provisions thereof. The Parties agree that exclusive jurisdiction and venue for any action arising under this Agreement shall be the state and federal courts located in New York County, New York. Both Parties irrevocably waive any objection to such jurisdiction and irrevocably waive the right to seek dismissal or transfer on the grounds of lack of in personam jurisdiction, improper venue, forum non conveniens or similar grounds. The prevailing party in any action shall be entitled to recover from the non-prevailing party the prevailing party's reasonable costs and expenses including, without limitation, attorney's fees.

The governing law provision of the agreement indicates which jurisdiction's laws will be applied and also typically includes an agreement by the parties to adjudicate any claims under the agreement in the courts of a certain jurisdiction. If either of the parties is particularly savvy, they may try to have the jurisdiction set in a location where the applicable law and/or the courts are more likely to decide in their favor or at least be more familiar with the issues that are likely to arise. More often, a party is interested in having the agreement's governing law and choice of forum set to be conveniently close to their offices.

## ARBITRATION

In the event that there shall be any dispute in any way arising out of or in connection with this Agreement, including any question regarding its existence, validity, or termination, the Parties shall make reasonable efforts to resolve such dispute amongst themselves, with or without mediation. Should the Parties fail to resolve such a dispute amongst themselves, such dispute shall be referred to and finally resolved by binding arbitration in the State of New York and City of New York by a sole arbitrator. Arbitration will be under the auspices of, and pursuant to the rules of, the American Arbitration Association's Commercial Arbitration Rules as then in effect, which rules are deemed to be incorporated by reference herein, or such other procedures as the parties may agree to at the time. The sole arbitrator shall be appointed by agreement of the parties. If the parties are unable to agree or fail to appoint the sole arbitrator within a period of thirty (30) days from the date when the claimant's request for arbitration has been received by the other party, the sole arbitrator shall be appointed by the American Arbitration Association. Arbitration must be concluded within thirty (30) days after the appointment of the arbitrator or such other time as agreed to by the parties. Any award issued as a result of such arbitration shall be final and binding between the parties, and shall be enforceable by any court having jurisdiction over the Party against whom enforcement is sought. A ruling by the arbitrator shall be non-appealable. Publisher and Company agree to abide by and perform any award rendered by the arbitrator. If either Party seeks enforcement of the Agreement or seeks enforcement of any award rendered by the arbitrator, then the prevailing Party (designated by the arbitrator) to such proceeding(s) shall be entitled to recover its costs and expenses from the non-prevailing Party, in addition to any other relief to which it may be entitled. Either Party may cause an arbitration proceeding to commence by giving the other Party notice in writing of such arbitration.

As an alternative to settling disputes in court, the parties to a contract may agree for disputes that they cannot resolve to be decided by binding arbitration. Arbitration is typically a less expensive and quicker option for resolving disputes and is generally seen as benefiting smaller parties in an agreement. The exception to the general idea that arbitration benefits smaller parties is the impression among the public that agreements with customers or users that require the resolution of disputes by arbitration may deprive the individual of the opportunity to bring their case to court, where they may be more sympathetic than a large company and potentially receive a larger award or negotiate a larger settlement. Arbitration clauses may also memorialize other details that assist in resolving issues quickly and cheaply, including the selection of a specific arbitration authority, the indication that only one arbitrator will be used, and setting deadlines by which an arbitration must be completed. In the interest of clarity, agreements do not typically include arbitration clauses like the one above *and* governing law/forum selection clauses like the one discussed before it, I've included both here for discussion purposes only.

### INDEPENDENT CONTRACTOR STATUS

It is understood and agreed that the Parties are and shall complete all obligations under this Agreement as independent contractors, and that neither Party shall be deemed to be an employee, partner, subsidiary, office, agent or representative of the other for any purpose. Each Party understands and agrees that: (a) it is not authorized to make any representation, contract or commitment on behalf of the other Party unless specifically requested or authorized by the other Party in writing; (b) its employees are not eligible to participate in any benefit plans, programs, or arrangements offered, or which may in the future be offered, by the other party to its employees; (c) it is responsible for its own taxes in connection with any amounts paid under this Agreement and the other Party will not withhold any taxes on its behalf; and (d) it is free to engage in other business activities and may offer services to other companies, organizations, or individuals, to the extent that such other business activities do not interfere with performance of the Services.

This clause is included to make clear that the parties enter into and perform their respective duties under this agreement as independent entities at arms-length from one another. In this way, the companies avoid any complications or obligations that could apply if either were a subsidiary, agent, or partner of the other. This clause sets an express limit on the connection between the two entities in order to remove any ambiguity that might result from one entity being principally engaged in performing services or creating content for the other for a significant period of time. That limitation is stated both in general, that the parties are independent contractors, and specifically, with the lettered clauses discussing subjects like the parties not representing each other or withholding taxes on the other's behalf.

### FORCE MAJEURE

In the event either Party is prevented from fulfilling its material obligations hereunder or said obligations are materially interfered with by reason of events of war, terrorism, fire, flood, earthquake, explosion or other natural disaster, or any other cause not within the control of such Party, such obligation which cannot be performed may be delayed until it can be performed. The Party claiming excusable delay must not have contributed to the delay and must promptly notify the other Party of such delay in writing. Moreover, the Party claiming excusable delay must take all steps reasonably necessary under the circumstances to mitigate the effects of the force majeure event upon which such notice is based. If the delay continues for more than forty-five (45) days, the other Party may terminate this Agreement by giving thirty (30) days prior written notice to the delaying Party; provided that the Agreement will not terminate if the Party claiming excusable delay substantially performs the material obligation which has been delayed within such thirty (30) day period.

Despite the exotic-sounding name, a force majeure clause simply identifies that certain circumstances are beyond the control of the parties and that if those circumstances prevent a party's performance under the agreement for an agreed-upon period of time, that failure to perform may be excused or the entire agreement may be terminated. While force majeure clauses are not common by any means, the importance of knowing what they are and how they work may be growing as the occurrence of natural disasters appears to be on the rise.

## SEVERABILITY

In the event that any restriction, covenant or provision of this Agreement should be found by a court of competent jurisdiction to be void, invalid, illegal or unenforceable in any respect, the validity, legality and enforceability of the remaining restrictions, covenants, and provisions contained herein shall not in any way be affected or impaired thereby. In the event that any restriction, covenant, or provision of this Agreement should be found by a court of competent jurisdiction to be unenforceable by the Party seeking to enforce it, such restriction, covenant, or provision shall apply with such modifications as may be necessary to make it valid and effective.

Contracts include severability clauses in order to keep a single problematic clause from sinking an entire agreement. For various reasons, an agreement provision that is perfectly legal and enforceable in one jurisdiction may be illegal or unenforceable in another jurisdiction. As an attempt to prevent a court presiding over a case involving an agreement that contains such a term from declaring the entire contract void, a severability clause memorializes the parties' agreement that, in such circumstances, the rest of the agreement should continue in full force. As in the excerpt above, a severability clause is often accompanied by a reformation clause, which generally states that if a provision of the agreement is determined by a court to be unenforceable, then it will essentially be modified ad hoc at the time of trial as needed to make it enforceable.

## ASSIGNMENT

This Agreement and the rights granted hereunder are personal to Publisher and Company. Neither Party may assign this Agreement by contract or by operation of law, without the other Party's prior written approval, provided either Party may assign this agreement as part of the acquisition or merger of the Party or the sale of substantially all of the assets of the Party. To the extent approval is given for an assignment, this Agreement will be binding on the Party's respective successors and permitted assigns. Publisher may assign this Agreement to an affiliate of Publisher without the permission of Company, provided that any such assignment shall not relieve Publisher of liability for any failure of performance or breach of this Agreement by such affiliate. Any attempt by either Party to sub-license, assign, mortgage or pledge this Agreement or any of its rights hereunder other than as permitted herein shall be of no force or effect and shall constitute a material breach of this Agreement.

In general, agreements that involve the performance of complex services or the creation of content typically prohibit the service performer/content creator from assigning their obligations to a third party. The hiring party likely selected the service performer/content creator to perform the services or create the content and those duties are rarely fungible. The above provision restricts either party from assigning the agreement without the other party's permission, except that permission is not required when the assignment is part of a merger or sale of the company, which is a fairly standard carveout. The exception included later in the paragraph, which would allow the publisher to assign the agreement to an affiliate without the company's permission, should raise questions that you may want answers to before agreeing to that language.

## WAIVER

No waiver by either Party, whether express or implied, of any provision of this Agreement shall constitute a continuing waiver of such provision or a waiver of any other provision of this Agreement. No waiver by either Party, whether express or implied, of any breach or default by the other Party, shall constitute a waiver of any other breach or default of the same or any other provision of this Agreement.

A "no waiver" clause is included in an agreement to prevent one party from claiming that the other party has permanently waived a provision of the agreement or must ignore repeated breaches or defaults, simply because the party has not required strict performance of all agreement provisions or correction of all breaches or defaults to date. In other words, the clause ensures that the terms of the agreement remain enforceable by the parties as written, even if one or both of the parties are occasionally lax in requiring the strict performance of some terms of the agreement or do not always require timely correction of all issues.

## NOTICES

All notices which either Party is required or may desire to serve upon the other Party shall be in writing, and addressed to the Party to be served at the addresses set forth below (or such other addresses as the Parties request by notice given pursuant to this section) and may be served by personal delivery, nationally-recognized delivery company (postage prepaid with tracking provided upon request), United States first class mail (postage prepaid with tracking provided upon request), or electronic mail. Notices to Publisher shall be sent to Publisher, Inc., Attention: John Empire, 350 5th Ave, New York, NY 10118, (jempire@publisher.com), with a copy to: General Counsel, same mailing address (legal@publisher.com). Notices to Company shall be sent to Company, LLC, Attention: William Flatiron, 175 5th Ave, New York, NY 10010 (wflatiron@company.com), with a copy to General Counsel, same mailing address (legal@company.com). Notices shall be deemed served at the time of delivery if delivered personally, two (2) days after deposit if sent via overnight delivery or United States mail, and upon sending if sent via electronic mail.

Notice provisions are not very contentions terms but they are a valuable reminder that, while the parties to an agreement may speak informally on a regular basis, communications concerning certain aspects of the agreement must be sent according to formal requirements. What communications require this heightened level of formality and notice will typically be indicated in the agreement, but at a minimum they usually include notifications of breach, termination, or change of address for sending formal notices. The notice provision should set forth the addresses for each party that required notices must be sent to, the methods by which such notices may be sent, and the number of days after sending that notices are considered served upon the other party. If physical deliveries are not reliable at your office then you may also want the notice provision to indicate that an electric copy of all required notices also be sent to a designated email address that is checked at least daily.

## ENTIRE AGREEMENT

This Agreement, along with any attachment, exhibits, and/or schedules, constitutes the entire agreement including all understandings, representations, conditions, warranties and covenants between the Parties concerning the subject matter hereof and supersedes any prior agreement between the Parties. Neither Party relies upon any warranties, representations or inducements not set forth herein. This Agreement may be amended only by a written instrument signed by officers of both Parties.

The entire agreement clause, also known as the integration clause, states that the agreement document (including any schedules and exhibits it references) is the entire bargain negotiated and agreed to by the parties, that all obligations, promises, assurances, warranties, and other terms relevant to the deal are included therein, and that nothing has been left out. This is largely a preventative measure to preclude either party from claiming that the bargain they negotiated included other terms or factors that didn't make it into the agreement. As an additional measure to prevent non-agreement materials from being considered binding, the entire agreement clause is followed by a succinct statement that the agreement can only be changed by a subsequent document that is also signed by both parties. The general point is that if it isn't here and it isn't signed, then it isn't going to be binding.

## COUNTERPARTS

This Agreement may be executed in one or more counterparts, including in scans, electronic transmissions, facsimiles, and other media, each of which shall be deemed an original, but all of which together shall constitute one and the same instrument.

The counterparts clause is a useful housekeeping measure to ensure that all parties are in agreement that the document is still a single enforceable contract even though it was executed electronically or using scans exchanged via email. The days of every important contract being executed in person followed by handshakes and brandy are gone and agreements must adapt.

# CHAPTER 6

# Privacy and Data Security in the Game Industry

## THE ONE THING WE KNOW ABOUT PRIVACY AND DATA SECURITY IS THAT WE HAVE NEITHER

Going forward, no company will ever have a finished privacy and data security program. Technology is rapidly changing, and the threats are continuous. In the early 2000s, privacy used to be a single task and that task was to write a privacy policy. California was the first and only state to require it after passing pioneering legislation in 2003. After the policy was written, no one ever read it again. Now "doing" privacy is a continuous process that involves resource allocation year-round, including assigned employees, financial commitments, and legal resources. The people currently responsible for privacy programs have grown up in a world where it was not important. For 20 or 30 years, they have done their jobs in games thinking privacy was something done by information technology (IT) or human resources (HR). Now, it is part of the daily lives of almost every department in the game industry. The technological hurdles are real, but the institutional complacency, political issues, and personal resistance to change are the biggest barriers to games becoming legally compliant and catching up to more sophisticated industries in terms of privacy.

As a first step, we should define privacy and data security. They are not the same thing, but are intimately related. Privacy refers to the safe, confidential, and compliant treatment of player or employee data. It can include marketing regulatory aspects like the CAN-SPAM Act for email and COPPA for children, and the TCPA regulating the use of a person's phone number. Outside of the game industry, and in some special cases, this might also include keeping a person's healthcare and financial information private. Data security is the physical, administrative, and technological measures that we use to prevent unauthorized access to data. This can be personal and private information on users or employees or it can be sensitive business information like contracts, price lists, and source code. Data security is a safe and privacy is the combination. The two topics are related because you might have data security without privacy, but you cannot have privacy without data security.

## DATA SECURITY: PHYSICAL, ADMINISTRATIVE, AND TECHNOLOGICAL MEASURES

Physical, administrative, and technical security measures are usually mentioned together in any discussion of data security. These terms refer to the three main classes of mechanisms we use to keep data safe. Physical measures are items such as locks on doors, secure server rooms, and desktop and laptop locks. Administrative measures are password requirements, a functioning Privacy Group, enforcement of a data lifecycle, and frequent audits. Finally, technical measures are software-based impediments to intrusion such as encryption, file tracking, and firewall technology.

## CREATION OF A PRIVACY AND DATA SECURITY PROGRAM

Your privacy and data security program starts with the creation of a Privacy Group within your game company.[1] Depending on the size of your company, this might have just a couple of people, but could be as many as a dozen in an international organization. Who is in the group? It is important that the Privacy Group be multidisciplinary because working toward the goals of the group will require coordination across different parts of the company that are not accustomed to working closely together. This, by far, is the most difficult part of implementing a program. You will need representatives from each department to understand their concerns, the concerns of others, and how these tie together as a whole. Then, they actually have to work toward implementation of your program. The core areas to start a Privacy Group are IT, HR, finance, marketing, and legal. Depending on the size of your game company, you may also have risk management, business affairs/procurement, and international representatives from overseas offices. As we move forward with this chapter, it will become obvious why each one of these departments needs to be represented.

Planning and pacing the group's progress is a key consideration. For companies with fewer than 50 employees, a basic program can be set up in as little as three or four months. For large game companies like publishers with offices in several countries, a program may take up to 24 months to reach the same level of maturity because of the complexities of departmental coordination, the volume of data, and institutional inertia. In either case, the Privacy Group should meet as often as it takes to implement the program. Normally, this meeting schedule is monthly, with concrete follow-up at the end of each meeting. I also recommend that the Privacy Group set goals on a monthly, quarterly, and annual basis.

Last, consider implementing rules and other practical elements to increase participation. Simple items like agenda creation and reporting add accountability. Another main administrative element that seems to increase participation is mandating that each representative department sends an empowered representative. This is first set up by circulating an agenda prior to every meeting to ensure that no one can be surprised about what topics are covered. Then, if a group is not in attendance, that department must abide by the decisions of other attendees. This type of purely parliamentary procedure increases involvement and attendance. It also furthers the managerial idea that the Privacy Group jointly governs privacy and data security issues across departments. Good Privacy Group procedures also apply pressure to the "fiefdoms" that oversee these issues—fiefdoms that can create the main corporate resistance to creating and implementing privacy and data security standards.

## WHAT DOES THE PRIVACY AND DATA SECURITY GROUP DO?

The Privacy Group has the following core responsibilities, which also serve as an outline for this chapter:

1. Reviewing and updating the Privacy Notice (privacy policy)

2. Data classification

3. Assigning data attributes

4. Auditing the game company's data collection, use, and storage practices

5. Vendor management, including vendor data audits

6. Setting internal policies regarding employee information

7. Creation of policies regarding confidential business information, including company and player financial information

8. Reviewing marketing communication issues and player information usage

9. Review of IT infrastructure, patching, and application security management

10. Responding to data incidents and data breaches.

Reviewing the list above makes it obvious why the Privacy Group has to have representatives from so many areas of the game company. It is impossible to talk to marketing or finance about data security and storage without having IT in the room to discuss what is technically possible. It is impossible to do any of the above without understanding the legal framework. All of those groups have to work together to make this happen. Furthermore, everything on the list above should be implemented consistently across the organization, which also implicates a cross-functional group. Sharing budgets to build or license communal privacy and security software products is a common result.

Taking each task above and reviewing a short summary of what is involved will further reinforce the necessity for a cross-functional group.

## REVIEWING AND UPDATING THE PRIVACY NOTICE (PRIVACY POLICY)

The company privacy policy is the one thing that almost anyone could guess that the Privacy Group will be responsible for. Regular reviews of the policy, reviews of the law, and, most importantly, keeping up with changes in business processes related to a game company's data collection, storage, and usage are the key to keeping the policy current.

People often ask which country's law a company should consider when going through any of the tasks above, and especially when reviewing and revising the privacy policy. The simplistic lawyer answer is that every country where the game company has customers, does business, or has an office should be reviewed. I call this the simple lawyer answer because, while it is technically correct, and would likely get an A on a law school exam, it is no way to run a business. That answer, a law student's answer, does not balance cost and risks.

The real answer is to look at rationalized compliance. With rationalized compliance, we consider: (1) Where are your players? (2) Where are your offices? (3) Where are your assets? and, finally, (4) What countries have had the most privacy enforcement, especially against foreign companies? Taking a look at these four areas will help your Privacy Group to decide which countries and laws should be used to inform the privacy policy. Beyond law, we should also mention that the consideration of industry best practices and self-regulation will also inform the privacy policy. An example of high-quality self-regulation that makes its way into a lot of privacy policies is the online behavioral advertising program created by the Interactive Advertising Bureau or the ESRB's efforts around privacy policies, especially children's privacy for games.

After assessing the relevant law as discussed above, the next item to consider in a privacy policy is maintenance of the company's data collection, use, and storage. Each of these are different areas that need to be fully understood by the Privacy Group and outlined in the company's privacy policy. This task leads us neatly to the next area of responsibility for the Privacy Group: company data classification.

## DATA CLASSIFICATION

This is fundamental to the success of each game company's privacy program. Before we can discuss how to protect information at all, we need to list the data types we have and then know how to classify the different types of information we possess. Data classification systems should be customized to each company by the Privacy Group. The description below is a common one, but your company may have more, less, or different categories, depending on your operations and risk tolerance.

- *Confidential business information*: This information is normal business-sensitive information like source code for your game, vendor contracts, pricing, and sourcing information.

- *Employee personal information*: Employee names, phone numbers, addresses, social security numbers, retirement plan information (including beneficiaries), banking information for direct deposits, health plan information, employee salary, and reviews.

- *Customer personal information*: Customer names, addresses, email addresses, birthdays, account user IDs, and passwords.

- *Customer financial information*: Customer credit cards, bank details, and other financial information.

- *Children's information*: This definition comes from the U.S. COPPA statute. This information includes any uniquely identifying information relating to children under 13 (in the US) including name, address, email address, geolocation information, unique numerical identifiers, and photos.

- *Other special types of information (that is healthcare)*: Unless you are focused on healthcare related games, health specifically is not going to apply to you outside of your employee and insurance records. In the United States, healthcare information is specially regulated by HIPAA and other statutes. More than anything else, this is mentioned as a reminder to think through the different types of information your game company has, to see if there is anything that needs to be changed to customize this list to your company.

- *Non-sensitive information*: Last, there is non-sensitive information in every business. The information on your website is non-sensitive. Information about the physical address of your company, information about where your company is incorporated, information on your state licensing and other registration, and information on the winners of public contests are all non-sensitive. Sometimes this non-sensitive information is private as well, but it can still be non-sensitive. Consider the number of paper cups you order each month or what brand of toilet paper is in the bathrooms. I suspect that information is not publicly known, but we should not work very hard to protect it. The question to ask in each department is: Do we care if this information gets out? If so, this is the only information that the Privacy Group should work to protect. Everything else can go into the non-sensitive category.

Now that we have the data type above, we move to the second step, which is to assign a classification. Another way to think about data classification is to ask what the attributes of that data should be. For instance, now that we have labeled the important types of data above, consider what that means for the company. Should that data be encrypted in storage; how about in transit? Does the data have limited access, and if so, what type of limited access? What is the life cycle for this data (i.e., how often is it destroyed)? Does the data have special back-up requirements?

Another frequent step in data classification is to take a list, like the one above, and expand those data types into buckets as follows.

- *Secret*: Data that is secret is core information for the company and is only known and freely accessed by a few people. This data might normally be encrypted all the time and will be accessible in very limited circumstances. Employee data, healthcare, salary, contracts, and children's personal information are good examples of data that is normally labeled secret.

- *Wide internal use*: This includes things like email, player non-public telemetry data, or game assets currently in development. There are probably some restrictions on use, but a larger number of people have access to this data. Some of the data, like game builds, may be encrypted when it leaves the building, but in the day-to-day operations of the company, this data type is not encrypted.

- *Public*: This label is used for items classified above as non-sensitive information and perhaps other similar information, like a company phone directory. Even if, strictly speaking, the information is not public, if we are not going to special efforts to protect the information, it may get this classification. This classification would include very few access controls, no encryption, and no other special protections.

## ASSIGNING DATA ATTRIBUTES

After the data is classified, what does that mean in practice? What makes secret data different from public data, or any two data classes different? The key difference is what attributes that data has in your management system. Data can have any number of attributes, generally speaking, but privacy and data security usually focus on a few key attributes more than any others.

- *Access*: Simply put, who has access to this data? For instance, HR records may be viewable by the individual employee and the HR department alone. Only the CEO or even the legal department may have access to HR records under special circumstances. How is the access controlled? Is there a physical security mechanism for a paper record, or perhaps a network drive with limited access?

- *Storage*: How is the data stored? Is it on a computer or network? Is it printed only?

- *Encryption at rest and encryption in transit:* Some but not all data should be encrypted. This depends on the organizational risk tolerance and data classification. Furthermore, you may choose to only encrypt data when it is being moved from one place to another, but after it is "safely" in a regulated system environment, for speed of access, cost, or other reasons, you may choose to leave it unencrypted. A customer email list is an example of something that may be unencrypted at rest, but encrypted when it is being moved.

- *Tracking*: Some data, like financial spreadsheets or game builds, will have tracking. You will want to know whenever a change is made and who accessed the materials. Other data is not as critical to track. Currently, we really cannot reasonably and cost-effectively track every bit of data and all data access, so choices have to be made around this attribute. Tracking also includes copying or moving files, including, most importantly, moving files over the internal network or internet, or on a removable drive.

- *Data life cycle*: The king of all data attributes is data life cycle. How long will the data live on your systems? "Forever" is the traditional and still most common answer. However, "forever" is always the wrong answer. All data should be deleted at some point for a number of reasons. Cost of storage comes immediately to mind. Larger publishers waste hundreds of thousands to millions of dollars per year storing worthless data. The second overriding reason to delete data is that you cannot lose what you don't have. Never in the history of the world has properly deleted data resulted in a data breach. Third, this allows a company to control the story in a litigation context. One of the most expensive parts of litigation is the production of documents, known as "discovery." A good data life cycle makes calculating discovery cost efficient and easy. Imagine if every project had a binder at the end, which only contained well-reviewed documents necessary for the project going forward. All of the cursory email communication and other material are automatically destroyed after a few years. Saving discovery cost pays for much of the cost of a privacy program in many large companies. Avoiding a litigation loss based on superior records is an unanticipated boon as well.

## AUDITING THE GAME COMPANY'S DATA COLLECTION, USE, AND STORAGE PRACTICES

At the start of the privacy program and every year (or two) thereafter, each company should separately consider the collection, use, and storage of information. By way of example, the information covered in this section includes the information collected by marketing and procurement departments. The HR group and employee information are covered in a separate section below. Each department with sensitive information should be surveyed first with a written form and followed up with a personal interview from someone either in the Privacy Group or another person designated by the Privacy Group to perform the audit.

The audit should include the information that is collected and stored in each department along with the protections for that information. Any changes from year to year should also be noted. The product of the audit should be a report to the Privacy Group that contains the information above along with a plan for any required remediation procedures.

## VENDOR MANAGEMENT, INCLUDING VENDOR DATA AUDITS

Vendor management includes setting requirements, on-boarding vendors, and then vendor monitoring or audit. The internal data audit tells a company about the types of information it deals with. Some vendors will not require any monitoring or special onboarding by the Privacy Group if they do not deal with any sensitive information. For vendors that have access to the sensitive information outlined earlier in this section, those vendors should be classified based on how sensitive that information is.

Audit frequency is almost self-explanatory. A normal game company may audit some vendors with access to sensitive information every year. Others may only be audited every two to three years or even as part of a randomly selected audit pool. The frequency determination is made based on the type of information the vendor has access to and the level of supervision the Privacy Group has mandated for those vendor classes.

As for audit type, audits can occur in three general ways: (1) self-certification, (2) first-party audits, and (3) third-party audits. Self-certification is similar to the first step of an internal audit. A form is sent out to a vendor containing the privacy requirements. This form is completed by the vendor, returned, and may be followed-up by a phone call, if necessary. First-party and third-party audits are reserved for vendors with more highly sensitive information. First party involves the publisher directly auditing the vendor. Third party involves hiring an outside company to audit the vendor. Those audits will often include forms and site visits, and may also include technical penetration testing.

After auditing, any report or aggregated report collection is given to the Privacy Group along with any necessary remediation plans. The Privacy Group directs these remediation efforts and sets additional audits or makes other changes in the vendor audit process as necessary. This remediation process should be stressed from the beginning with vendors to support their honesty in self-reporting and their cooperation in the audit. The audit is not about termination, though it can lead to that in unusual situations. The audit is about knowing where the risk is and working to fix it. In some cases, the Privacy Group and business stakeholders should be comfortable that this may come with increased pricing, which is often less expensive than changing vendors.

Privacy is not a "cost of doing business," especially when a company has very specific privacy requirements. Privacy is often part of a specification that a vendor will build specifically for a company. The alternative is to work within the boundaries of the vendor system and accept some protections that are less than, or different to, what the game company would have requested.

## SETTING INTERNAL POLICIES REGARDING EMPLOYEE INFORMATION

One of the most sensitive types of information that every game business has is employee information. This includes employee onboarding documents, their reviews, health insurance, salary, tax, and other associated information. Clearly, this type of information is confidential and should only be shared with other people and entities on a need-to-know basis. Data breaches in this area, even lost HR laptops containing employee data, are one of the most common and expensive data breaches.

HR could be considered one of, if not the most important area, of the internal audit because of the risk level and impact of a breach in this department. This area should be tightly reviewed for physical, administrative, and technical security procedures. The compliance in this group should fit both legal requirements and the requirements of the Privacy Group.

A core component of data inventory and audits in this environment is ensuring that everyone in the company has completed the proper onboarding paperwork, such as confidentiality and intellectual property agreements. Secondarily, the proper paperwork for employees departing the company is equally important to confirm. Encouraging consistent procedures for hiring and removing employees along with mandating appropriate paperwork is one of the best outcomes of an internal HR audit.

## CREATION OF POLICIES REGARDING CONFIDENTIAL BUSINESS INFORMATION, INCLUDING COMPANY AND PLAYER FINANCIAL INFORMATION

Another key type of sensitive information held by every game company is confidential business information. This includes things such as vendor agreements, pricing, and game analytics. It can also include heavily regulated as well as confidential information, such as player financial information.

As with HR, the physical, administrative, and technical safeguards should be reviewed annually and each department with access to this information should be audited. Depending on the Privacy Group's risk tolerance, and the sensitivity of the information, policies can be set in each area. As with HR, data audits in this area also serve the additional function of providing an inventory. Vendors without completed contracts are discovered and potential issues with player financial information may be uncovered as well.

## REVIEWING MARKETING COMMUNICATIONS ISSUES AND PLAYER INFORMATION USAGE

This is one area that is really best described as a crossroads in privacy and data security. So many of the areas above come together in this section. For instance, earlier tasks deal with reviewing the privacy policy for a game. Here is where that policy becomes a tactical reality.

Compare the privacy policy for player information against what is actually being done. Are we collecting, storing, using, and sharing in the way we describe it online? Do we think we have data for a person from any country where we don't meet the data requirements? For instance, do we have EU players without completing the GDPR requirement? Do we have personal information for children under 13 without COPPA compliance? Do we engage in behavioral advertising? Are we following FTC guidance as well as self-regulatory guidance?

## REVIEW OF IT INFRASTRUCTURE, PATCHING, AND APPLICATION SECURITY MANAGEMENT

In coordination with the IT department, the Privacy Group should review the overall IT structure within the organization. This includes basic server information, hardware upgrades, and the software patching schedule as well as data archiving and password standards. The Privacy Group should also create a disaster recovery plan as part of this function. This area integrates with other areas in this document as well because any IT systems required to implement the plans in other areas are designed under this function. For instance, the vendor audit and vendor interactions with the game company's internal systems are also provided for in this function.

## RESPONDING TO DATA INCIDENTS AND DATA BREACHES

The difference between a breach and an incident is that a breach is more serious. An incident is any potential loss or misuse of data. The loss may not be confirmed and the data may not be sensitive personal information. The incident may not require notice to consumers under a statute. A breach is a confirmed loss or misuse. It is also usually the type of loss that would implicate state statute's consumer notice requirement. The word "breach" is used for a loss or misuse of information as defined in a statute.[2] This loss or misuse will require notice to the people affected and may require additional steps to be taken as well. These steps could also include notice to a data regulatory authority. For reading ease, throughout this section, I will refer to "incident" as a term that covers both an incident and a breach.

The key to successful incident management is having an incident response plan in place prior to the incident. An incident response plan will always have the following parts.

A list of internal people to contact to report the incident. This is often easily done by setting up an email address like "incident@gamecompany.com." This way, the members of the group can be changed as the organization changes. Who is normally on this list? The CEO, CFO, GC, CTO, an outside privacy attorney contact, and a third-party forensic company to aid in diagnosing and repairing the incident.

Contacting the parties above is a good first step, but what happens next when responding to an incident?

First, we need to stop the incident. How do we know the incident is not ongoing? This is where third party forensics comes in. There is going to be a strong inclination to use internal resources and to not engage an outside party. Internal IT may say, "We understand what happened and have it under control." We cannot stress enough that this is literally always the answer from internal IT regardless of the severity of the incident. It is critical to not trust internal IT with this because they are at a psychological disadvantage. They want to take responsibility and contain the issue. It is not a malevolent wish, but it is not in the best interests of the company. Internal IT usually cannot objectively consider what occurred or how to fix it. It's human nature to resist criticizing your own systems. As a result, IT must be told politely that they may not be "at fault" for the incident, but they are responsible for it, and the company needs a fresh set of eyes, working with internal IT, to fully diagnose the problem. An outside forensic company has the advantage of being objective and requiring an explanation of the game company's systems. This forces everyone involved to look at each piece of the puzzle carefully.

During the investigative process, beware of hacker tools that may be left in the system. It is a common tactic by hackers to continue to damage systems and steal information after an incident has occurred. The hack may be ongoing or lie deliberately dormant waiting to re-activate these tools when the company has become complacent. Fully stopping the breach may actually require wiping systems and/or replacing hardware.

After we are certain the incident is over, we need to assess the extent of the damage. What, if anything, was accessed, modified, or is missing? An incident does not require the destruction or theft of information. Damage may be done by merely accessing or modifying existing information. These breach types may be the most insidious. After you know what has happened, there are (hopefully) backup files to compare and repair any damage done.

The next stage of incident management is user communication. If personal information such as account IDs and passwords are lost, this type of communication is mandatory in many U.S. jurisdictions. The statutes will discuss what is required in the notice and may also require that administrative agencies or other governmental bodies within the state are notified. The tougher cases are those that do not require notice. What would you do if the users noticed there was an incident and what would you do if they did not notice? In my experience, incidents go more smoothly with more communication. People often distrust companies that keep things from them. If there was an incident and nothing was damaged or accessed, it will not hurt to communicate that. Most important, every incident communication, mandatory or not, should use the words "we are sorry." It is not an admission of any failure and it is extraordinarily humanizing. Every department will make efforts to remove those words, but put yourself in the consumer's shoes. Receiving a generic, whitewashed, incident notice usually gives very little information and no comfort to the consumer. Be the exception to the rule—look at the situation and ask what would you want to know as a consumer, what can we be certain of at this stage, and what actually puts the company at risk if it is disclosed?

## A WORD ON COPPA COMPLIANCE[3]

Entire books have been written on COPPA compliance and it would be outside the scope of this chapter to recreate those excellent resources here. This section is a short introduction to a complex area of the law. Today, with behavioral advertising and the analogues between COPPA and certain elements of the GDPR, working with an attorney is more important than ever for children's information.

The trigger to COPPA compliance is knowingly collecting data from children under the age of 13 or having a game/website/application directed at children under the age of 13. If either of those things are true, a game publisher is likely collecting some form of personal information under COPPA. Personal information includes a child's name, email address, unique identifier (including unique advertising identifiers), phone number, photo, geolocation information, or any other information that can be used and matched to a child.

The first compliance pillar for COPPA is age-gating. If your game is directed toward children, you must present a neutral age gate to players prior to their entering any area where information is collected. The most common neutral age gate only asks a person's birthday. If they are 13 or over, they go into the game experience. If they are 12 or under, they get asked for a parental email and they must undergo the parental consent mechanisms below prior to the collection of any information. Furthermore, a game company cannot just move them out of your game to another website or service. They should be tracked into another game-related experience that does not collect information until their account is verified. A game company also cannot give them any hints that they failed a birthday screen. The company must set a session cookie that won't allow them to just use a browser's back button or similar to enter another birthday.

COPPA is one of the most complex areas of game industry law (or privacy law) in existence. The fines related to COPPA routinely exceed $100,000. Simply put, it is a law with real teeth. The second compliance pillar after age-gating is parental consent. The two main forms of parental consent are called email plus and verifiable parental consent.

Email plus is used when the child's information is only used for internal purposes, such as tracking game-play. The most common way to set up email plus is to send an email to a child's parent explaining that the child has asked to play your game. The email should broadly describe your game with links and include a link to your privacy policy. The parent must click through and "opt in" to allow the child to play the game. A few days later, this email is re-sent to confirm the parent's consent. The parent does not have to opt in a second time.

Verifiable parental consent can be obtained through a phone call, signed form, video interview, or, most commonly, through a credit card transaction. Verifiable parental consent is used whenever a child's information is used for any purpose beyond "internal use."

Lastly, the FTC maintains a helpful FAQ that is always an excellent first step prior to contacting an attorney (https://www.ftc.gov/tips-advice/business-center/guidance/complying-coppa-frequently-asked-questions).

## THE LARGEST BARRIER TO A PRIVACY AND DATA SECURITY PROGRAM

People unfamiliar with the process will say that the most difficult thing about creating a privacy and data security program is budget or technology implementation. Nothing could be further from the truth. Costs and timing are almost entirely within the control of the organization. The technology is well known and readily available.

The largest barrier to creating a privacy and data security program is managing people and their psychological resistance to change.

Most privacy regulation and enforcement began around the turn of the last century. These regulations became more prevalent with increasing enforcement after 2010, so we have lived in a privacy-laden world for less than a decade. The recency of the development has led to a number of difficulties in adoption, especially in the game industry, which values creative laissez-faire management and resists regulation more than other industries. Healthcare and finance have lived with similar restrictions for some time and they have adapted to new laws more readily than media and games. This means that most senior people in the game industry have been trained in a world without substantial privacy protections. Consciously or unconsciously, they devalue privacy and its regulation as sand in the wheels of commerce. Of course, very few people openly admit this, but when the time comes for meeting, organization, budget, and implementation, watch what they do instead of listening to what they say.

## COMMON POLITICAL AND PSYCHOLOGICAL BARRIERS TO IMPLEMENTATION

Everyone is in favor of a privacy and data security program until they find out it is going to change how they do things. The subsection below presents the three most common problems in the implementation of a program. Every objection below is another way of saying that people do not want to (1) recognize that privacy is important and (2) change anything about how they work.

- *We have a privacy program*: This is one of the first mantras of the people resistant to the implementation of a mature program. They will point to spots of privacy like firewalls or locked cabinets in HR. They will talk about a prior breach and how it was handled as an example of their privacy program. They do not really understand the scope or purpose of a privacy program and it is just another way of expressing their resistance to change. It is not uncommon during an audit to find a pocket or department insisting that the company has a comprehensive privacy program in place. However, if other core departments in the company, such as legal, finance, HR, marketing, or IT do not know about the isolated privacy program, that alone is a sign of an immature or inadequate program.

- *Privacy is either (a) "not my job" or (b) "all my job"*: This is also referred to as the "privacy within or privacy without mentality." At first glance, it is hard to see how this is the same problem because it leads to opposite, but equally wrong, conclusions. The error is still the same and that error is fundamentally misunderstanding the scope of a privacy program. Secondarily, the error is misunderstanding a department's role in that scope.

  Examples of the "privacy within" mentality are departments like IT and HR that think privacy and data security begins and ends with their department. They falsely believe that they independently control privacy autonomously in their department, which is common for HR. Other department types, commonly IT/information security, believe that they run privacy for the organization as a whole from their department. In both of these situations, the fact is that they run a critical component of a full privacy program, but a small portion of the program as a whole.

  An example of the "privacy without" mentality is usually found in the marketing department. It is not uncommon for that group to have almost no sense of the privacy or data security laws that apply to them. Further, they are usually blissfully unaware that a large number of COPPA, FTC, and other non-breach privacy violations usually originate in marketing departments. This group controls advertising, including behavioral advertising. The group also has the most access, storage, and use of player personal information in the company. Despite these two critical privacy tasks, the department often designs advertising and communications programs that violate every principle of privacy and data security. As a result, after auditing a marketing department, it is a common result for privacy and data security to be viewed as a burden or a task that rests entirely outside of the department.[4]

- *We must protect our fiefdom*: People see a Privacy Group as a threat to their department's autonomy. How dare IT have any say in how HR records are stored?[5] Marketing cannot believe legal is going to review their promotional texts. No one understands why we need to audit and save records related to pixel tracking on our site and in our advertising. They do not understand why we cannot send our player contact information to five new Russian/Chinese vendors a year. IT does not understand why any other department can ask about, let alone influence, software patch schedules. People like to operate independently and like to believe they are independently competent at their jobs. This is usually true, but some tasks are complex, dependent, organizational tasks—like privacy.

## OVERCOMING POLITICAL AND PSYCHOLOGICAL RESISTANCE

Given that the real resistance to the creation of a privacy program is not technology or cost, what can we do to overcome those managerial problems?

- *Publicity*: A good first tool is doing a publicity tour. A privacy program should not be a corporate surprise. In the months leading up to the start or reinvigoration of a privacy program, a game company should make a concerted effort to spread the word that the program is coming. This mentally prepares people and helps remove the resistance attributable to surprise and overcome all of the resistance mechanisms above.

- *Education*: Related to the publicity tour is education. Education is similar to publicity in that it is widespread, but it has a different substance and purpose. Publicity is about raising awareness, but education is explanatory. Education answers the questions: Why do we need a privacy program? How does it affect your department? What will we be doing? And what is the timeline? Beyond addressing the objection that there is already a privacy program, along with the privacy within and privacy without mentalities, education begins to erode the fiefdom issue. Education plus publicity starts to set up a cultural expectation that a program is going to happen and starts to set internal accountability.

   Game companies can start to explain that it is true that other departments will have some operational input on privacy matters in your department, but it is also true that your department will have operational input across the company on privacy as well. This erodes the fiefdom resistance because it frames the privacy program as a compromise, reducing power and autonomy in some areas but increasing influence in other areas. The Privacy Group is a cross-functional group and that does not mean other departments will run yours, but it does mean that you will be able to exchange meaningful input between departments.

- *Buy-in*: Education and publicity will only go so far if people do not want to implement the program. I assure you that people do not want to implement the program. I have not met them, but I have met hundreds like them. They do not want to do it, but they will not express it. They will just show you through their actions.

One way of overcoming this is to generate buy-in. Buy-in is most successfully generated through input gathering and molding. Even if the end goal is and the requirements are known, work hard to gather input through a few rounds of contact and involve departments in the decision-making around implementation. The managerial effect is to streamline implementation by working within current process. In addition, the psychological effect is that people feel included in the program rather than feeling that the program is thrust upon them.

## SUMMARY

Privacy and data security, outside of payment processing and hacking game code, were largely ignored for the first 40 years of the game industry. Now, through national and international regulation and player demand, we are forced to deal with a new standard. The growing pains are real. The technical challenges exist to a degree, but they are far outweighed by the political and ideological challenges as management adjusts to the new environment. Still, we can and must adjust. Properly supervising vendors and educating our own people are important to a holistic approach. By forming cross-departmental groups, performing data audits, and consciously managing our data, internally and externally, we will eventually reach the industry maturity our players deserve for investing billions of dollars and hours into our games.

## NOTES

1. Privacy Group is a general title for the group, but some companies have found success by changing the title to increase interest and perceived prestige. For instance, attending the Privacy Group meeting may seem like a burden, whereas being named a member of the Risk Group looks like a promotion, though the tasks and scope are exactly the same.
2. Yes, different states and countries define breach differently. However, if you have an incident that requires consumer and/or regulator notice in either Germany or California, that incident has risen to the level of a breach.
3. The chapter on Advertising and Video Games (Chapter 9) contains an additional and expanded discussion on COPPA.
4. I write this paragraph with love and a deep understanding of marketing departments and advertising agencies. In fact, they are my primary legal focus in the game industry and outside of it.
5. HR will never give up the most beloved sign and symbol of their guild, the disorganized, insecure, 1960s-era metal file cabinet. They will often argue it is much more secure than having this information just "out there in the cloud" and will inform an auditor that a file cabinet cannot be hacked.

# CHAPTER 7

# Free Money!

## *Making Use of Video Game Tax Incentives*

THE YEARLY REVENUE FROM the current video game market is estimated to be $100 billion. This number is projected to grow over the next few years by somewhere between 7% and 10% a year. To put this into perspective, estimates of the global film box office for 2016 was around $38 billion, not even half of the video game revenue. While a comparison of these industries is not apples to apples, it does give an indication of a shift in the consumption of media from a passive viewer to a more active participant. This interest in being part of the action has supported the growth of eSports as a legitimate method to sell out a sports stadium.[1] As the growth of the video game sector continues, many states are seeking ways to become part of this cutting-edge industry. As opposed to the temporary nature of many jobs created by a film shoot, which might last only three months or more and which may involve a significant number of transient workers, most positions in the video game industry are more permanent in terms of time and location. These factors make video game development and publishing an especially attractive industry in many locations and are fueling competition among various states.

Some states have a natural head start in the video game world, as they already have significant technological and creative industries in place and pools of skilled workers for companies to draw from. As an example of this, California is the state with the most video game companies but does not have an incentive program focused on the industry. Other locations benefit from existing colleges and universities which focus on teaching the necessary skills to foster technology development in general or specifically in video game design and production. Still other states are seeking to generate interest in video game development in their territory by providing favorable business incentives. Many locations have learned successful lessons by enticing movie and television shoots and are now seeking to capitalize on the same benefits to generate interest from the video game industry.

Interestingly enough, many of the same state-based production and business incentives that film and television studios have taken advantage of for years have now been extended to the production or development of video games. As film, television, and video games are all "audiovisual works," various states have easily transitioned their incentives from the former categories to also include the latter. Unfortunately, there are certain states where the laws or acts creating their incentive program were so focused on television and film that they have not, and cannot, be applied to the video game industry without being amended or replaced. While considerable attention has been focused on incentives offered in places like Texas and Louisiana, these are only two of a number of locations that offer incentives to spur the development of video games and interactive entertainment. In the United States, 17 such state programs currently exist in various forms.

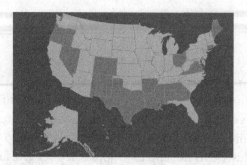

While the nature and applicability requirements of these video game incentives differ, some can be quite significant (e.g., 25% transferable tax credit or a cash rebate for qualified expenditures). As the international market witnesses the continued paradigm shift of consumer spending habits from movies and television to video games, more locales are instituting or increasing the available incentives for development. However, not "everything is coming up roses" when it comes to the expansion of incentives for video game production. In the past few years, several states have eliminated their incentive programs or no longer allow for video game development to be part of them.[2]

That said, understanding the nature and requirements of these potentially substantial financial benefits is valuable to both established game companies and new development teams. Whether a decision involves where to locate a new video game production start-up or where an established company should base a new development team, it may be of paramount importance to know if there are incentive programs the project may be able to take advantage of.

Whether you are a video game start-up or an established company, the potentially substantial financial benefits from a state incentive may be the difference between your game being made or not. If additional investment in your project is needed, the incentives can make an investment in your project more attractive. For example, an investor may be able to invest less funds in the project, thereby reducing his or her risk and potentially increasing the rate of return. If additional investment is not needed, the extra funds from these incentives can increase the profitability of a video game. Below is a list of the current states offering video game production incentives and a summary of the description, requirements, and nature of such incentives.[3]

## ALABAMA

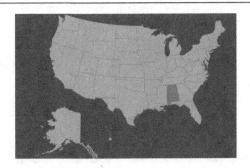

Alabama enacted the Entertainment Industry Incentive Act of 2009[4] ("Alabama Rebate"). The Alabama Rebate, which was amended in 2012, specifically includes interactive games and video games and offers companies up to 25% of qualifying expenditures, excluding payroll expenses. Additionally, the Alabama Rebate will offer up to 35% on all payroll paid to state residents. In order for a video game production to qualify for the Alabama Rebate, expenditures must be more than $500,000 but less than $20 million. The rebate will be first applied to any income tax liability the company incurs and any excess amounts will be paid directly to the company. The rebate is fairly inclusive and will cover almost all video game production expenses paid in the state of Alabama. Specifically, most preproduction, production and postproduction costs, payroll expenses, music, equipment, and facilities qualify. However, postproduction marketing costs are not included in the definition of covered expenses. Additionally, a qualifying company intending to spend more than $150,000 in a year may apply to be exempted from state sales, use, and lodging taxes for funds expended in Alabama.

To take advantage of the Alabama Rebate, the video game company is not required to be an Alabama corporation, only a corporation, partnership, limited liability company (LLC), or other business entity that is a qualified production company under the act. The Alabama Rebate is administered by the Alabama Film Office, and as is often the case with state-sponsored programs, any video game which includes content that is sexually explicit, or involves gambling or wagering, does not qualify for this benefit. Obtaining the Alabama Rebate involves applying to the Alabama Film Office to be considered as a qualified production at least 30 days prior to the commencement of the production activities on the project.[5]

The contact information for Alabama is below:
Alabama Film Office
Alabama Center for Commerce
401 Adams Avenue, Suite 170
Montgomery, Alabama 36104
Phone: (334) 242-4195

## ARKANSAS

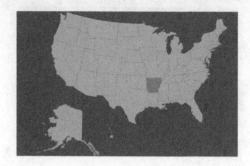

Arkansas replaced its Motion Picture Incentive Act of 1997 by enacting the Digital Product and Motion Picture Industry Development Act of 2009 ("Arkansas Rebate").[6] The Arkansas Rebate, which specifically includes interactive games and video games among the entertainment media it is intended to support, offers development companies a non-transferable rebate against qualified production costs of up to 20%, so long as these expenditures add up to more than $200,000 within a six-month period. The Arkansas Rebate also offers an additional 10% on payroll paid to certain types of employees who are full-time state residents. Almost all expenses incurred in Arkansas that are directly related to the preproduction, production, or postproduction of a video game qualify, including developer compensation (for salaries under $500,000). Even the purchase or optioning of intellectual property relating to the development of the game will generally qualify. However, most marketing, media, and public relations costs are not considered qualified production costs.

To take advantage of the Arkansas Rebate, the video game company must be a corporation, partnership, LLC, or other entity principally engaged in a qualifying production that is registered with the Arkansas Secretary of State to engage in business within the state. The Arkansas Film Office, which is part of the Arkansas Economic Development Commission, administers the tax credit. To obtain the rebate development, companies must first apply to the Arkansas Film Office for approval prior to incurring any production expense, and then certify the total costs of the production within 180 days after the last production expense is incurred in the state. The commission will then review the supporting documentation and prepare and send a recommendation for rebate to the Arkansas Revenue Division of the Department of Finance and Administration. Within 120 days, the Revenue Division will certify the amount of rebate due to the production company and issue the rebate (within an additional 10-day period).[7]

The contact information for Arkansas is below:
Arkansas Economic Development Commission
Arkansas Film Office
900 West Capitol Avenue
Little Rock, Arkansas 72201
Phone: (501) 682-7326

## COLORADO

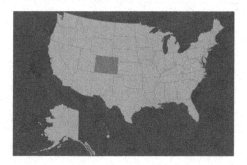

In 2012, the 2009 Colorado Film Incentives program was amended ("Colorado Rebate").[8] The Colorado Rebate, which specifically includes video games, offers development companies a non-transferable rebate against up to 20% of qualifying expenditures in Colorado, so long as these expenditures add up to more than $100,000 for a Colorado company or $250,000 for an out-of-state company. In addition, Colorado residents must comprise at least 50% of the workforce on the project. Essentially, all expenses paid in Colorado that are directly related to the production of a video game will qualify, including developer compensation (up to $1 million per employee), and the purchase or licensing of intellectual property.

To take advantage of the Colorado Rebate, a video game company is not required to be a Colorado corporation. Any corporation, partnership, LLC, or other entity principally engaged in a qualifying production may apply. However, an out-of-state company must register with the Secretary of State as a "foreign entity." The Colorado Office of Film, Television and Media administers the rebate. To obtain the Colorado Rebate, the development company must submit a "Statement of Intent" to the Office of Film, Television and Media for approval prior to commencement of the project. Once a "Notice of Conditional Approval" has been received by the developer, the state will thereafter enter into a formal contract concerning the video game project. When the development company has finished the project, it must submit "Proof of Performance" and have all financial documents audited by a Certified Public Accountant. Upon approval by the Office of Film, Television and Media, a rebate check will be issued to the company.[9]

The contact information for Colorado is below:
Colorado Office of Film, Television and Media
1625 Broadway
Ste. 2700
Denver, Colorado 80202
Phone: (303) 892-3840

## CONNECTICUT

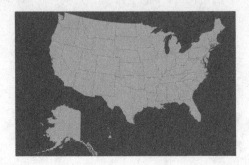

To promote the production of video games and other digital media within its borders, Connecticut enacted the Connecticut Digital Media and Motion Picture Tax Credit in 2006 ("Connecticut Tax Credit").[10] The Connecticut Tax Credit, which specifically includes video games among the entertainment media it is intended to support, offers development companies a transferable non-refundable tax credit against business taxes of up to 30% of qualifying expenditures made over the course of producing a game, so long as these expenditures add up to more than $100,000. The legislation is permissive, and essentially all expenses paid in Connecticut that a developer can demonstrate were directly related to the production of a video game will qualify, including developer compensation, design and preproduction costs, development equipment and software, and certain postproduction and marketing costs. Even the purchase or optioning of intellectual property on which to base one's game qualifies under certain circumstances.

To take advantage of the Connecticut Tax Credit, the video game company is not required to be a Connecticut corporation. Any corporation, partnership, LLC, or other entity principally engaged in a qualifying production may apply. To qualify, the development company must also register with the Connecticut Secretary of State. The Digital Media and Motion Picture Division of the Connecticut Commission on Culture and Tourism administers the tax credit. As mentioned in connection with other state-sponsored programs, any video game which includes content that is obscene, as defined in the applicable state statute, does not qualify for this benefit. To obtain the Connecticut Tax Credit, the development company must apply to the Digital Media and Motion Picture Division of the Connecticut Commission on Culture and Tourism for an eligibility certificate (within 90 days after the first qualified production expense or cost is incurred). Next, the development company must apply for a tax credit certificate (within 90 days after the last production expense is incurred in the state). No credits may be claimed before the production tax credit certificate is issued.[11]

The contact information for Connecticut is below:
Department of Economic and Community Development
505 Hudson Street
Hartford, Connecticut 06106
Phone: (860) 270-8000

## GEORGIA

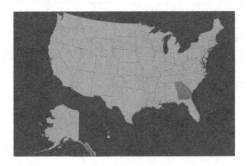

Georgia has sought to position itself as a fertile ground for game development over the last few years. To demonstrate its support of game development within its borders, Georgia passed the Entertainment Industry Investment Act in the spring of 2008 ("Georgia Act"),[12] offering producers of qualifying video games a transferable non-refundable tax credit of 20% of in-state expenditures against state tax liability. Game production companies can increase the tax credit by an additional 10% (to a total of 30%) by including a Georgia promotional logo in a prominent position within the game or credit roll. To be eligible for tax credits, production companies must first be certified by the Georgia Film, Music & Digital Entertainment Office. The certification process generally takes only a few days. Additionally, companies may also qualify to obtain a Georgia sales tax exemption.

To qualify for the tax credit, game developers do not have to be incorporated in Georgia—they only have to spend a minimum of $500,000 within the state on one project or across several projects in the course of a single year. For the purposes of calculating the $500,000 spend, game developers can include all expenses paid within the state for materials, services, and labor "directly used" in the video game production. Under the Georgia Act, "directly used" is expansive, including rental of facilities and equipment, leasing of vehicles, food and lodging costs, and even airfare expenses if purchased through a Georgia-based travel agency or travel company. In calculating labor expenditures, game developers can include payments made to both resident and out-of-state employees working in Georgia. However, marketing and distribution costs will not be included as qualifying expenditures.[13]

The contact information for Georgia is below:
Georgia Film, Music & Digital Entertainment Office
75 Fifth St., N.W., Suite 1200
Atlanta, Georgia 30308
Phone: (404) 962-4000

## HAWAII

In 2013, the Hawaii legislature expanded Hawaii's film production tax credit program by enacting Act 88/89 ("Hawaii Tax Credit").[14] Administered by the Hawaii Film Office and the Hawaii Department of Taxation, the Hawaii Tax Credit offers video game developers with a minimum of $200,000 in qualified production expenditures a refundable tax credit for 20% of those costs. (The amount may be raised to 25% for productions located in certain less-populated counties.) Unlike the non-refundable tax credits already discussed in connection with other jurisdictions, Hawaii applies a refundable tax credit to reduce tax payments due, but if the incentive is greater than any tax liability, the Hawaii Department of Taxation will make a direct cash payment to the development company. Qualified expenditures under the Hawaii Tax Credit include both resident and non-resident compensation for the time that the employee is physically working in Hawaii and subject to Hawaii income tax. Other qualifying expenditures must be subject to Hawaii's general excise or income tax and can include travel and shipping costs both between islands and from Hawaii to the mainland.

In addition to including Hawaii among the production credits of the final product, game development companies that wish to take advantage of the Hawaii tax credit must make reasonable efforts to hire Hawaiian employees and also make a financial or in-kind contribution to education or the interactive media workforce in Hawaii. Contributions have specific requirements but may generally include hardware or software donations to Hawaii public schools, offering on-site internships to public school students, or planning or participating in seminars or educational programs that benefit local unions and industry members.[15]

The contact information for Hawaii is below:
Hawaii Film Office
State of Hawaii, Department of Business, Economic Development and Tourism
250 South Hotel St., 5th Floor
Honolulu, Hawaii 96813

Mailing Address:
P.O. Box 2359
Honolulu, Hawaii 96804
Phone: (808) 586-2570

## LOUISIANA

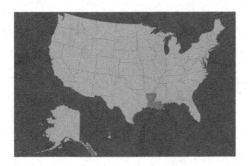

With the stated objective of encouraging "development in Louisiana of a strong capital base for the production of digital interactive media," Louisiana passed the Louisiana Digital Media and Software Act in 2005 and amended it in 2009 and 2011 ("Louisiana Act").[16] The Louisiana Act offers the developer a tax credit for labor performed in the state of Louisiana and for production equipment purchased through Louisiana businesses. The tax credit is refundable, but does not contain any transferability or carryover provisions. The enacting legislation contemplates both video games designed to be sold through regular marketing channels and projects involving virtual worlds and online games with long-term producer involvement. The tax credit offered by the Louisiana Act is equal to 25% of the investments made in those years, with no minimum spending requirements. An additional 10% may be awarded based on labor costs paid to Louisiana residents. The tax credit may be claimed for 100% of its value at the end of each year, or for 85% of the value at any other time during the year. Since being enacted, the Louisiana Act has drawn various video game companies to open up or expand their presence in the state.[17]

To receive the benefits offered under the Louisiana Act, a video game or other digital interactive media production must first submit an application to the Louisiana Office of Entertainment Industry Development. This application must contain details about the production, including the budget, anticipated employment, schedule, and intended distribution plan for the finished product. The Louisiana Office of Entertainment Industry Development reviews the application and provides an initial certification if applicable. Prior to final certification, the developer must submit a cost report of production expenditures, performed by a CPA. The Louisiana Department of Economic Development makes a final tax credit certification decision based on this report.[18]

The contact information for Louisiana is below:
Louisiana Economic Development
1051 North Third Street
Baton Rouge, Louisiana 70802-5239
Phone: (225) 342-3000

## MAINE

Adopted in 2006, the Maine Attraction Film Incentive program ("Maine Incentive") includes two incentives available to qualified companies that develop video games intended for a national audience: the Certified Media Production Credit[19] and the Certified Media Wage Reimbursement.[20] To qualify for the dual benefits of the Maine Incentive, a video game developer must spend a minimum of $75,000 in Maine over the course of one year on one or more video game productions that have been certified by the Maine Film Office, a division of Maine's Department of Economic and Community Development (the "Film Office"). To certify a video game production, the game developer must apply for and receive a media production certificate from the Film Office prior to beginning work. After completion of each certified video game production, the development company must then request from the Film Office a Tax Reimbursement and Credit Certificate.

The Certified Media Production Credit is a non-refundable, non-transferable credit equal to 5% of a developer's visual media production expense related to the production of a certified video game. The Certified Media Wage Reimbursement portion of the Maine Program applies to compensation paid by qualified developers for work done within Maine on certified video game productions. Qualifying game developers are generally reimbursed in an amount equal to 12% of total wages and salaries paid to Maine residents and 10% for total wages and salaries paid to non-residents. The Certified Media Wage Reimbursement and the income tax credit are separate applications.[21]

The contact information for Maine is below:
Maine Film Office
59 State House Station
Augusta, Maine 04333
Phone: (207) 624-9828

## MISSISSIPPI

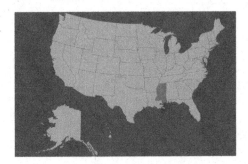

The Mississippi Film Office offers two incentive programs to video game developers. The first is a rebate on eligible expenses and the second is a reduced sales tax on equipment that is used directly in the creation of a video game.

The Mississippi Motion Picture Production Incentive Program ("Mississippi Incentive")[22] provides video game developers with a cash rebate on a portion of eligible expenses. To qualify for the Mississippi Incentive, a developer must spend at least $50,000 in their base investment or employee payroll expenses, or both, in Mississippi. The base investment is defined broadly, and includes expenses such as housing, food, and equipment rental, as long as the expense is related to the production. Employee payroll expenses are defined as salary, wages, or other compensation including benefits. The rebate amount on the base investment is 25%. For employee payroll expenses, the rebate is 30% of the payroll for Mississippi residents and 25% of the payroll for non-residents. An additional 5% bonus rebate is available for payroll made to honorably discharged veterans. The rebate amount for a particular project is capped at $10 million, and the Mississippi Incentive's annual rebate amount cannot exceed $20 million.

Projects seeking incentives must be approved by the Mississippi Development Authority before production begins. After production is completed, the developer must submit a rebate request to the Mississippi Department of Revenue which may, upon review and approval, issue a rebate check. A video game will not be eligible for the Mississippi Incentive if it contains "any material or performance deemed obscene" under the applicable Mississippi statute.

Video game developers may also participate in the reduced tax rate program available to film producers. Under this program, certain production equipment that is used directly for the project is taxed at the reduced sales tax of 1.5%. Eligible equipment includes audio equipment and editing equipment.[23]

The contact information for Mississippi is below:
Mississippi Film Office
Woolfolk State Office Building
501 North West Street, 5th Floor
Jackson, Mississippi 39201

Mailing Address:
P.O. Box 849
Jackson, Mississippi 39205
Phone: (601) 359-3297

## NEVADA

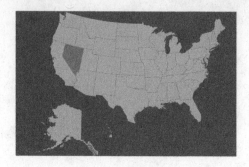

The Nevada Film Office offers video game developers a transferable tax credit on eligible expenses ("Nevada Tax Credit").[24] The amount of the tax credit on eligible production costs and on resident wages, salaries, and fringe benefits is 15%. The amount of the tax credit on wages, salaries, and fringe benefits to non-resident above-the-line personnel is 12%, but there is no similar incentive for non-resident below-the-line personnel. A developer can also receive a 5% bonus on the tax credit if more than 50% of the below-the-line personnel are Nevada residents. To be eligible for the Nevada Tax Credit, a developer must have incurred over $500,000 in qualified production costs in Nevada, and over 60% of the total production costs must have been incurred in Nevada. The Nevada Tax Credit amount for a particular project is capped at $6 million, and the annual rebate amount cannot exceed $20 million. Additionally, unused Nevada Tax Credits can be carried over for up to four years.

To apply for the Nevada Tax Credit, a developer must send in an application at least 90 days prior to the start of development. All accountings and other documents must be submitted within 30 days of completion of the video game development project. A CPA audit by a CPA licensed in Nevada is also required to claim the Tax Credit.[25]

The contact information for Nevada is below:
Nevada Film Office
6655 West Sahara, Suite C106
Las Vegas, Nevada 89146
Phone: (702) 486-2711
Fax: (702) 486-2712

## NEW MEXICO

New Mexico's Refundable Film Production Tax Credit ("New Mexico Tax Credit")[26] pro-vides developers with a 25% refundable but non-transferable tax credit on all direct pro-duction expenditures. As an added benefit for small to mid-sized video game productions, unlike incentive programs in other states that require minimum in-state expenditures to qualify, the New Mexico Tax Credit has no minimum in-state spending requirement. The New Mexico Film Office and the New Mexico Taxation & Revenue Department jointly administer the New Mexico Tax Credit. To apply, a developer must submit a registration form and tax agreement prior to the start of production. After production is complete, the developer must submit the tax application along with backup documentation to the Film Office. The Tax and Revenue Department then conducts a review of the submission and determines the tax credit amount.

The New Mexico Tax Credit does place a few limits on what expenditures are eligible to receive a 25% reimbursement. While most of the in-state expenditures contemplated by programs already discussed qualify for the New Mexico Tax Credit, a video game devel-opment company will not be reimbursed for any portion of compensation for employ-ees who are not residents of New Mexico, nor will they receive a rebate on expenses for advertising, marketing, or distribution. Additionally no rebate will apply to expenditures which were not subject to New Mexico taxation, which includes purchases made over the internet from non-New Mexico companies, purchases made on tribal lands, and pur-chases of intellectual property from non-residents. Finally, for a video game producer to be reimbursed for expenditures made on a video game, the game's script must not contain obscene material.[27]

The contact information for New Mexico is below:
New Mexico Film Office
1100 Saint Francis Drive
First Floor, Suite 1213
Santa Fe, New Mexico 87505
Phone: (505) 476-5600

## OHIO

For the purpose of "encouraging and developing a strong film industry," in 2009 Ohio enacted its Motion Picture Tax Incentive ("Ohio Tax Credit").[28] The Ohio Tax Credit specifically includes interactive games and video games within the definition of a "motion picture." It offers development companies a non-transferable but refundable tax credit against business taxes of up to 30% of qualifying expenditures made over the course of producing a game, so long as these expenditures add up to more than $300,000. Eligible production expenditures include most goods and services purchased and consumed in Ohio, including wages, facilities, and equipment. The Ohio Tax Credit will not cover any product which depicts digital images of actual sexually explicit conduct, as defined in the applicable federal statute.

To take advantage of the Ohio Tax Credit, a video game company must first register and file an application to be considered a tax credit-eligible production. Once the development company has been certified, it will receive an award letter stating the maximum amount of the eligible tax credit. There is also an application fee equal to 1% of the award amount up to a maximum of $10,000. Thereafter, within 90 days after certification as a tax credit-eligible production, and at any time thereafter at the Ohio Film Office's request, the development company must submit sufficient evidence of the progress of the project. The developer must, upon completion of the project, submit an audited report of the developer's expenses. Once the report is approved, the Ohio Office of Film will issue a tax credit certificate to the development company.[29]

The contact information for Ohio is below:
Ohio Development Services Agency
Ohio Film Office
77 South High Street, Floor 28
Columbus, Ohio 43215
Phone: (614) 644-5156

## OREGON

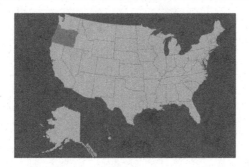

In 2013, the Oregon legislature expanded two state incentives to video game developers: the Oregon Production Investment Fund ("OPIF") and the Indigenous Oregon Production Investment Fund (iOPIF).[30] Unlike many states' programs, the Oregon incentives are cash rebates and not tax credits. OPIF applies to any project that spends a minimum of $1 million in Oregon, while iOPIF applies only to local developers whose crew is composed of at least 80% Oregon residents and whose in-state spending is at least $75,000. Both OPIF and iOPIF provide a 20% cash rebate on eligible production costs and a 10% rebate on any payroll that is subject to Oregon's state withholding tax. The iOPIF rebate applies only to the first $1 million expended on a project.

In order to apply for the OPIF and iOPIF rebate programs, a developer must submit an application to the Oregon Film and Video Office prior to the commencement of production. If the project is approved, the developer and the Oregon Film and Video Office must enter into a contract within 30 days of the eligibility approval. When the video game project is complete, the developer must submit all required paperwork to the Oregon Film and Video Office, and a rebate check will be paid pursuant to the terms of the contract.[31]

The contact information for Oregon is below:
Governor's Office of Film & Television
123 NE 3rd Avenue, Suite 210
Portland, Oregon 97232
Phone: (971) 254-4020

## RHODE ISLAND

Rhode Island's Motion Picture Production Tax Credit[32] was created in 2006 and is administered by the Rhode Island Film and Television Office. It was created for the express purpose of promoting and encouraging the production of entertainment media within the state of Rhode Island, including video games ("Rhode Island Credit"). The Rhode Island Credit offers a transferable but non-refundable tax credit to qualifying production companies equal to 25% of expenditures directly attributable to certified video game productions within the state. Rhode Island expenditures that may be counted toward a production's tax credit are expansive, including wages and other compensation to both residents and non-residents (so long as the work is done in Rhode Island), rental of facilities and equipment, leasing of vehicles, and even airfare expenses incurred to bring an employed person to Rhode Island. Notable expenditures for which the game developer cannot receive a tax credit include travel expenses for persons departing Rhode Island and any costs associated with the postproduction promotion or marketing of a video game. Moreover, the Rhode Island Credit will not cover any product containing actual sexually explicit conduct, as defined in the applicable federal statute.

To qualify for the Rhode Island Credit, a video game production must spend a minimum of $100,000 in the state. In addition, 51% of the production budget must be spent in-state (including employing at least five individuals). The Rhode Island Credit amount for a particular project is capped at $5 million, and the annual rebate amount cannot exceed $15 million. To apply for the credit, a developer must submit an initial application to the Rhode Island Film and Television Office. The Film and Television Office will review the initial application and certify the project. When production is completed, the developer must submit a final application with supporting documents, which must be reviewed and approved before the Rhode Island Division of Taxation can issue the tax credit. The video game production company must also be incorporated or organized under the laws of Rhode Island to qualify for the Rhode Island Credit. Benefits received under the Rhode Island program can only be applied for in the year in which the production is completed, but can thereafter be transferred, sold, or carried forward for up to three years.[33]

The contact information for Rhode Island is below:
Rhode Island Film and Television Office
One Capitol Hill
Providence, Rhode Island 02908
Phone: (401) 222-3456

## TEXAS

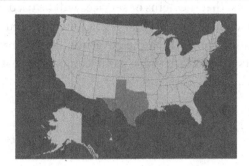

The Texas Film Commission offers two incentive programs that are specifically applicable to video game development: a rebate on eligible in-state spending under the Moving Image Industry Program and a tax exemption for the purchase or lease of qualifying items and services used in the development and manufacture of a finished video game.

Under the Moving Image Industry Program, a video game production can qualify for a cash rebate up to 20% of all eligible in-state spending so long as a minimum of 60% of the production days are completed in Texas, and at least 70% of the development team are Texas residents. The rebate amount varies with the amount of eligible spending: a development company is eligible to receive a rebate of 5% if it spends between $100,000 and $1 million, 10% if it spends between $1 and $3.5 million, and 20% if it spends a minimum of $3.5 million. Video game productions can also receive an additional 2.5% rebate on all qualifying expenditures across the entire span of the production if at least 25% of the production days are spent in an underused area of Texas (generally defined as locations outside of Dallas or Austin). Expenditures which qualify for the rebate and may be counted toward the $100,000 minimum in-state spending include wages and compensation to in-state residents (within limits), payments to Texas companies for goods and services directly attributable to the production of the video game, shipping within Texas, and air travel to or from Texas on a Texas-based airline (with exceptions). Some pre-production expenses may also qualify, but cannot exceed 30% of the project's combined Texas expenditures.

Expenditures which will not count toward the $100,000 minimum in-state spending requirement, and on which the game developer will not receive a rebate, include all wages and compensation paid to non-Texas residents and any lease or mortgage payments on facilities that are part of an ongoing business. Notably, rebates are unavailable or will be denied for video games directly used for gambling or which "contain inappropriate content or content that portrays Texas or Texans in a negative fashion."

Developers of video games also qualify as software manufacturers under Texas law and as such are eligible for a tax exemption on items or services the use or consumption of which are "necessary and essential" to the production of the completed game. These items include software that will be used in game production and computers or other equipment used solely for game development. Services which would rise to the level of "necessary and essential" include repairs to qualifying items, sound recording, and motion capture. By claiming the tax exemption, the game developer is stating, under risk of future tax penalties, that the items or services will be used directly and exclusively in the development of the video game.[34] The Texas Enterprise Fund also includes a $200 million "deal closing fund" from which the governor, lieutenant governor, and speaker together can offer grants to applicant video game companies that will bring new jobs to Texas.[35]

The contact information for Texas is below:
Texas Film Commission
P.O. Box 13246
Austin, Texas 78711
Phone: (512) 463-9200

## UTAH

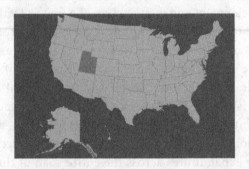

Effective as of 2015, Utah offers the Motion Picture Incentive Program to video game development companies ("Utah Incentives").[36] The Utah Incentives were created to promote Utah's resources, including its workforce, and to encourage digital media production in order to grow the state's economy. The Utah Incentives' enacting legislation, administered by the Utah Film Commission, specifically envisioned "digital media projects" as a covered production category and offer a non-transferable but refundable tax credit of 20% of qualifying new in-state expenditures. Wages and salary payable to Utah residents may be included in calculating such new in-state revenue. That said, the incentive may not exceed 100% of the new state revenue generated by the digital media project. Generally, in any given fiscal year, Utah may not issue more than $6,793,700 in tax incentives under the program. However, if the tax incentives authorized in any particular year are less than the above amount, Utah may roll the remainder over and issue it in subsequent years.

To qualify for the Utah Incentives, a digital media company must submit an application to the Utah Film Commission which includes a report detailing the qualified new in-state spending and provides for the disclosure of relevant tax returns and other auditable information. The information will be shared with the Utah State Tax Commission and the Tax Commission will determine the amount of any incentive due for the digital media project and issue a tax credit certificate in that amount. Only upon the receipt of such a tax credit certificate may a company claim the credit.[37]

The contact information for Utah is below:
Utah Film Commission
300 North State Street
Salt Lake City, Utah 84114
Phone: (800) 453-8824

## VIRGINIA

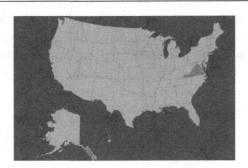

Since 2013, video game developers have been eligible to participate in the Virginia Motion Picture Tax Credit Program ("Virginia Tax Credit").[38] The Virginia Tax Credit, administered by the Virginia Film Office, was created in part for the purpose of promoting and encouraging digital interactive media production. The Virginia Tax Credit offers a non-transferable but refundable tax credit to qualifying production companies equal to 15% of expenditures (20% if development occurs in an economically distressed area) directly attributable to certified digital interactive media productions within the state during the specific tax year. Virginia expenditures that may be counted toward a production's tax credit are expansive, including goods and services leased or purchased and compensation and wages (for employees earning less than $1 million). A development company may be allowed an additional 10% tax credit of the total aggregate payroll for Virginia residents for projects costing between $250,000 and $1 million and 20% for projects over $1 million. Developers may also be eligible for an exemption to Virginia's state sales tax.

To qualify for the Virginia Tax Credit, a production must incur a minimum of $250,000 of in-state expenditures directly attributable to the video game. The Virginia Tax Credit will not cover any product containing obscene material. To apply for the Virginia Tax Credit, an eligible video game developer must submit an application to the Virginia Film Office prior to the start of production. The Virginia Film Office will decide whether to approve the project and notify the developer about the approval status within 30 business days.[39]

The contact information for Virginia is below:
Virginia Film Office
901 East Byrd Street
West Tower, 19th Floor
Richmond, Virginia 23219-4048
Phone: (804) 545-5530

## CONCLUSION

The above analysis demonstrates that many states in the U.S. are interested in bringing video game production to their particular territory. As the incentives run the gamut from the non-refundable variety to transferable (or even saleable) credits or cash rebates, it is important to fully understand their benefits and requirements. Additionally, while the application processes for certain state incentives are insignificant, others can be quite burdensome. However, if a company picks the right location to engage in video game development, the benefits related to the incentives will likely far outweigh the effort in applying for them. In the end, incentives are basically "free money" for a video game development company. They can allow for an increased level of profit on a game or allow for more funds to make a better game without increasing your overall budget. Therefore, developers should look into what programs are available in their state or keep these programs in mind when looking where to locate a development team.

## APPENDIX I: UNITED STATES TAX INCENTIVES FOR VIDEO GAME PRODUCTION

| State | Offers Incentives? | Type of Incentive | Is the Incentive Transferable or Refundable? | Minimum Expenditure Required to Qualify for Incentive | Maximum Amount of Expenditures that can Qualify for Incentive | Prior Approval Required to Claim Incentive?[a] |
|---|---|---|---|---|---|---|
| Alabama | Yes | • 25% tax rebate of qualifying expenditures, excluding payroll expenses; and • 35% tax rebate of payroll paid to AL state residents | | $500,000 | $20 million | Yes, at least 30 days prior to the start of production |
| Alaska | No | | | | | |
| Arizona | No | | | | | |
| Arkansas | Yes | • 20% tax rebate of qualifying expenditures; and • An additional 10% tax rebate for payroll paid to certain state residents | Non-transferable | $200,000 within a six-month period | | Yes, prior to incurring any production expense |
| California | No | | | | | |
| Colorado | Yes | • 20% tax rebate of qualifying expenditures so long as 50% of the workforce are residents of the state | Non-transferable | $100,000 for a state company or $250,000 for an out-of-state company | $1,000,000 per employee for developer compensation; no maximum for all other expenditures | Yes, prior to start of production |
| Connecticut | Yes | • Up to 30% tax credit of qualifying expenditures | Transferable; non-refundable | $100,000 | | Yes, within 90 days after the first qualified production expense or cost is incurred |
| Delaware | No | | | | | |
| Washington, D.C. | No | | | | | |
| Florida | No | | | | | |
| Georgia | Yes | • 20% tax credit of qualifying in-state expenditures; and • Additional 10% tax credit for products that include a state promotional logo | Transferable; non-refundable | $500,000 | | Yes, within 90 days of the start of the project |

*(Continued)*

| State | Offers Incentives? | Type of Incentive | Is the Incentive Transferable or Refundable? | Minimum Expenditure Required to Qualify for Incentive | Maximum Amount of Expenditures that can Qualify for Incentive | Prior Approval Required to Claim Incentive?[a] |
|---|---|---|---|---|---|---|
| Hawaii | Yes | • 20% tax credit of qualifying expenditures (25% for productions located in certain less-populated counties) so long as game developers make reasonable efforts to hire Hawaiian employees and also make a financial or in-kind contribution to education or the interactive media workforce in Hawaii | Refundable | $200,000 | | Yes, at least five days prior to the start date |
| Idaho | No | | | | | |
| Illinois | No | | | | | |
| Indiana | No | | | | | |
| Iowa | No | | | | | |
| Kansas | No | | | | | |
| Kentucky | No | | | | | |
| Louisiana | Yes | • 25% tax credit of qualifying expenditures; and • An additional 10% based on labor costs paid to state residents | Non-transferable; refundable | | | Yes, application and preliminary budget must be submitted[b] |
| Maine | Yes | • Certified Media Production Credit equal to 5% of qualifying expenditures; and • Certified Media Wage Reimbursement equal to 12% of total wages and salaries paid to state residents and 10% of total wages and salaries paid to non-state residents | Certified Media Production Credit is non-transferable and non-refundable | $75,000 | | Yes, prior to the start of production |
| Maryland | No | | | | | |

(Continued)

| State | Offers Incentives? | Type of Incentive | Is the Incentive Transferable or Refundable? | Minimum Expenditure Required to Qualify for Incentive | Maximum Amount of Expenditures that can Qualify for Incentive | Prior Approval Required to Claim Incentive?[a] |
|---|---|---|---|---|---|---|
| Massachusetts | No | | | | | |
| Michigan | No | | | | | |
| Minnesota | No | | | | | |
| Mississippi | Yes | • 25% cash rebate on base investment, 30% cash rebate on payroll for state residents, and 25% cash rebate on payroll for non-residents; • Additional 5% cash rebate on payroll made to honorably discharged veterans; and • Reduced sales tax on eligible audio and editing equipment | | $50,000 | | Yes, prior to the start of production |
| Missouri | No | | | | | |
| Montana | No | | | | | |
| Nebraska | No | | | | | |
| Nevada | Yes | • 15% tax credit of qualifying expenditures and resident payroll, 12% tax credit of non-resident payroll; and • 5% bonus tax credit if more than 50% of "below-the-line" personnel are state residents • 5% bonus tax credit on qualified expenses if more than 50% of development days performed in a rural area | Transferable | $500,000 | | Yes, within 90 days prior to the start of production |
| New Hampshire | No | | | | | |
| New Jersey | No | | | | | |
| New Mexico | Yes | • 25% tax credit of qualifying expenditures | Non-transferable; refundable | | | Yes, prior to the start of production |

(Continued)

| State | Offers Incentives? | Type of Incentive | Is the Incentive Transferable or Refundable? | Minimum Expenditure Required to Qualify for Incentive | Maximum Amount of Expenditures that can Qualify for Incentive | Prior Approval Required to Claim Incentive?[a] |
|---|---|---|---|---|---|---|
| New York | No | | | | | |
| North Carolina | No | | | | | |
| North Dakota | No | | | | | |
| Ohio | Yes | • 30% tax credit of qualifying expenditures | Non-transferable; refundable | $300,000 | | Yes, prior to the start of production |
| Oklahoma | No | | | | | |
| Oregon | Yes | • 20% cash rebate on qualifying production costs and 10% cash rebate on any payroll subject to the state withholding tax (note: these rebate percentages apply to both the Oregon Production Investment Fund (OPIF) and the Indigenous Oregon Production Investment Fund (iOPIF), which applies only to local developers) | | Minimum expenditures vary based on the applicable fund. The OPIF requires a minimum amount of $1 million. The iOPIF requires a minimum amount of $75,000 | There is a maximum amount of $1 million for the iOPIF | Yes, prior to the start of production |
| Pennsylvania | No[c] | | | | | |
| Rhode Island | Yes | • 25% tax credit of qualifying expenditures so long as 51% of the principal photography took place in-state | Transferable; non-refundable | $100,000 | | Yes, an initial application must be submitted[d] |
| South Carolina | No | | | | | |
| South Dakota | No | | | | | |
| Tennessee | No | | | | | |

(Continued)

| State | Offers Incentives? | Type of Incentive | Is the Incentive Transferable or Refundable? | Minimum Expenditure Required to Qualify for Incentive | Maximum Amount of Expenditures that can Qualify for Incentive | Prior Approval Required to Claim Incentive?[a] |
|---|---|---|---|---|---|---|
| Texas | Yes | • Up to 20% cash rebate so long as a minimum of 60% of the production days are completed in-state and at least 70% of the development team are state residents; and<br>• An additional 2.5% rebate on qualifying expenditures if at least 25% of the production days are spent in an underused area<br>• Developers are also eligible for a tax exemption on items or services that are "necessary and essential" to production | | $100,000 | | Yes, no earlier than 60 days and no later than five business days prior to the first day of production |
| Utah | Yes | • Up to 20% tax credit on qualified in-state expenditures and salary<br>• However, this only applies to new state revenue as opposed to existing in-state spending | Non-transferable; refundable | | Utah allocates a maximum of $6,793,700 for the program in any fiscal year | Yes, prior to the start of production |
| Vermont | No | | | | | |
| Virginia | Yes | • 15% tax credit of qualifying expenditures (20% if development occurs in an economically distressed area); and<br>• An additional 10%–20% tax credit of payroll to state residents | Non-transferable; refundable | $250,000 | | Yes, prior to the start of production |

(*Continued*)

| State | Offers Incentives? | Type of Incentive | Is the Incentive Transferable or Refundable? | Minimum Expenditure Required to Qualify for Incentive | Maximum Amount of Expenditures that can Qualify for Incentive | Prior Approval Required to Claim Incentive?[a] |
|---|---|---|---|---|---|---|
| Washington | No | | | | | |
| West Virginia | No | | | | | |
| Wisconsin | No | | | | | |
| Wyoming | No | | | | | |

[a] This column notes whether prior approval is required to claim the incentive or whether submission upon completion is sufficient.

[b] It is unclear when the application and preliminary budget for the project must be submitted. More information about the application is available at: http://www.opportunitylouisiana.com/page/digital-interactive-media-and-software-development-incentive.

[c] Legislation creating a $1,000,000 digital media tax incentive was passed in 2016. While the legislation was anticipated to be enacted sometime following July 2017, it has not received budget approval. Therefore, the details of any Pennsylvania incentives remain uncertain.

[d] It is unclear when the initial application must be submitted. More information about the application is available at: http://www.film.ri.gov/taxinfo.html.

## NOTES

1. Paul Tassi, League of Legends Finals sold out the Los Angeles Staples Center in less than an hour, *Forbes*, August 24, 2013: https://www.forbes.com/sites/insertcoin/2013/08/24/league-of-legends-finals-sells-out-las-staples-center-in-an-hour/#66d3ed3232b8

2. Florida, Kentucky, Michigan, New Jersey, and North Carolina have eliminated incentives for video games over the last few years.

3. Appendix I contains a state-by-state chart noting where incentives are (and are not) available and providing an overview of the type of incentives and the rules and regulations surrounding said incentives.

4. The enacting legislation for the Entertainment Industry Incentive Act is available at: http://www.alabamafilm.org/downloads/New_Rules_And_Regulations.pdf

5. Further information about the Alabama incentives is available at: http://www.alabamafilm.org/2010/Summary_of_Film_Incentives2.pdf

6. The enacting legislation for the Digital Product and Motion Picture Industry Development Act is available at: http://www.arkleg.state.ar.us/assembly/2009/R/Acts/Act816.pdf

7. Further information about the Arkansas incentives is available at: http://www.arkansasedc.com/incentives

8. The enacting legislation for the Colorado Film Incentives is available at: http://www.leg.state.co.us/CLICS/CLICS2012A/csl.nsf/fsbillcont3/C7612C556131464D8725798500062B10?Open&file=1286_ren.pdf

9. Further information about the Colorado incentives is available at: http://coloradofilm.org/incentives/incentive-faqs/

10. The enacting legislation for the Connecticut Digital Media and Motion Picture Tax Credit is available at: http://www.cultureandtourism.org/cct/lib/cct/TaxCreditLegislation.pdf

11. Further information about the Connecticut incentives is available at: http://www.ct.gov/ecd/cwp/view.asp?a=3880&q=454828

12. The enacting legislation for the Entertainment Industry Investment Act is available at: https://gov.georgia.gov/sites/gov.georgia.gov/files/related_files/document/143729.pdf

13. Further information on the production incentives offered by Georgia is available here: http://www.georgia.org/industries/entertainment/georgia-film-tv-production/production-incentives/

14. The enacting legislation for Hawaii's production tax credit program is available at: http://www.capitol.hawaii.gov/session2013/bills/GM1189_.pdf

15. Further information on the production incentives offered by Hawaii is available here: http://filmoffice.hawaii.gov/incentives-tax-credits/

16. The enacting legislation for the Louisiana Digital Media and Software Act is available at: https://www.legis.la.gov/Legis/Law.aspx?d=321886

17. Electronic Arts employs hundreds of video game professionals at its location on Louisiana State University's campus. Additionally, High Voltage Software, InXile Entertainment, and Gameloft have all opened offices in Louisiana.

18. Further information on the production incentives offered by Louisiana is available here: http://opportunitylouisiana.com/page/digital-interactive-media-and-software-development-incentive

19. The enacting legislation for the Certified Media Production Credit is available at: http://www.mainelegislature.org/legis/statutes/36/title36sec5219-Y.html

20. The enacting legislation for the Certified Media Wage Reimbursement is available at: http://www.mainelegislature.org/legis/statutes/36/title36ch919-Asec0.html

21. Further information on the Maine incentives is available here: http://www.filminmaine.com/incentives/default.aspx

22. The enacting legislation for the Mississippi Motion Picture Production Incentive Program is available at: http://billstatus.ls.state.ms.us/documents/2013/pdf/SB/2400-2499/SB2462SG.pdf

23. Further information on the production incentives offered by Mississippi is available here: http://www.filmmississippi.org/incentive-rebate-program-home.php

24. The enacting legislation for the Nevada tax credit is available at: https://nevadafilm.com/wp-content/uploads/2014/08/Transferable_Tax_Credit_Regulation_120-13_FINAL_2013-12-23.pdf

25. Further information on the production incentives offered by Nevada is available here http://www.nevadafilm.com/incentives

26. The enacting legislation for the New Mexico Refundable Film Production Tax Credit is available at: http://nmfilm.com/uploads/files/HB0641.pdf

27. Further information on the production incentives offered by New Mexico is available here: http://nmfilm.com/Overview.aspx

28. The enacting legislation for the Ohio Motion Picture Tax Incentive is available at: http://codes.ohio.gov/orc/122.85

29. Further information on the production incentives offered by Ohio is available here: http://www.ohiofilmoffice.com/Incentives.html

30. The enacting legislation for the Oregon Production Investment Fund and the Indigenous Oregon Production Investment Fund is available at: http://legiscan.com/OR/text/HB3367/id/870729

31. Further information on the production incentives offered by Oregon is available here: https://oregonfilm.org/incentives/

32. The enacting legislation for the Motion Picture Production Tax Credit is available at: http://www.film.ri.gov/MPProdTaxCredi2012.pdf

33. Further information on the production incentives offered by Rhode Island is available here: http://www.film.ri.gov/taxinfo.html

34. Further information on the Texas Sales Tax Exemptions is available here: https://gov.texas.gov/film/page/sales_tax_exemptions

35. Further information on the Texas Enterprise Fund is available here: https://businessintexas.com/services/texas-enterprise-fund

36. The enacting legislation for the Utah Motion Picture Incentives is available at: https://le.utah.gov/xcode/Title63N/Chapter8/63N-8-S101.html?v=C63N-8-S101_2015051220150512

37. Further information on the production incentives offered by Utah is available here: https://film.utah.gov/incentive-info/

38. The enacting legislation for the Virginia Motion Picture Tax Credit Program is available at: http://leg1.state.va.us/cgi-bin/legp504.exe?101+ful+SB257ER

39. Further information on the production incentives offered by Virginia is available here: http://www.film.virginia.org/incentives/

# CHAPTER 8

# Beyond Goldfarming

## *Virtual Property Regulations*

M ANY TITLES TODAY ARE designed to allow gamers to level up their in-game characters by earning virtual property/currency and developing skills that make them more powerful. Virtual items may be earned/created through game-play or can be purchased for real-world fiat currency. As such, the in-game society works much like that of a real-world society. Research currently estimates that billions of dollars are being spent annually on the purchase of in-game virtual items worldwide. Since intangible intellectual property can have real-world value and virtual items can be relatively easily converted to the fiat currency of various nations, the question arises: Should a legal standard be applied? The answer to this and other questions may turn on whether virtual items are property and whether players are allowed to own virtual items obtained or created in-game. Certain proponents of property rights argue that allowing creator ownership of virtual items will foster creativity, which is the interest copyright protection was first enacted to protect. Others say that judicial determination of the ownership of a *World of Warcraft* "Bonecrusher Mace" or *Clash of Clans* "Gems" is just a waste of time. This chapter will seek to address the regulation of virtual items from a variety of perspectives. By the end of this chapter, you will also have a better concept of what industry best practices exist.

## THE NATURE OF VIRTUAL PROPERTY AND OWNERSHIP

Historically, property was easy to define: it was considered a thing that belonged to someone—a physical possession. If someone took it from me, that meant that I did not have it any longer. As time and technology progressed and concepts became more complex, we began to look at the scope and ownership of property differently. More than 150 years ago, Joseph Story, an Associate Justice of the Supreme Court, called intellectual property "the metaphysics of law" and described its distinctions as being "almost evanescent." In the modern age, property does not just mean physical possession of an item.

In fact, the most valuable companies today did not generate value from their physical property but from their intangible intellectual property. Today, property rights are often referred to as a "bundle of sticks." I can hold most of the bundle but still give, sell, or lend one or more of those "sticks" to someone else without affecting my rights to the rest of the bundle. Add intangible virtual property elements to this bundle and things get even more interesting.

Likewise, if you ask someone to explain what constitutes currency, you will likely get a simple description about the money they have in their pocket, but not about the credits they purchased in *Candy Crush Saga*. However, the United States' Financial Crimes Enforcement Network's ("FinCEN") definition of "currency" (also referred to as "real" currency) is more complex than mere pocket change and includes "[t]he coin and paper money of the United States or of any other country that is designated as legal tender and that circulates and is customarily used and accepted as a medium of exchange in the country of issuance. Currency includes U.S. silver certificates, U.S. notes and Federal Reserve notes. Currency also includes official foreign bank notes that are customarily used and accepted as a medium of exchange in a foreign country" (31 C.F.R. § 1010.100(m)). While that is a real mouthful, it is also quite broad if you look at the strict language. What is currently accepted as a "medium of exchange" has well surpassed the mere physical "coin of the realm" and now also can include intangible items often referred to as Digital Currency. Digital Currency, among its various names, is electronic money that acts as an alternative to real currency. According to FinCEN, "convertible virtual currency" is the type of Digital Currency which "either has an equivalent value in real currency, or acts as a substitute for real currency."[1] Digital Currency can exist in a form that can be used in transactions with real goods and services—not just circulation within games. Early versions of such digital currencies were often backed by a promise to pay a set amount of gold or silver bullion in exchange for each of its units. Alternatively, there are other forms of Digital Currency which can only be used in-game or within some predefined system. There are many types of Digital Currencies on the market and their features and uses vary greatly. Many in-game virtual currency systems use a dual currency model which includes both earned and purchased forms. "Credits," "coins," "points," "tokens," etc. are purchased with real money, or earned by playing or gaining experience. Additionally, virtual currency may be provided by the issuer to an end user pursuant to a loyalty, award, or promotional program for free.

Cryptocurrency is a type of Digital Currency that relies on cryptography in order to create and manage the currency. Cryptocurrency is generally designed to have no inflation (once all the currency has been produced), in order to maintain scarcity and, hence, value. Cryptocurrencies are also designed to ensure that funds can neither be frozen nor seized. *Bitcoin* is one of the most well-known cryptocurrencies where the creation and transfer is based on an open-source cryptographic protocol that is independent of any central authority. The concept was introduced in a 2008 paper by a pseudonymous developer known as "Satoshi Nakamoto," which referred to it as "a peer-to-peer, electronic cash system." The Bitcoin miner servers communicate over an internet-based network and confirm transactions by adding them to a ledger which is updated and archived periodically using peer-to-peer file-sharing technology.

The majority of games today include intangible objects or elements which may be purchased, created, earned, or used by a player. The industry has seen a change in the business model for games over the past few years. The traditional model of selling a game for $59.99 has expanded, and in some cases been supplanted by, games that are being made available for free (or for a nominal sum) and monetized by sales of in-game virtual items or Digital Currency. Given his early predictions about intellectual property, I would love to hear what Justice Story would have had to say about the legal status of in-game virtual property in today's world. Given the regulations that surround FinCEN's definition of currency, it is important for game publishers to understand where the line is between virtual items used as a "medium of exchange" and an item or point system existing merely as a licensed entertainment feature of a game. Failing to appreciate the distinction or failing to comply with applicable requirements can have a significant impact on a game designer or publisher.

One of the questions that may affect whether a virtual item can act as a "medium of exchange" may turn on who actually owns it. As stated, publishers often offer virtual items for in-game use. These items can be purchased, earned through playing, or provided for exposure to offers or advertisements. The providers of games that include virtual items predominantly take the position that any items available in-game are not (and cannot be) owned by the users. Through the use of well-crafted end-user license agreements, players accept a definition of virtual property and virtual currency as a limited license (or service) to access some feature of the game. Specifically, virtual property or virtual currency is stated as not being a form of currency. To the game providers, there is no legal significance to virtual property or virtual currency so the players cannot have any rights or ownership related thereto. Both are merely part of the code-base for the game and indistinguishable from all other game elements owned by the publisher.

However, some games include Digital Currency or other virtual items that make the legal distinction and application a little murkier, even with the existence of a broadly drafted end-user license agreement. Many in-game virtual property or virtual currency systems only allow the items to be used within a single game or only with the entity from whom it was acquired. This is done to avoid any argument that it is a "medium of exchange." This is typically referred to as a "closed-loop" system and is generally safer from a legal compliance perspective. However, other games allow virtual items to be used with unrelated third parties or games, or to be exchanged for real currency or used to purchase real goods or services. This variation is often referred to as an "open-loop" system and is more likely to implicate FinCEN's regulations. Markets have also arisen outside of the relevant games as mechanisms by which virtual items, and even entire user accounts, are bought, sold, or traded for real-world money or other value. These markets have been encouraged by certain open-loop systems and litigated against by many publishers offering closed-loop games. The publisher's approval or disapproval of these markets may significantly impact the legal treatment their virtual items may receive.

**OPEN-LOOP: ACCEPTED AT MULTIPLE LOCATIONS**
- Can be transferred between individuals and accounts
- Can be converted into cash
- Certain game cards (single issuer but redeemable across different game platforms).

**CLOSED-LOOP: CAN ONLY BE USED WITHIN A PUBLISHER'S GAME(S)**
- Cannot be redeemed for cash
- Cannot be traded/sold
- Usable at a single location.

## THERE ARE MANY LEGAL ISSUES TO CONSIDER!

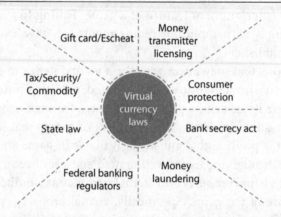

While publishers may be looking to create a fun, exciting, and immersive experience that takes a player out of the real world, this does not mean that the real world will permit it. Depending on the type of virtual property or virtual currency systems employed, a panoply of legal concerns can arise. Unfortunately, the law is written broadly and sometimes can be applied even to areas that were never foreseen when the law was enacted. Only when a law has been applied by a court (or specifically not applied) do we have a better idea of a law's scope. This can mean that a publisher may have to assume that a specific law governs their game and make design changes accordingly, or ignore that law and risk the consequences. Below are some common laws that potentially apply to games and services featuring virtual property or virtual currency.

## BANKING AND MONEY LAUNDERING LAWS

When you designed your game and virtual currency and virtual property systems, you probably weren't thinking about terrorists, right? Well the government looks at these things differently. Many state laws and the federal Bank Secrecy Act (BSA) require Money Services Businesses (MSBs) to develop, implement, and maintain policies, procedures, and internal controls reasonably designed to prevent the risk of money laundering and the financing of terrorist activities. These requirements include establishing a written anti-money-laundering program and a customer identification program, filing government reports, creating and retaining records, and responding to law-enforcement requests. The BSA's implementing regulations define an MSB as "a person wherever located doing business … wholly or in substantial part within the United States, in one or more of the capacities listed in paragraphs (ff)(1) through (ff)(7) of (31 C.F.R. § 1010.100)," one of which capacities is a money transmitter. In general, a "money transmitter" is an entity that provides "money transmission services" or is otherwise engaged in the transfer of funds (see 31 C.F.R. § 1010.100(ff)(5)). "Money transmission services" means the acceptance of currency, funds, or other value that substitutes for currency from one person and the transmission of currency, funds, or other value that substitutes for currency to another location or person by any means. "Any means" includes the use of an electronic funds transfer network or an informal value transfer system. FinCEN's Guidance notes that the definition of "money transmitter" does not differentiate between the transmission of real currencies and convertible virtual currencies, which it defines as virtual currency that either has an equivalent value in real currency or acts as a substitute for real currency. Therefore, depending on its design, a video game virtual currency system could be considered a "money transmitter" under the regulations. This can also be complicated by whether the in-game system falls within the open-loop or closed-loop models.

## Is a Player an MSB?

Under FinCEN's Guidance, a "user" of virtual currency is a person that obtains virtual currency to purchase goods or services. FinCEN recognizes that a person may "obtain" virtual currency by, for example, earning, harvesting, mining, creating, auto-generating, manufacturing, or purchasing it. The Guidance confirms that someone who only qualifies as a "user" of virtual currency is not an MSB under the BSA's implementing regulations because such activity does not fit within the definition of "money transmission services." Accordingly, a user of virtual currency is not subject to FinCEN's registration, reporting, and recordkeeping requirements for MSBs. That at least takes the burden off the player of a game, but does not address the publisher's role and responsibilities.

## Is the Publisher an MSB?

FinCEN's Guidance defines an "exchanger" of virtual currency as a person engaged as a business in the exchange of virtual currency for real currency, funds, or other virtual currency, and an "administrator" of virtual currency as a person engaged as a business in issuing (putting into circulation) a virtual currency, who also has the authority to redeem (to withdraw from circulation) such virtual currency. FinCEN concludes that, in contrast to "users" of virtual currency, an "exchanger" or an "administrator" that accepts and transmits a convertible virtual currency or buys or sells convertible virtual currency for any reason is a "money transmitter" and therefore is an MSB under the BSA's implementing regulations, unless the person qualifies for a limitation to or an exemption from the definition of a money transmitter.[2]

How does one determine whether they qualify for a money transmitter exemption? The BSA's implementing regulations specify that a person is not a money transmitter, despite accepting and transmitting currency, funds, or value that substitutes for currency, if that person only (1) provides prepaid access or (2) accepts and transmits funds only integral to the sale of their own goods or the provision of their own services. Therefore, in the absence of an exemption, a game publisher may be considered an MSB. In practice, this means that closed-loop systems are generally safe while open-loop systems may need to comply with the regulations.

## TAX LAWS APPLICABLE TO VIRTUAL ITEMS

It is not completely clear how virtual currency transactions should be taxed. "[A] recent trend among states, as digital consumption has become more commonplace, is the inclusion of digital goods in the sales and use tax base."[3] So a publisher should take the time to understand whether they are offering their virtual items in a state that requires the collection of sales tax.

Moreover, there are three different revenue recognition models that a publisher may consider using for the sale of virtual goods: the Game-Based Revenue Model, the User-Based Revenue Model, and the Item-Based Revenue Model. Under the Game-Based Revenue Model, a company recognizes the revenue generated from the sale of virtual goods ratably over the estimated remaining life of the game, and no distinction is made for the "characteristics" of the virtual good. Characteristics of the virtual good includes whether the item is a "one-time" or limited-time use, like a token or power-up, which is categorized as a "consumable." Alternatively, there are virtual items that, once obtained, can be used indefinitely in the game and are usually referred to as "durable." Under the User-Based Revenue Model, the presumption is that the period of delivery for the virtual good is the estimated average user life. Generally, the average user life is a shorter period than the expected game life as player attrition is common in games, resulting in the recognition of revenue over a shorter period. Finally, the Item-Based Revenue Model takes into consideration the characteristics of the virtual good sold to determine the (implied or explicit) period that the virtual good is made available to the user—otherwise known as the "delivery obligation period." The delivery obligation period will vary depending on whether the virtual goods are consumable or durable. Once the delivery obligation period has been established, revenue is recognized ratably over that period of time. In the case of a consumable virtual item, the estimated delivery obligation period would be shorter than the estimated user life. The tax obligations and benefits of these different strategies are important, and should be part of your business strategy. However, given that every company's position is different, this is something that should be discussed with and considered by your accountants and/or tax advisor.

## GIFT CERTIFICATE/GIFT CARD LAWS

*I am just adding a "Mighty Eagle" to my tower defense game—not sending out little plastic cards, so why should I worry about gift card law?* As one commentator has noted, "[b]roadly speaking, state and federal gift certificate laws apply when consideration is paid for a record evidencing a promise to provide goods or services of a certain value to the bearer of the record. State and federal definitions vary, but can apply to virtual currency. Gift certificate laws could restrict a publisher's ability to expire virtual currency or impose inactivity or service fees on virtual currency accounts and otherwise require the conspicuous disclosure of key terms, and require an issuer to provide cash refunds of unused virtual currency. Certain exemptions apply, however, for gift certificates provided on a promotional basis without payment of money or other consideration from users."[4]

Commonly known as the "CARD Act." the federal regulation prohibits the expiration of gift certificates, store gift cards, and general-use prepaid cards within less than five years and restricts fees, including dormancy, inactivity, and service fees, unless the gift certificate or gift card has not been used for at least 12 months, unless excluded from the CARD Act.[5] Gift certificates, store gift cards, and general-use prepaid cards may be in the form of a "card, code and other device." The language, which very clearly does not require any physical card or certificate, may thus cover certain types of in-game systems. When explaining the application of expiration date provisions after the redemption of a card, code, or other device, FinCEN explained that "[t]he requirement that funds underlying a certificate or card must not expire for at least five years from the date of issuance or date of last load ceases to apply once the certificate or card has been fully redeemed, even if the underlying funds are not used to contemporaneously purchase a specific good or service." By way of example, it noted that "some certificates or cards can be used to purchase music, media, or virtual goods." It confirmed that "[o]nce redeemed by a consumer, the entire balance on the certificate or card is debited from the certificate or card and credited or transferred to another 'account' established by the merchant of such goods or services. The consumer can then make purchases of songs, media, or virtual goods from the merchant using that 'account' either at the time the value is transferred from the certificate or card or at a later time." It further confirmed that "[u]nder these circumstances, once the card has been fully redeemed and the 'account' credited with the amount of the underlying funds, the five-year minimum expiration term no longer applies to the underlying funds." However, it further confirmed that "if the consumer only partially redeems the value of the certificate or card, the five-year minimum expiration term requirement continues to apply to the funds remaining on the certificate or card."

The CARD Act also imposes strict disclosure requirements. Disclosures must be "clear and conspicuous" (i.e., the location and type size are readily noticeable and not obscured by a logo or indentation from embossed type), and generally must be in writing in a form the consumer may keep. State laws that are consistent with the CARD Act are not preempted by the CARD Act, which means that the CARD Act provides a minimum floor. In practice, this means that if a publisher designs its virtual item systems to allow for prepayment of monies into a "virtual wallet" that can later be used by the player, the company may be subject to gift card regulations.

Nearly every state has its own complementary laws covering the issuance and use of gift cards. Not all of these state laws are similar in their construction and coverage. Most state gift card laws prohibit or restrict the imposition of expiration dates or service fees on some form of gift cards. Several states have amended their laws to follow more closely the CARD

Act, including expanding the definitions of gift certificate and gift card to include gift certificates, store gift cards, and general-use prepaid cards. A handful of states currently require merchants to, upon request, redeem gift cards with less than a specified balance for cash. For example, in California, any gift certificate with a cash value of less than ten dollars ($10) is redeemable in cash for its cash value.[6]

## ESCHEAT LAWS

Many states have also enacted what are commonly referred to as "unclaimed property laws" or "escheat laws" to require the holders of both tangible and intangible property that has been abandoned, unused, or unclaimed by the owner to transfer the property to the state for safekeeping after a specified period of time. Often, the definition of property is quite broad. For example, New Jersey defines "property" to mean tangible property or a fixed and certain interest in "intangible property that is held, issued, or owed in the course of a holder's business... and all income or increments therefrom, and includes property that is referred to as or evidenced by: money, a check, draft, deposit, interest, or dividend; credit balance, customer's overpayment, security deposit, refund, credit memorandum, unpaid wage, unused ticket, mineral proceeds or unidentified remittance..."[7] This broad language is only from one of the many states that have escheat laws on their books. As it was intended to strengthen the coffers of the particular state, it intentionally covers many forms of property, including arguably virtual items. However, being required to track the use or abandonment of virtual items and potentially turning them over to a particular state would undoubtedly be a burden on the providers of the items. "Breakage" is a term often used to describe a situation where a buyer purchases, for example, a gift certificate, gift card, or virtual currency but thereafter fails to redeem its value. "This industry term means that users pay for an amount of virtual money, but abandon it after a period of time, and thereby forfeit it to the company... Laws covering breakage differ between states and countries."[8] Laws covering breakage may include a state's unclaimed property law. Time frames for turning over property to the state vary, ranging from one to seven years.

Some states exclude certain types of property. At least one state expressly excludes from its definition of intangible property "gaming chips or tokens, or gaming award points."[9] California, and other states, exempt gift certificates subject to California's gift card law, but do not exempt "any gift certificate that has an expiration date and that is given in exchange for money or any other thing of value."[10]

If the virtual currency is "property," and it is not otherwise exempted, then abandoned, unused, or unclaimed virtual currency may be subject to remittance to a state. The second complexity related to the escheatment of virtual currency is how to define its value. While some virtual currency can be used like cash at numerous locations, other virtual currency may be redeemed only for goods or merchandise. The escheatment framework must contend with how to value this latter virtual currency, and whether to impose upon issuers the obligation to turn over to the state the full face value of the virtual currency. A game publisher can face the prospect of losing the profits in the event that the owner never attempts to redeem the virtual currency or virtual property or reclaim the value from the escheating state. The states have taken various approaches to value gift cards that may be redeemed only for goods or merchandise. Similarly, the Uniform Unclaimed Property Act (UUPA) provides for the escheat of gift certificates, "but if redeemable in merchandise only, the amount abandoned is deemed to be (60) percent of the certificate's face value."[11] Similarly, under the 1981 UUPA, the amount of a gift certificate presumed abandoned was the price paid by the purchaser for the gift certificate. Escheat is another area where a provider of virtual items may have significant regulatory compliance concerns depending on whether they choose to pursue an open-loop versus closed-loop system.

## CONSUMER PROTECTION LAW

Consumer protection law is another tricky area of law potentially applicable to virtual property or virtual currency. Myriad state laws protect users from being misled or abused in some way. Given the number and range of laws that can fall into this category, it would be counterproductive to discuss them all. Moreover, as these laws are all designed to protect a user's experience when dealing with a publisher, it is better to just err on the side of fairness and disclosure. Including a clear, specific, and well-drafted terms of service or end-user license agreement that covers the acquisition, ownership, use, and redemption of virtual items will go a long way to avoiding a consumer protection claim. Moreover, it is wise to include disclosures at the time a user pays for or otherwise acquires the virtual item. A game publisher would do well to include additional disclosures at the time the virtual item or virtual currency is used. If a user encounters disclosures in connection with use of virtual items in the game, it becomes very difficult for the user to argue later that they were somehow mislead or not treated fairly.

## GAMBLING, SWEEPSTAKES, AND LOTTERY LAWS

Many companies are offering virtual property or virtual currency as a prize in a sweepstakes-type contest, or are allowing customers to use virtual items as a wagering device to participate in online gaming. This is a highly regulated area and including such elements in a game should not be done lightly without giving considerable thought to the potential legal consequences. For more information on the laws governing gambling, sweepstakes, and lotteries, see Chapter 10.

## INTERNATIONAL LAWS

*Now that I have an understanding about the United States laws and regulations that may be applicable to my virtual items, are there any other laws that I should consider?* Unfortunately, yes. When virtual items move among different countries, international laws may also apply. Given the complexity and differences between international laws, it would be impossible to cover them in this section (or even in one book for that matter). Therefore, if you anticipate that your virtual items will be made available in jurisdictions outside the United States, it would be wise to discuss the ramifications with counsel who know the law in all the markets that you will offer your products. Alternatively, publishers can consider whether to offer their products only in a select group of territories, versus worldwide. Having researched the salient issues in approximately 200 territories, I can tell you that the answers differ significantly from country to country and will be very specific to the actual design of the particular virtual item system.

## BEST PRACTICES

As you have seen so far in this chapter, the current state of the law is confusing at best. I expect that by this point you are wondering what, if anything, you can do to protect yourself fully. If that is your goal, then my advice would be to not include *any* virtual items in your game. Unfortunately, there is no reasonable way to do business and comply with every law and regulation that might be applicable to the issuance of virtual property and virtual currency. Even the most conservative companies have had to take a wait-and-see approach on how their virtual items will be treated by regulators or the plaintiff's bar. As there has been very little application of these legal concepts to in-game virtual items, we are without clear guidance on which paths are best to take. Moreover, in today's litigious society, a publisher of a game can be investigated or sued with little or no provocation. As U.S. courts do not generally require the filer of specious suits to pay for the costs of the winner's legal fees, there is often not much downside to a plaintiff bringing such a claim either through a regulator or private attorney. But there are certain strategies that can help to minimize any potential exposure if a lawyer or regulator does come calling. Below are some proposed best practices to minimize your risks associated with offering virtual currency or virtual property. These are generally the steps that most publishers are enacting to provide potential protection, coverage, or at least defensible arguments in support of their actions.

### User-Facing Documents

Be sure to put sufficient thought and resources into designing and drafting your user-facing agreements, including terms of service and end-user license agreements. Confirm that proper language exists for disclosing, describing, and limiting your risks in connection with offering virtual items. Don't cut-and-paste another company's policy for a similar service. First, the terms may not properly describe or cover the virtual property or virtual currency system that you have included in your game. Second, someone else's policy may not provide you with the types of exclusions for the regulations mentioned above. Third, improperly describing your systems may give rise to a consumer protection claim. Finally, copying someone else's policy may also constitute copyright infringement.

Assuming that you take the correct approach and work with someone to craft your user-facing agreements properly, you will want to ensure that there is language stating, among other things, that the virtual property:

1. Has no real-world value

2. Is not to be considered stored value (i.e., a gift card)

3. Is owned by the publisher

4. Can be terminated, nerfed, or devalued

5. Is a "limited license"

6. Is not available in all jurisdictions

7. Cannot be cashed-out, sold, transferred, etc.

8. Cannot be refunded

9. Has its virtual item balance calculations controlled by the publisher.

It is important to set up any virtual item system as a limited license for the player to access a feature of the game, rather than an actual exchange of goods, and to limit the license in the ways listed above. Additionally, any terms of service and/or end-user license agreements should also specify that the license for the virtual property or virtual currency can be terminated at any time at the issuer's option. As it is often necessary to tweak items in-game for balancing purposes, it is important to make it very clear that a publisher can take any action, including those that may have the effect of reducing or eliminating the value of any item, character, or account. Additionally, it is important that no marketing or advertising statements are made which may be contrary to such rights.

## Use a Single In-Game Virtual Item System

In-game virtual items should have an original, distinctive name that does not include currency key words such as "money," "currency," "coins," or "dollars." PAC-MAN® Championship Edition Power Pellets would be a good example of this. Also, any icons or images used to depict the virtual items should preferably not resemble dollars or coins. Wherever possible, the value of the in-game virtual items should not directly reflect the purchase amount (i.e., value should not constitute dollar-for-dollar or one-to-one purchases or cash equivalents). For example, if a player spends $5 on virtual currency, they should not receive five units of the applicable virtual currency. Additionally, virtual items should be game-specific wherever possible (closed-loop) and not transferable or otherwise useable in other games and on other platforms (open-loop).

## No Cashing Out

Virtual items should be redeemable for goods and services in-game only and should not be redeemable for cash, monetary value, or other convertible virtual currency by either the purchaser or any third-party recipient. Notwithstanding the foregoing, funds used to purchase virtual items can be returned to the original purchaser at the same location and in the same account used to make the purchase, such as a credit card refund to the credit card used to make the original virtual item purchase.

## No Player-to-Player Transfer

Ideally, virtual items should be a part of a closed-loop system and not be transferable— meaning a player cannot transfer virtual items to another player or trade or sell the virtual items. However, if the issuer wants to allow the appearance of transfers, then once an item is "dropped" (i.e., abandoned in-game and potentially available for alternate player pick-up/transfer), the item should actually revert to the issuer and then the issuer can reissue the virtual item to any other player under another license. This could appear as a seamless exchange to a player, but would ultimately avoid direct transfers between the players. A publisher can also limit transfers so that a dropped item will disappear if not picked up by another player before (1) a designated time limit, (2) all players leave the virtual location where the item was dropped, or (3) all players leave the gaming session. Any limitations on transferring, trading, or gifting virtual items should be clearly included in the terms of service and end-user license agreement in addition to the language suggested above that grants the issuer the right to terminate any license for virtual items. In general, however, allowing a player to transfer, trade, or gift virtual items between that player's own various "Alt" characters is typically fine.

## No Third-Party Exchanges

If a publisher wants to strengthen its closed-loop virtual item system argument it should institute a policy barring players from selling virtual items through the use of third-party online auction systems or barter houses. The issuer should have a program to monitor offers to sell/transfer any of its game-based virtual currency, characters, virtual items, etc. and send takedown notices or take any other necessary actions to ensure that such sales are not allowed. Otherwise, these third-party platforms will arguably have a market and set real-world values (albeit unauthorized) for the virtual items.

## Immediate Deposit of Virtual Items

Broadly speaking, state and federal gift card/certificate laws apply when consideration is paid to a record evidencing a promise to provide goods or services of a certain value to the bearer of the record. State and federal definitions vary, but can apply to virtual currency digital records and account balances. Therefore, in order to avoid such laws, if a player purchases virtual items, those items should be deposited into the player's account immediately and directly without any further intervening steps. In other words, an issuer should not allow players to store paid value in an account for a period of time, which could implicate gift card/certificate laws. To constitute a true license, the virtual items should be converted immediately after a player purchase. Additionally, if another business is processing a sale on the issuer's behalf (e.g., Apple), the virtual item should likewise be deposited immediately and directly into the player's account, just as it would be if purchased directly.

## Subscriptions

Instead of allowing players to make separate purchases of virtual items, a publisher may want to consider a subscription/VIP account or prepaid option (e.g., pay $5/month for various perks including a set amount of virtual items per month). Pairing paid-value virtual items with other perks and incentives may mitigate the risk of the virtual items coming within the purview of the BSA, the CARD Act, or other state laws regulating monetary transactions.

## Tracking Virtual Items

As stated above, virtual item issuers should use best efforts to shut down any unauthorized, third-party reselling/trading markets that allow users to circumvent a closed-loop system and transfer virtual items for real-world money or other value. The publisher should also implement a back-end tracking system that tracks any virtual item transfers or "drops" and compares this with any third-party trading platform offers or sales. The issuer should also implement a back-end system that differentiates between earned virtual items from any purchased virtual items and tracks when such virtual items were earned or purchased. Many games will allow earned virtual items to be used in certain ways while purchased virtual items can be used in other ways. This may be to ensure that a player cannot buy his/ her way to success in the game or to allow the "free" earned virtual items to be exchanged between players in ways that would trigger legal concerns for the exchange of purchased virtual items. Additionally, to combat stored value arguments, certain games have tracked purchases and implemented a "first in, first out" approach for purchased virtual items (i.e., purchased virtual items must be spent before more purchased virtual items can be obtained, or the older purchased virtual items are used first before any newly acquired virtual items may be used).

## Apply Earning Limits in Open-Loop Systems

Earning limits are not necessary for a true closed-loop system, but the issuer may want to consider placing certain limitations on closed-loop virtual items, such as limiting the total amount of virtual items that can be obtained or purchased during a particular period (e.g., each month) or creating a general cap on the amount of virtual items that any player can have in his/her account at any time. However, if the issuer allows for an open-loop system or prepaid access, then limits should be placed on any virtual items in order to comply with certain exceptions that may exist under federal and state laws.

## Ways of Spending

Players are often able to spend virtual items in a number of ways in-game. The following categories are generally acceptable ways that players can spend virtual items in-game: durable items (e.g., clothing, character customization, property, weapons, and vehicles), consumable items (e.g., ammunition, food, armor, and NPC services), and as entry fees to access locked levels, features, or more competitive modes in-game.

## Notice to Players When Canceling Virtual Items

Whenever possible, a publisher should include any "shut-down" date for a game in the terms of service or end-user license agreement from the outset. For example, if an issuer knows that it will shut down a server supporting a game at a predetermined date in the future to make room for a planned game sequel or another game, the issuer should notify players from the outset. If there is no planned shut-down date or a publisher needs to terminate all player virtual items, with or without a reason, it should provide players with advance notice regarding the expiration of their virtual items, default to allowing players to spend any purchased virtual items before any earned virtual items, and shut off any player's ability to purchase or earn more virtual items closer to the effective expiration date. If possible, I would suggest six months' initial notice (requiring player acknowledgment of some sort), followed by monthly and weekly reminders as the final date approaches. Moreover, the publisher may want to consider adding some virtual currency-required features or other "VC sinks" into the game as a method to entice players to spend what virtual currency they may still have. While somewhat weakening its closed-loop system argument, a publisher could also notify the players that any virtual items may be used in another game made available by the publisher. So long as the virtual items remain solely usable in publisher's games, and not any third-party games, the publisher would likely still fall within the gift card/certificate exception for virtual currency which can only be used with the issuer.

## CONCLUSION

The law related to the use of virtual currency and virtual property in video games is truly at a nascent stage. It is evolving daily and often changes at a rapid pace in response to lateral movement in regulations and public policy. This chapter is based on industry norms and best practices and it is intended only as an overview of the relevant legal and business issues. While the practices we advocate in this chapter should strengthen a publisher's legal defenses and reduce risk, we cannot guarantee that federal, state, or local officials in any particular jurisdiction may not take a different view of the virtual item issues discussed herein. Therefore, while following these best practices is advisable, you should know that nothing is foolproof. You need to weigh the value of having a virtual item system against the potential compliance burden. However, if you are like most companies in the industry, you will find that the potential benefits of offering virtual items, in terms of customer acquisition, retention, game-play, and revenue, far outweigh regulatory risk.

## NOTES

1. The Guidance follows FinCEN's issuance of a Final Rule amending definitions and other regulations relating to money services businesses ("*MSBs*"), 76 F.R. 43585 (July 21, 2011) (the "*MSB Rule*"), and a Final Rule amending definitions and other regulations relating to prepaid access, 76 F.R. 45403 (July 29, 2011) (the "*Prepaid Access Rule*"). The Guidance explains the regulatory treatment of "persons" engaged in "convertible virtual currency" transactions under the Bank Secrecy Act and its implementing regulations.
2. The determination of whether a person is a money transmitter is a matter of facts and circumstances. 31 CFR § 1010.100(ff)(5)(ii).
3. J. Robert Schlimgen, *Virtual World, Real Taxes: A Sales and Use Tax Adventure through Second Life Starring Dwight Schrute*, 11 Minn. J.L. Sci. & Tech. 877 (Spring 2010): https://scholarship.law.umn.edu/cgi/viewcontent.cgi?referer=http://www.google.com/url?sa=t&rct=j&q=&esrc=s&source=web&cd=1&ved=0ahUKEwiL1riA-OvaAhWHyoMKHSCVAl4QFggnMAA&url=http%3A%2F%2Fscholarship.law.umn.edu%2Fcgi%2Fviewcontent.cgi%3Farticle%3D1182%26context%3Dmjlst&usg=AOvVaw1CGni1WPnl9azqyDO1h2mX&httpsredir=1&article=1182&context=mjlst
4. M.E. Kabay, Real legal issues with virtual currencies, *Network World*, May 12, 2010: https://www.networkworld.com/article/2207996/software/real-legal-issues-with-virtual-currencies.html
5. The six exemptions are cards, codes, or other devices: (1) useable solely for telephone services; (2) reloadable and not marketed or labeled as a gift card or gift certificate; (3) that are part of loyalty, award, or promotional programs; (4) not marketed to the general public; (5) issued in paper form only; or (6) redeemable solely for admission to events or venues at a particular location or group of affiliated locations, or to obtain goods or services in conjunction with

admission to such events or venues, at the event or venue or at specific locations affiliated with and in geographic proximity to the event or venue. The Board indicated that the statutory exemptions should be interpreted narrowly to ensure consumers receive full protection contemplated by the CARD Act.

6. Cal. Civ. Code § 1749.5(b)(2).
7. N.J. Rev. Stat. § 46:30B-6(r).
8. Eric Eldon, As Facebook continues testing credits, some developers worry about costs, *AdWeek*, June 21, 2010: http://www.adweek.com/digital/as-facebook-continues-testing-credits-developers-worry-over-costs/
9. Colo. Rev. Stat. § 38-13-102(7).
10. Cal. Code of Civ. Proc. § 1520.5.
11. UUPA § 2(6) (1995).

# CHAPTER 9

# Advertising and Games

A N OFTEN-OVERLOOKED LEGAL TOPIC is advertising regulation in video games. People routinely think of advertising as doing whatever it takes to get more people to play your game and extract more revenue from it. However, there are many rules around advertising practices. Though not as often discussed, advertising should be thought of as a regulated area of game development like tax, intellectual property, privacy, or human resources.

While there are many advertising regulations, all or almost all of them can be reduced to two simple rules. When in doubt, consider these guides and honestly ask yourself if you in line with the following:

*Rule 1*: Tell the truth.

*Rule 2*: Don't rip anyone off.

In the United States, advertising is regulated on the federal level by the Federal Trade Commission (FTC).[1] The FTC gets its authority from a statute that allows it to regulate practices that are considered "unfair or deceptive." That authority is very broad and allows the FTC to police activities ranging from television commercials to online tracking and privacy breaches.

State law also comes into play for regulating advertising, and has equivalent protections for consumers as federal law. In addition, state law requirements are often more specific. State law might answer these questions: What kind of return or refund policies are required? What kind of warranties must be included with a product? What constitutes a sweepstakes versus gambling? What are the requirements for collecting money from consumers, including payment plans for larger purchases?

## RULE 1 EXPLAINED: TELL THE TRUTH

The primary purpose of advertising regulation is to protect consumers from lies about a product. The policies are set up to prevent people from being deceived by advertising. Deception can come in a variety of forms. Colloquially, this is normally called "false advertising." The cases below are illustrations of the rule at work.

## Advertising Features and Graphics

It is OK to talk about potential features in an interview or public presentation, but by the time real advertisements are being created, including social media influencer and press packets as well as actual advertisements (billboard, print, online, or TV), you should not show or imply features that do not exist. For instance, do not show real-time mobile multi-player over a cellular network unless that is actually available over most cellular networks.

Consider graphics as our first example. There is no such thing as a "neutral platform" for game footage. Whenever anyone suggests that you record on a "neutral platform," they always mean the same thing. They want to record the best game footage we have and then advertise it for all platforms. Perhaps they believe that this can be fixed with a disclaimer at the bottom that says "test footage" or "development footage," but it cannot. Text at the bottom of an advertisement is meant to further explain what people are seeing, not contradict it. So, we cannot show our best development machine footage with all the bells and whis-tles turned on in the national advertising campaign, even with a very truthful text under it saying, "We wish it looked this good, but it doesn't." The only time development footage is legitimate is when the game is in development. After launch, you should use the actual game running on a platform. You can show the best platform you have for multi-platform ads; for instance, if a game is available on Xbox, PlayStation, and PC, you can show the best one and say "PC footage shown." Sometimes, with focused captive advertising on an individual platform, you have to advertise for just that one platform (i.e., advertising the Xbox version on the Xbox Network). In those cases, the footage must match the platform advertised.[2]

Substantiation and truth in advertising can apply to hardware- as well as software-related graphical issues. Consider a recent graphics card case where the NVIDIA GTX 970 originally advertised 4 MB of high-speed RAM. In fact, the card only had 3.5 MB of high-speed RAM and the remaining 0.5 MB of RAM ran 80% slower. This resulted in a class action case in the Northern District of California. The NVIDIA GTX 970 overstated its graphical capabilities and ultimately settled the class action, paying consumers for false advertising. The settlement was $30 per consumer that had purchased the graphics card.

## Substantiation and Hardware: Waterproof Devices

Substantiation is another way to describe telling the truth. Substantiation in advertising means asking whether an advertiser has the proof to back up claims in a commercial. Are the product claims true and are we able to show those claims are true with evidence and tests? This applies to both software and hardware, but the effects in hardware are particu-larly striking. Above, we discussed showing graphics that were realistic to the consumer experience as well as accurately describing video card technical features. Now consider other hardware attributes, like a device being waterproof.

As waterproof devices become better and more common, I suspect that this advertising trend will fade because it will no longer be a special feature of the devices, but it is important now and will be illustrative for any hardware attribute going forward. When we have paper-thin phones, or in-home teleportation devices, we will still use the same advertising standards.

If a device is advertised as waterproof, the advertisements must show the device submerged in the same conditions it was tested in. For instance, waterproof devices are normally tested by being submerged in clean fresh water for 30 minutes, at 21 degrees Celsius (about 71 degrees Fahrenheit) in about three feet of water.[3] The advertisements have to show something similar to the testing conditions.

Why use those as the normal testing conditions? Mainly because those are obvious, easy, and commonly available. That temperature is about room temperature. That depth is the depth of easily available waterproof containers, and 30 minutes is enough time to do several test runs in one day. It is also longer than most people would leave the device in the water, because they would fish it out. Lastly, those testing conditions are related to an international electronics manufacturer standard called IEC60529, also referred to as the IP Code (Ingress Protections Code), which rates devices on their resistance to both dust and liquid.

The harder question is: Why are devices not tested in more conditions? Waterproofing has and will be a core selling feature in national advertising campaigns where tens of millions of dollars spent are on creative materials, production, and media buys. I have never once been given device specifications for a waterproof device that was tested in conditions substantially different from the above.[4] It is as if companies are paralyzed by convenience and the IEC60529 standards rather than what people actually want to know about their phones. Compare this testing reality to the ads people want to run and the lives of real people. We take showers and we want to listen to our playlists on our phones. That water is hot and soapy. Sometimes you want to be in there for 45 minutes. How about pools? That water is filled with chlorine (at least). How about the beach, or when you want to take snorkeling and diving photos? What about the sink, when I am washing dishes, or at a dinner party, spilling wine, liquor, or soft drinks on a phone? For years now, advertising agency creatives have been taking devices that are supposed to be "waterproof" and trying to make advertisements like the above when the device was never or not adequately tested in those common conditions. Most of these proposed commercials in the shower or pools or the ocean are stopped prior to production, but occasionally some get through, to the great embarrassment of the people involved.[5]

## Substantiation: Whose Job Is It and How Is It Done?

Advertising should be reviewed for substantiation, legally as well as on an engineering level. Substantiation for game software or hardware is *always* conducted at the game company or by a qualified third-party testing service. Substantiation is never properly performed at the advertising agency. It is the game company's responsibility to only approve pitches that can be substantiated. There should never be a creative brief issued to an agency for unsubstantiated claims. Asking the advertising agency to perform substantiation testing or research is essentially an admission that engineering was entirely disconnected from the marketing plan. It is a suggestion that the product or software is being marketed beyond the intended attributes and benefits. Lastly, it is evidence of incompetence that regulators justly revel in uncovering.

Unfortunately, engineers do not work in the game company marketing department. This leads to failures in understanding the true product functionality, which results in litigation and regulatory action. It is critical that engineering and development communicate with marketing on substantiation because the consequences of making unsubstantiated marketing claims are so severe, including litigation costs, regulatory fines, and customer refunds. The only thing worse than unchecked substantiation coming from the marketing department alone is asking the advertising agency to do its own testing. Advertising agencies are known for their service-oriented structures, flexibility, and broad skill set. Still, they should never be performing substantiation like estimating frame rates, testing video cards, or submerging mobile devices in differing liquid conditions. To say that it is a recipe for disaster is an understatement.

So, what should a game company do if it receives a pitch from its agency that makes unsubstantiated claims? The company itself should do the testing internally or commission a qualified third party to perform the testing necessary to substantiate the claim—*in advance* of the advertising being made. This common sense, but uncommon practice, can literally save millions of dollars.

## Influencers and Disclosure

One novel area where telling the truth is especially important is with social media influencers. An influencer is a person on social media that has a robust following. Usually this following is at least tens of thousands of people, and may be tens of millions or more. These people may be on YouTube, Twitch, Instagram, Twitter, or another social media platform. The marketing proposition is that people interested in an influencer have common interests and demographics. Furthermore, they will likely be persuaded to make buying decisions by the influencer. They consider the influencer a trusted endorser of a game or other hardware. Some influencers have become bona fide celebrities entirely through social media.

So, when an influencer is paid to discuss a game or piece of game hardware, we have to consider another aspect of telling the truth. Telling the truth includes making sure consumers fully understand the relationship between people talking about the product and your company. The FTC started regulating this area in the radio and television era before the internet and before video games achieved the popularity they enjoy today. The original rules still apply, with some important additions. The core rules are:

1. Influencers must give their honest opinion about a product

2. Influencers must disclose their association with the game company.

In person, on television, or the radio, this was easier than in social media. An endorser in the 1990s would thank a particular company for supporting him or her and providing the endorser with products. Today, social media has very little room for text. Video platforms only offer several seconds of time, and Twitter launched with only 140 characters until it generously doubled that number in November 2017. Even six seconds or 280 characters is not a lot of room for an advertisement and a disclosure.

## Disclosure: Content and Placement

What is the correct placement of an influencer disclosure, and what should it say? The FTC does not say where exactly a disclosure should be, but we have guidelines that say the disclosure should be "clear and conspicuous." What about social platforms that have limited text and limited room? The FTC has addressed this, and stated that if you do not have room for the disclosure then you should not use the platform.

The social content company Machinima was sanctioned by the FTC and the New York Attorney General in 2016 for a program related to influencers and disclosure. Microsoft and its ad agency Starcom paid Machinima to run an influencer campaign around the launch of the Xbox One. In that campaign, Machinima paid a small number of influencers to post material about pre-release versions of the Xbox One. Secondarily, it offered to pay a larger group of influencers a bounty of $1 for every 1000 views of any video about the Xbox One. Machinima influencers uploaded over 300 videos that generated more than 35 million views. The FTC found that the influencers were not required to disclose their relationship with Microsoft or that they were being paid to produce the videos. The New York Attorney General levied a $50,000 penalty on Machinima and the FTC issued a 20-year consent order that required disclosure going forward on social media campaigns and an audit of influencer materials for the next five years.

Assuming that there is room for disclosure on social platforms, how do we know what works? In 2017, the FTC sent a letter to 90 influencers and brands, explaining that they were not adequately disclosing their relationship. Later in the year, they sent 21 follow-up letters to influencers, warning that they had still not adequately disclosed the relationship. From these letters, we can derive several attempted disclosures that were not sufficient and can avoid those in the game context. In the table below, the insufficient disclosures are provided along with some improved examples of disclosures the author considers compliant in most contexts.

| Non-Compliant Disclosure | Author-Suggested Improvements (Normally Compliant) |
|---|---|
| #sp | #ad |
| #spon | #sponsored |
| #collab | #Brand Ambassador |
| #ambassador | #Thanks to Brand for your support |
| #Thanks brand | Put all disclosure above the fold (before "more") |
| #Thanks to my friend at brand | Disclosures on an image itself |
| Any disclosure after the "more" | Disclosures in the voiceover or actual content of a video |
| Disclosures that do not travel with the content | Disclosures in text several times in a video in a readable |
| Disclosures in a comment section | form |
| Disclosures in an About section or Bio section | |

The game industry may claim the dubious honor of being the first industry in which the FTC had an action against the influencers themselves. Previously, any enforcement was limited to brands and a warning to the influencers. The line was crossed by two founders of a *Counter-Strike: GO* skins trading business. Those founders, Trevor "TmarTn" Martin and Thomas "Syndicate" Cassell, were widely followed in the online game community. They deceptively endorsed the online gambling service CSGO Lotto while failing to disclose that they jointly owned the company.[6] They also allegedly paid other well-known influencers thousands of dollars to promote the site on YouTube, Twitch, Twitter, and Facebook, without requiring those influencers to disclose the payments in their social media posts. The Commission order settling the charges required Martin and Cassell to clearly and conspicuously disclose any material connections with an endorser or between an endorser and any promoted product or service.

### Two for One Example: Sony Vita Substantiation and Disclosure Combined

In 2015, the FTC settled an enforcement action against Sony Computer Entertainment America and its advertising agency, Deutsch LA. There were two core problems with the campaign for Sony's new product, the Sony Vita. First was a substantiation problem, and this was made worse by a lack of disclosure in some of the advertising agency's communications.

The issue with new product creative briefs is that we often do not fully understand the product prior to launch. Yet, advertisements take months to make and we need them to be ready at or before product launch. That was the case with the Sony Vita. There were two controversial features touted by the Vita. First was that a player could play games on a PlayStation and then move immediately to a Vita as the player went on about their day. This essentially promised that consumers would have a portable console experience. Second was the idea that people could play real-time multiplayer games over a cellular network—another groundbreaking technological feat. Game industry companies constantly promise features like these at trade shows, but a satisfying, bug-free experience has never been delivered on either of them. So, to promise both of these features in one piece of hardware was questionable from the start.

Unsurprisingly, it turned out that neither claim was actually true in the way it was shown in the commercials. A player could not just pause the console and any point and walk out of the house with his or her Sony Vita, continuing to play. This functionality was limited to a small number of games and was limited to certain special times within the game. The real-time multiplayer functionality was also not true. It was available over Wi-Fi, which was not innovative, and was also available over a cellular connection for turn-based games and to review leaderboard displays in games, which was also not innovative.

In retrospect, some of the ads were deliberately vague on these points, but that made it worse. At root, the issue to consider is: What does a reasonable consumer take away from the advertisements? Vague is always going to be the wrong answer because it can be misinterpreted. In the final analysis, just as we discussed with waterproof devices above, the client has to substantiate their claims. This is true for all product properties, but it is especially true for claims about innovation or market superiority. Those claims are the most likely to get consumers to make a buying decision. Launch-related unknowns and timing exigencies are not an acceptable excuse. The requests of a creative brief or a client's instructions are no reason to break the law and will not save the company or the ad agency when a regulator reviews the advertisements.

The ad agency made the investigation worse when one of the Deutsch assistant account executives wrote the following email to all of the ad agency employees:

Fellow Deutschers—

The PlayStation Team has been working hard on a campaign to launch Sony's all-new handheld gaming device, the PS Vita, and we want YOU to help us kick things off! The PS Vita's innovative features like 3G gaming, cross platform play and augmented reality will revolutionize the way people game. To generate buzz around the launch of the device, the PS Vita ad campaign will incorporate a #GAMECHANGER hashtag into nearly all creative executions. #GAMECHANGER will drive gamers to Twitter where they can learn more about the PS Vita and join in the conversation. The campaign starts on February 13th, and to get the conversation started, we're asking YOU to Tweet about the PlayStation Vita using the #GAMECHANGER hashtag. Easy, right?…

In response, Deutsch agency employees used their personal Twitter accounts to hype the PlayStation Vita through tweets like:

One thing can be said about PlayStation Vita … it's a #gamechanger
PS Vita [ruling] the world. Learn about it! us.playstation.com/psvita/# GAMECHANGER
Thumbs UP #GAMECHANGER—check out the new PlayStation Vita
This is sick … See the new PS Vita in action. The gaming #GameChanger
Got the chance to get my hands on a PS Vita and I'm amazed how great the graphics are. It's definitely a #gamechanger!

It is clear that the request had an effect on the marketplace and the agency was helping to seed the hashtag without disclosing the material connection between the brand and the ad agency employees. This type of fake grassroots movement is referred to as astroturfing.

After the FTC settlement, Sony had to offer every Vita purchaser $25 in cash or a voucher $50 worth of Sony merchandise. The ad agency was barred from making misleading advertising claims and required to disclose any future material relationship between a brand and an influencer (including any ad agency employee). The agency also had to submit to five years of monitoring of its advertisements.

## RULE 2 EXPLAINED: DON'T RIP ANYONE OFF

There are two main variations on Rule 2—Don't Rip Anyone Off. First, and most important, do not take advantage of consumers. Regulators are on the lookout for anything that harms consumers. This facet of Rule 2 is tightly intertwined with Rule 1 (Tell the Truth). In fact, some of the examples in this section clearly overlap.

A second way to look at Rule 2 is: do not steal advertising material from other advertisers or brands. When you latch on to the goodwill and social currency that another brand has built, you are free-riding. You are stealing from their hard work and using it to artificially elevate your game brand. It might sound like a terrific idea to advertise your new fantasy role-playing game with the launch of the new *Game of Thrones* season, complete with references to Winterfell, but that would violate Rule 2.

The intellectual property violation aspects of Rule 2 are more fully discussed in the intellectual property chapter of this text. For this chapter, we will focus on the aspect of the rule related to taking advantage of consumers.

One prominent example in recent years surrounds microtransactions. Games supported by microtransactions can easily mislead consumers. The game looks "free to play," but it is really just an evolution of the original "free to try" game model back in the early days of the game industry. The evolution is, of course, that people not only have to pay to play the game well, they can often pay hundreds or thousands of dollars a month to excel at the game.

Originally, the Apple App store and Google store labeled microtransaction-supported games as "Free" when they were downloaded from the store. In 2014, both companies yielded to pressure from the European Commission to change the labeling of those games. Now, the reader is probably familiar with "Get" next to those titles in the store. Going forward, all applications were required to clearly disclose in-app purchases.

## Specific Examples: Microtransaction Disclosure

In 2014, the UK version of the FTC, the Advertising Standards Association (ASA), found that the Electronic Arts (EA) application for *Dungeon Keeper* had issued an email ad that was deceptive for consumers. It wrote "GET DUNGEON KEEPER ON MOBILE FOR FREE!" The ad did not adequately disclose that microtransactions were necessary for the average player to progress in the game.

In some cases, a regulator does not need to step in for consumer harm to be recognized. The marketplace itself can complain so loudly that it generates a change. In 2017, EA launched *Star Wars Battlefront II*. That game launched with a retail price of $79.99 and included microtransactions. Worse, the character-advancement microtransaction monetization strategy was tied to the "loot box" concept.

Loot boxes are randomly generated virtual property. A player buys a loot box for a chance to get some item or advancement, but may only get something of limited value (or of no value). Loot boxes are not currently regulated in the United States because game systems that use them are essentially cash-in systems with no payout. They are not slot machines, but are merely digital versions of the arcade games we have been familiar with for almost 100 years. Analogously, you put in a quarter to play the game, and luck has a huge effect on the outcome. We have allowed that type of pay-for-amusement in the United States, going all the way back to physical carnival games and electro-mechanical games. However, *Star Wars Battlefront II* finally brought loot boxes to the attention of regulators and irritated consumers. In November 2017, after the launch of the game, the Belgian Gaming Commission described loot boxes as gambling aimed at children and called for their elimination from Belgium and Europe.[7] The fundamental problem in that case was greed. Traditionally, loot boxes had been part of microtransaction games or a small part of AAA titles. This has been acceptable from a social and regulatory perspective since the start of "free-to-play" games. EA actually tried to incorporate an AAA retail price of $80 with a requirement to purchase loot boxes in addition to that retail price for basic character advancement. The system and associated initial EA response also resulted in the most down-voted Reddit post of all time, with a score of negative 683,000 as of this writing. The result was that loot boxes were pulled from the game literally overnight.

The general theme here is that we should not say that a game is free or otherwise forget to mention in-game purchases. If in-game purchases such as currency or items are an important part of the game, or otherwise substantially help people to make progress in the game, then they should be disclosed in all of the game advertising. Not disclosing those elements is a way to "bait-and-switch" customers. They thought they were buying something of high value, but found out they were buying something of lower value where they had to spend more to have the high-value experience.

## KEY ADVERTISING LAWS

In addition to telling the truth and not ripping anyone off, there are a few core statutes that are part of many advertising campaigns. Below is a brief summary of the most important advertising laws.

### Email Marketing Compliance: CAN-SPAM Act

All email marketing in the United States has to fit within this system. The statute covers all commercial messages, but not simple transactional messages. A transactional message is something simple like a purchase confirmation or a customer service email. You are not trying to sell the consumer anything and the message is mainly for the benefit of the consumer.

On the other hand, commercial messages are defined as "any electronic mail message, the primary purpose of which is the commercial advertisement or promotion of a commercial product or service," including content on a website operated for a commercial purpose. Generally, the test to determine if something is a commercial message is whether a recipient reasonably interpreting the subject line would likely conclude that the message contains an ad or promotion for a commercial product or service, or whether most of the message's non-commercial content does not appear at the beginning of the message.

Each email violation of CAN-SPAM is subject to penalties of up to $40,654. This is rarely enforced in the United States and does not have a private right of action. Still, the potential loss is enough to keep legitimate companies in line and compliant.

The basic requirements of CAN-SPAM are:

- Do not use false or misleading header information. The "From," "To," "Reply To," and routing information (including the originating domain name and email address) must be accurate and must identify the person or business who initiated the message. Do not use fraudulent transmission data, such as open relays and false headers.

- Do not use deceptive subject lines. The subject line must accurately reflect the content of the message.

- Identify the message as an ad early in the message. Initiators of a commercial email must clearly and conspicuously disclose that the message is an ad. The message should contain at least one sentence.

- Tell recipients where you are located. The message must include your valid physical postal address, which can be a current street address, registered post office box, or a registered private mailbox.

- Tell recipients how to opt out of receiving future email from you. Your message must include a clear and conspicuous explanation of how the recipient can opt out of getting email from you in the future. Give a return email address or another easy internet-based way to allow people to communicate their choice to you. You may create a menu to allow a recipient to opt out of certain types of messages, but you must include a "global" option to stop all commercial messages from you. Make sure your spam filter does not block these opt-out requests. The current industry gold standard is an unsubscribe button with the unsubscribe happening automatically or one click away through a dashboard.

- Honor opt-out requests promptly. Any opt-out mechanism you offer must be able to process opt-out requests for at least 30 days after you send your message. You must honor a recipient's opt-out request (however received) within 10 business days. Here, the industry standard (exceeding the statutory requirement) is 24–48 h. You cannot charge a fee, require the recipient to give you any personally identifying information beyond an email address, or make the recipient take any step other than sending a reply email or visiting a single page on an internet website as a condition for honoring an opt-out request. Once people have told you that they do not want to receive more messages from you, you cannot sell or transfer their email addresses, even in the form of a mailing list. The only exception is that you may transfer the addresses to a company you have hired to help you comply with the CAN-SPAM Act.

- Monitor what others are doing on your behalf. Even if you hire another company to handle your email marketing, you cannot contract away your legal responsibility to comply with the law. Both the company whose product is promoted in the message and the company that actually sends the message may be held legally responsible.

## TCPA: The Most Dangerous Law in Advertising

We are saturated by advertising in so much of our lives. One place we are not is text messages. The Telephone Consumer Protection Act (TCPA) is one of the main reasons our text messages are not as flooded with commercial messages as our email is. Traditionally, text message plans were not unlimited and people often paid for each text message. In this way, text messages were similar to faxes (which are also regulated by the TCPA). Since there was a real cost for each text, it made sense to substantially limit what advertisers could do with the medium. Now that most text plans are unlimited, consumers are still grateful that there is one place in their life where advertising is an opt-in experience.[8]

Unlike the CAN-SPAM Act, there is a private right of action and a potential $500 fine per text message. These numbers become astronomical quickly. The private right of action means that the plaintiff's bar (contingency fee attorneys) are always on the lookout for a chance to be paid. As mercenary as this sounds, it essentially privatizes enforcement and makes most companies enormously careful when using text marketing.

Another effect of the private right of action is that there are a huge number of cases each year, probably more than any other type of advertising case. In 2016, there were almost 5000 TCPA cases. Plus, because of the $500 per message penalty, the damages can be large. For example, in just the past few years, Capital One Financial Corp. settled a TCPA class action for $75 million. Several cruise lines settled claims for $76 million and AT&T Inc. and Bank of America Corp. settled cases for $45 million and $32 million, respectively.

The key requirements of the TCPA are as follows:

Prohibited call times and numbers. No person or entity may initiate any telephone solicitation to (1) any residential telephone subscriber before the hour of 8 a.m. or after 9 p.m. or (2) a residential telephone number on the national do-not-call registry. Calls and text messages have the same protection under FCC rules. However, please note that telemarketing laws are regulated on a state-by-state basis in addition to the TCPA.

Caller contact information. FCC rules require anyone making a telephone solicitation call to a consumer's home to provide his or her name, the name of the person or entity on whose behalf the call is being made, and a telephone number or address at which that person or entity can be contacted. For texting purposes, you can just identify the sender in the opt-in information.

You must obtain consent for prerecorded or autodialed messages. Companies using autodialers ("robocall") or prerecorded messages for a marketing call or text are required to obtain the prior express written consent of the called party.

A consumer's written consent must be signed (electronic or digital form of signature is acceptable, to the extent this form of signature is recognized as a valid signature under applicable federal or state law) and be sufficient to show that the consumer (1) received "clear and conspicuous disclosure" of the consequences of providing the requested consent, that is, that the consumer will receive future calls/texts via an autodialer, or receive prerecorded messages by or on behalf of a specific seller, and the frequency of the recorded messages; and (2) having received this information, agrees unambiguously to receive such calls at a telephone number the consumer designates.

In addition, the written agreement must be obtained "without requiring, directly or indirectly, that the agreement be executed as a condition of purchasing any good or service" and must state as much.

Game companies should watch out for reassigned numbers. Callers are liable for robocalls to reassigned wireless numbers when the new subscriber to (or customary user of) the number has not consented, subject to a limited, one-call exception for cases where the caller does not have actual or constructive knowledge of the reassignment. This rule is particularly disconcerting to many people, but the requirement in practice is to include a reasonable mechanism for identifying and filtering out reassigned numbers.

One of the keys overall and to identifying reassigned numbers is honoring opt-out requests. Telemarketers must provide an automated, interactive "opt-out" mechanism during each robocall or text so that consumers can immediately tell the telemarketer to stop calling. Generally, this is done by including an option to text "STOP" or some similar phrase in the initial message. Consumers may revoke consent to receive robocalls or texts at any time and through any reasonable means. A calling company cannot require someone to fill out a form and mail it in as the only way to revoke consent.

Internet-to-phone messages are also considered "robocalls" for the purposes of the statute. They also require consumer consent.

## TCPA Consent Exception

There is an on-demand text exemption, also called a one-time exception. This is for "on-demand" text messages sent in response to a consumer request and they are not subject to TCPA liability. This exception applies only if the message (1) is requested by the consumer; (2) is a one-time-only message sent immediately in response to a specific consumer request; and (3) contains only the information requested by the consumer with no other marketing or advertising information. This exception would allow a marketer to publish an ad with a clear call-to-action to consumers (such as "text COUPON to obtain a 20% off coupon"), along with the appropriate disclosures, and then respond with a single text to any consumers who followed the call-to-action by texting the marketer with a request for information. Another common example would be "text HELLO to receive a link to (Information)."

As you can see above, the TCPA is complicated and there are severe penalties for non-compliance. Game companies interested in text marketing or automated calling should be aware of these rules and follow them carefully.

## Sweepstakes and Contests

Sweepstakes and contests are some of the most popular ways to advertise video games or any product. They build community. They are engaging. We have a long history of data that show they drive product sales and awareness. However, they are also right next to gambling in most state statute books. It is easy to design them in a way that crosses over the line into gambling and give rise to penalties and potential criminal liability.

This section will set out the core elements of sweepstakes and contests. Furthermore, it will alert the reader to where they may make a mistake and have a promotion cross the line into the gambling realm.

## WHAT IS GAMBLING?

Gambling is any game that contains *all* three of the following three elements:

- *Chance*: States disagree on how much chance is required to trigger this element. It could be that it depends to a material degree on chance or it could be stronger and state that chance is the dominant factor in the outcome. Either way, if there is luck involved in the promotion, this element may be met.

- *Consideration*: Consideration providing anything of real value. It can be paying money to play. It could also be taking substantial effort to play.

- *Prize*: A prize is something of real value received for participating in the promotion. A cash-out system in a game would certainly trigger this. Physical prizes also trigger this element. An interesting point going forward is whether prizes in game will also trigger it. Traditionally, we have allowed game mechanics like loot boxes to be unregulated, but this may change in the coming years.

You will see in the summary descriptions below that sweepstakes and contests are carefully designed so they do not contain all three elements.

## WHAT IS A SWEEPSTAKES?

- In a sweepstakes, the winner is determined by chance, that is, at random, like drawing a name out of a hat.

- A sweepstakes cannot require "consideration" from entrants, such as payment or extensive effort, for the chance to win a prize. Therefore, the game company cannot charge a fee to consumers or require them to buy a product in order to enter a sweepstakes. The game company also cannot require entrants to incur text messaging or extensive data charges. Entrants also cannot be required to invest a substantial amount of time or effort to enter, such as completing a lengthy survey. All of these methods of entry may be used, but if they are, there must also be a free (from cost and substantial effort) alternative method of entry ("AMOE"). Typical AMOEs include mail-in entries and online entries. The AMOE must be disclosed in the official rules and those entering via the AMOE must be given "equal dignity" in the promotion.

- Other names for a sweepstakes include "giveaway" and "drawing." Note that the word "raffle" should not be used in any promotion: only charities are allowed to conduct "raffles" (in accordance with specific state requirements), requiring entrants to buy tickets for a chance to win a prize.

## WHAT IS A CONTEST?

- In a contest, the winner is determined by his or her skill, such as writing the best essay or taking the best photograph.

- In most states, the sponsor can charge a fee for entry (or require a purchase of a product) if it is running a bona fide contest. (If charging a fee or requiring the purchase of a product, some states will have to be voided.)

- Sometimes, advertisers will conduct "hybrid" promotions. For example, to increase the number of entries received in a contest, an advertiser will sometimes offer an entry into a random drawing to anyone who submits an entry into the contest. In this scenario, the advertiser must also provide a "non-contest entry" method of entering the sweepstakes portion of the promotion, in order to avoid requiring "consideration" (see Sweepstakes, above).

## WHAT IS A SURPRISE AND DELIGHT?

- In a true "surprise and delight" promotion, the prizes awarded to consumers must truly be a surprise: there can be no pre-promotion or hint that "prizes" will be awarded if the consumer responds to the call-to-action in the post or advertisement. Otherwise, the promotion is a sweepstakes (if the winner is selected at random) or a contest (if the winner is selected based on the quality of his or her post) and, therefore, the requirements for such promotions must be followed.

- To maintain the element of surprise, a surprise and delight promotion must be done on an infrequent basis and cannot always be done in connection with the same or similar call-to-action. For example, a sponsor cannot run a Twitter promotion as a surprise and delight every Friday at noon with a call-to-action requesting posts about weekend plans and awarding prizes to the funniest responses. (Such a promotion could, however, be conducted as a contest.)

- If truly a surprise and delight, the promotion does not require Official Rules or other promotions disclosures.

One last very important word on modern sweepstakes and contests is that they usually require some form of moderation. By that I mean that most promotions require players to do something that displays user-generated content. This can be a video of them playing the game or their character in the game or something as simple as their username displayed in a list. All of these can be abused. As of 2017, software is not enough to filter out every way the human mind can imagine thwarting those censors. In fact, some people enjoy the publicity around getting something offensive posted on an official channel more than they enjoy your game or the contest. Do not rely on platforms like Facebook, Instagram, or Twitter either because they are far from perfect. Moderation can be done in-house, but is better outsourced. There are companies that specialize in moderation. So, please consider some type of delay in posting with a human approval for sweepstakes and contest entries (especially winners).

### Children's Online Privacy Protection Act[9]

COPPA applies to all websites, games, and applications, directed toward children under the age of 13 or where a game operator knowingly has personal information of children under 13. For the purposes of this section, the word "game" should be interpreted as any digital presence including websites, applications, VR, console, portable, and PC games. These games require some form of parental consent before allowing the game company to collect, store, and process that information.

### Is Your Game Directed Toward Children?

Here, a holistic analysis of the game is required. There is no one factor that determines it, but they should all be considered together. What is the subject matter of the game? Do you use cartoonish animated characters? What is the audio like? Are there child celebrities or child heroes in the game? What are the activities in the game and the language used in the game? Each of these and more will generate a sense of whether or not the game is child-directed.

## What Is Personal Information in the Context of Children, and Do You Collect it?

Personal information from children includes first name, last name, home or other address, online contact information like an email, screen name, telephone number, social security number, photograph, video, audio files, geolocation information, or a persistent identifier. Generally speaking, the list above is much broader than most people consider personal information. The rule of thumb is that any information collected about a child will likely qualify, even if it is simple technical information that would qualify under a persistent identifier.

## General COPPA Principles

Your privacy policy and procedures must be COPPA compliant to collect, store, and use children's information. This includes reasonable security for that information. This is an FTC requirement for adults, but it is viewed even more seriously for children. The privacy policy must describe the types of information collected and how it is used within the game company and by third parties. Parents must have the right to view, edit, and opt out of game company collection and use of the information.

## Getting Parental Consent

Your game must have a neutral age gate before allowing children to enter. It must ask a neutral question like: "What is your birthday?" It cannot say: "Click here if you are over 12," or give other hints. If the child puts a birthday in that shows they are 12 or under, the game must set the online equivalent of a session cookie. This must not allow the child to go back and change their birthday to gain access to the game. There are two main types of parental consent. The first type is referred to as verifiable parental consent. This is the highest standard, and the following are the acceptable ways of obtaining that consent:

- Sign a consent form and send it back via fax, mail, or electronic scan

- Use a credit card, debit card, or other online payment system that provides notification of each separate transaction to the account holder

- Call a toll-free number staffed by trained personnel

- Connect to trained personnel via a video conference

- Provide a copy of a form of government-issued ID that you check against a database, as long as you delete the identification from your records when you finish the verification process

- Answer a series of knowledge-based challenge questions that would be difficult for someone other than the parent to answer

- Verify a picture of a driver's license of other photo ID submitted by the parent and then compare that photo with a second photo submitted by the parent using facial recognition technology.

These are high bars and there is a lower standard that can be used if the children's information is going to be used internally only. That standard is called email plus. The email plus verification works by sending a parent an email, having the parent respond with their consent, and then sending a follow-up communication via email (or other contact information) so that the parent is reminded that they have consented to the information collection. The emails must also give a link to the privacy policy and describe the core parts of information collection and use by the game. Importantly, it must also show the parent how to opt out of information collection in the future.

## BEYOND STATUTES: SOME FINAL CONSIDERATIONS

### Introduction

There are so many bits and pieces to advertising regulation in the game industry. It honestly is hard to know when to stop writing detailed sections. However, I am confident that the major areas have been covered above, but please indulge a few sentences on each of the following topics. They are too important to be left out entirely.

### Game Advertising and the ESRB

When advertising your game, it also important to remember that if your game has been rated by the Entertainment Software Rating Board (ESRB), then you may be obligated to comply with certain rules and requirements concerning packaging, advertisements, videos, and any other materials that promote your game. Depending on how your game was rated by the ESRB, you may be subject to a detailed set of guidelines and requirements that you can access through the ESRB website or a shorter set of guidelines provided or linked to on your rating certificate. The ESRB's Advertising Review Council (or "ARC") works with publishers to ensure compliance with applicable requirements and will even review draft advertisements that a game company submits to determine whether they comply with applicable requirements. Additional information concerning ARC requirements, including potential penalties for non-compliance, can be found in the ESRB section of the game ratings chapter of this book.

### Children's Advertising Review Unit

In addition to COPPA, the Children's Advertising Review Unit (CARU) is a second area where children's advertising regulation occurs. CARU actually controls advertising in all media, including games, online, and television. Generally speaking, CARU guidelines cover truthful advertising and ensure that advertising is appropriate for children given their developmental stage. For instance, children have a difficult time discerning the difference between content and advertising. So, one of the CARU rules is that characters from a show may not advertise products. Another rule is that the advertisements cannot generate a sense of urgency, like "buy now!" The CARU guidelines are a substantial text, and summarizing all of the rules is outside the scope of this chapter. They are also updated as more research comes out on children's capacities as well as the monitoring of new developments in advertising technology.

The CARU program is not a state or federal governmental office. It is an industry-sponsored self-regulatory program where compliance is essentially ensured by the intimate cooperation of the state and federal governments. If CARU sanctions a game company, it has the right to refer that game company's case to a regulator if the company does not correct its errors. This is very motivating for most private companies because the regulators pay special attention to CARU. Consider that CARU is out there making the regulator's job easier. So, if a company is ignoring CARU, the regulator is motivated to act swiftly with the force of law to bring the company into line.

## Behavioral Advertising

Another area that is self-regulated is behavioral advertising or interest-based advertising. Behavioral advertising is tracking a person across sites or across devices in an effort to learn about their interests and buying habits or to pull them back toward a site or purchase they had previously considered. This type of advertising is why you might look at some shoes on one site or even put them in a cart and then later in the day, you may get an advertisement for those shoes. That ad may appear on your phone, even if you had previously looked on your desktop. This is also the technology that offers you hotels in a city later in the day after you have previously booked a flight to that city. This new technology has a much more invasive feel than prior advertising technologies. It is so personal that many people have described it as "creepy."

The guidelines for using this type of technology are that three steps are required. First, the game company or its advertising agency must license the AdChoices icon from the DAA (a trade association). This symbol is the blue "i" in a triangle that you see. Second, the company must place the AdChoices icon on its ads that use behavioral advertising. Third, the company must include a disclosure in its privacy policy that it uses behavioral advertising, which includes a functioning method to opt out of that advertising.

## Coupons and Discounting

One might think that a discussion on coupons and discounting is out of place in the high-tech media world of video games. Nothing could be further from the truth. The oldest possible promotional method is one of the most effective—the discount is immortal and will always have a place in advertising. As long as humans are humans, we love a deal. A discount or perceived discount sells more of anything, from apples to Apple Computers. So, what are the rules of discounts and coupons that we need to keep in mind? First, the discount or coupon needs to be true. That rule of advertising, all the way from the beginning of this chapter, applies here and in everything else.

If we say virtual property is 50% off this weekend, it should be 50%. What about a range of discounts? Can we say "up to 50% off virtual property this weekend?" We cannot lie to people or say "up to 50% off" when only one item is 50% off. It has to be a substantial number, including items people normally buy, so that it represents the normal user experience.

Lastly, a sale has to be a sale. Something cannot always be 25% off or 50% off. You can rotate sales, but there must be some realistic time that the items are sold at the retail price.

Coupons in a newspaper insert, in a physical store, or digital coupons all have the same rules. Those rules are fairly simple. They have to disclose the material terms of the coupon. What would a person using the coupon want to know? How much is the discount? Where can I use the coupon? Is there a limit to using this coupon with other discounts? When does the coupon end? All of those pieces of information plus any other bit of information specific to your coupon that an average consumer would think is relevant should be included on the coupon terms.

## CONCLUSION

People think of advertising as a fluid, creative, relatively unregulated field. Nothing could be further from the truth. Advertising and the law have been intertwined since the 1950s and before. There is a thread around truth and consumer protection that runs from coupons and radio advertising all the way to influencers and behavioral advertising. Product claims have to be scientifically supported. Certain areas like texting, sweepstakes, contests, children, and influencers are particularly highly regulated to protect consumers. Technology related to A/B testing and consumer metrics is developing advertising into a near-quantitative field. The industry is being infiltrated with people trained in mathematics, economics, and other hard sciences and is achieving a certain growing respect it has not received in the past. With this influx of technology and optimization, we should be more thoughtful than ever about how advertising complies with the law. As we get better at tracking and persuading consumers to buy our games, we should be more vigilant that the monitoring is transparent and the commercial messaging is true.

## NOTES

1. Other countries have similar regulatory bodies such as the Advertising Standards Association (ASA) in the United Kingdom and the German Deutscher Werberat or the Wettbewerbszentrale.
2. The UK equivalent of the FTC is the Advertising Standards Authority (ASA). In 2017, the ASA reviewed the advertising for *No Man's Sky* related to graphics quality, game footage, and features. It ultimately found that *No Man's Sky* was not deceptively advertised.
3. You can easily find out how your device was tested by reading your owner's manual. It usually shows the conditions under which the device was tested as being waterproof. You will be surprised how a company can spend hundreds of millions of dollars on development and manufacturing of an electronic device then spend almost that much on advertising where one of the key features of the device is that it is waterproof. Then, when you look at the owner's manual, the waterproof testing looks like they spent a couple of days and a few dollars on one mildly varied testing condition.
4. This is changing, but slowly. Starting in 2018, I have seen testing with water dripping, light spray, heavy spray, and submersion. I have still not seen salt, chlorine, or large temperature/depth variations.
5. The Sony Xperia line of tablets and phones is a good example. The company even made apps that were supposed to only be used underwater. As of 2017, Sony was the subject of a class action lawsuit where the plaintiffs were requesting 50% of the phone's retail value and a 6–12-month warranty extension (*Landes vs. Sony Mobile Communications*, EDNY).

6. CSGO allows people to bet virtual items known as "skins" on the outcome of gameplay. In an echo of the loot boxes discussion in this chapter, in December 2017, the UK Gambling Commission published a report on young people, stating that the exposure of children as young as 11 to video game skin betting was detrimental to their development and qualified as an early exposure to gambling.

7. It may be years before we know the effects of this request. The Belgian Gaming Commission does not have the power alone to outlaw loot boxes.

8. The TCPA does *not* apply to push notifications in apps. Still, Apple and Google have taken a similar approach as the TCPA, with push notifications only allowed on the platforms with opt-in consent.

9. Six steps to COPPA compliance from the FTC: https://www.ftc.gov/tips-advice/business-center/guidance/childrens-online-privacy-protection-rule-six-step-compliance. General FTC COPPA compliance FAQ: https://www.ftc.gov/tips-advice/business-center/guidance/complying-coppa-frequently-asked-questions.

# CHAPTER 10

# Gambling in Games

Y OUR ROOMMATE FROM JUNIOR year at college plays online poker religiously. His Facebook status announces that he's "running the table" or "taking a beating" at least once a week. The polyester suit sitting next to you on the bus is fuming as he taps away at his phone; you suspect he's ruining a subordinate's day, or maybe his wife's, until a sideways glance reveals he's losing at blackjack on his iPhone. A former co-worker just emailed to ask if you're interested in a fantasy football league he's setting up on a website for the fall—the winner gets $3,000. The fact is, people are gambling online, legally or illegally. How they do it and what they play is their business, unless of course, you're planning on making it your business.

Whether you're thinking about creating a new game that includes gambling elements, integrating wagering[1] into an existing game, or determining whether aspects of a game you are already operating qualify as an illegal game of chance, a foundational knowledge of what gambling is and how it is treated under the law can mean the difference between laughing all the way to the bank and standing up when the judge calls your name.

Most federal statutes focused on gambling do not contain their own definitions for illegal games of chance and instead make it a federal offense to operate a game that affects interstate commerce and violates gambling laws in the state where the game or its players are located. This is why the first step in avoiding criminal and civil liability for gambling offenses is a clear understanding of the elements that comprise a game of chance under state laws and whether the activity contemplated by your game will be considered gambling based on the presence or absence of those elements. Once you can recognize the elements of a game of chance, you can begin to understand how individual elements can be minimized or eliminated to reduce the likelihood that a game's activity will qualify as gambling. Applying these methods to existing games allows you to understand how other members of the video game industry are operating games that include some gambling elements without running afoul of existing gambling laws.

On the other hand, if your goal is to offer a game that will be defined as gambling under state law, or if the parameters of your game do not lend themselves to minimizing or eliminating one or more of the elements of a game of chance, then it is in your best interest to understand the entire legal landscape with respect to games of chance. Specifically, it would be wise for a developer contemplating operating such a game to become familiar with relevant federal laws that criminalize certain gaming activities, and also the regulations that permit games of chance in limited circumstances and territories.

Finally, the laws and positions of regulators with respect to games of chance are constantly evolving. What those laws are now versus what they may become only a few years from now could mean a world of difference regarding what types of gambling or gambling-like activities your game can legally include. This chapter will close with a discussion of where the law with respect to games of chance may be going and what that might mean for your video game business.

## STATE RESTRICTIONS

In most states, for an activity to be defined as an illegal game of chance, three elements must be present: consideration, chance, and a prize. In plain English, and using a spin on a roulette wheel as an example, the dollar amount wagered on a specific number is the consideration, the potential for the white ball to land on the selected number or another is the chance, and the payout that results if the white ball settles on the selected number is the prize. If "don't create a roulette game" is the message you take away from that example, then it is good that you find yourself reading this book. The trio of consideration, chance, and prize can be found in some of the most unlikely of places.

For an example that might be more familiar, let's look at a hypothetical subscription-based online game that offers a marketplace for the sale of in-game items for actual money. Applying the same elements discussed above, the subscription amount paid by the user to play the online game could be the consideration, the potential for an in-game activity (e.g., slaying an orc) to reward the player with a randomly generated in-game item (e.g., a battle-axe of smiting) could be the chance, and the real money that the player can exchange the item for at the in-game marketplace could be a prize. Several of the features described above are fairly common in video games and one could argue that, by including all of these features in an online game, a developer could be exposing itself to some degree of risk that the game could potentially qualify as a game of chance in some jurisdictions.

### WHAT HAPPENS IN VEGAS...

While video game developers take steps to prevent their games from including gambling elements, gambling device manufacturers are racing to add video game elements to their products in order to attract younger clients to casino floors. However, pre-existing laws in some jurisdictions where gambling is permitted prohibit gambling devices from basing winnings on entirely skill-based activities. In order to add video game elements to their products without violating these laws, some gambling device manufacturers have begun introducing skill-based arcade-style mini-games as bonus levels for additional winning opportunities following a chance-based activity (e.g., an asteroid shooting mini-game following a successful pull on a slot machine). That being said, Nevada and New Jersey have recently legalized gambling on entirely skill-based games, paving the way for cash payouts in casinos in Las Vegas,

Reno, and Atlantic City based entirely on a player's success in a video game. Multiple casinos are also contemplating adding non-player wagering on e-sports tournaments to their existing facilities for betting on traditional sporting events. These two developments point to video games having a much larger presence in real-world casinos in the coming years.[2]

Now, before you begin looking for potential consideration, chance, and prize elements in every game you have ever played or worked on, let's keep things in perspective. At the time of this writing there have been no official investigations or prosecutions in the United States, at either the federal or state levels, alleging that multiplayer online games like *World of Warcraft*, *EVE Online*, or other video games that are not merely digital recreations of casino games constitute illegal gambling. The above example is primarily provided to illustrate the potentially expansive applicability of the consideration, chance, and prize elements. The ease with which these elements might be applied to some online games, which are conceptually far removed from "casino-style" gambling, should drive home the point that the line between gambling and gaming[3] may be thinner than it appears.

Knowing how malleable the elements of consideration, chance, and prize can be, what can a developer do to minimize the likelihood that their game could qualify as a game of chance in some jurisdictions? It's simple: take concrete steps to reduce the presence of one or more of the three elements in the game being developed. You can have consideration and prize while reducing the reliance upon chance, consideration and chance while minimizing the prize, or, in certain circumstances, you can even have chance and prize with only limited consideration. The careful publisher may try to reduce each of these elements to the greatest degree practicable with respect to their game. To do that properly, it pays to look at the methods for minimizing each element in turn.

## CHANCE

Where an activity requires consideration from a player before entry and may result in the player receiving a prize, applicable legislation varies from one jurisdiction to another regarding the degree of chance that may control the outcome of the game or activity before it is deemed a prohibited game of chance. In the Unites States, different states apply different standards regarding the amount of chance that a game may include before it qualifies as illegal gambling. Most states apply the "dominant factor" test, under which an activity will not qualify as illegal gambling if chance is not the dominant factor in determining the outcome of the activity. Skill (and not chance) will be considered the dominant factor if the activity provides information and the possibility for players to exercise skill, the players are aware of and have the skill required to participate, and the players' skill sufficiently determines the outcome of the activity. While this concept may seem simple enough in theory, in practice it conjures up a spectrum that has entirely skill-based activities on one end, perfectly chance-based activities on the other, and any activity which falls too close to the chance side of the spectrum possibly qualifying as an illegal game of chance in some jurisdictions.

So how much chance is too much? A developer may have a gut feeling about how much chance figures into a particular outcome in a game, but that feeling can often be colored by the game's story elements or the programmed difficulty of achieving an outcome (please note that whether a task is skill-based does not rely solely on its difficulty). To objectively determine whether elements of chance are material or dominant in whether a prize will be awarded for an activity, it helps to break the activity down into the elements that determine its occurrence and result. Let's look at an example of an in-game hunter felling a deer:

- Tracking deer to their territory requires skill and knowledge of the in-game landscape

- Within their territory, deer are generated at random so the appearance of a particular deer is controlled by chance

- Targeting and striking a deer with a bow and arrow requires skill

- The meat and pelts acquired from the felled deer are always the same.

There is some element of chance to hunting a deer, but because tracking and striking the deer and the rewards for doing so are not controlled by chance, it is unlikely that chance would be determined to be a dominant factor in this activity. For a less obvious example, let's look at a simple dungeon quest:

- The location of the dungeon is static and known to all players

- The number of enemies faced within the dungeon is determined at random within parameters ranging from easily dealt with to barely survivable

- The minor enemies and the final boss of the dungeon require significant skill to defeat

- The number and level of items dropped by the final boss of the dungeon are selected at random from a long list of in-game weaponry and armor.

This example includes chance-dominated elements as well as elements in which chance is not a factor. If the consideration and prize elements could not be eliminated or significantly reduced with respect to this activity, then a careful developer would reduce the degree to which the outcome of this activity relies on chance. For example, the developer could design the quest so as to not vary either the number of enemies faced within the dungeon or the value of item(s) dropped upon defeating the final boss.

If a game involves a significant degree of skill, a publisher may gain an additional layer of protection by structuring it as a tournament of skill. In some jurisdictions, entry fees for tournaments of skill do not qualify as consideration wagered in an illegal game of chance if several other factors are also present. Specifically, entry into the tournament must be for a fixed fee, the prize must come from the company offering the tournament (as opposed to from the contributions of other entrants), and the amount of the prize must not vary with the number of participants.[4]

## PRIZE

While it may seem counterintuitive, removing or minimizing the prize element (i.e., "the potential benefit") from an in-game activity is conceptually simple and typically the safest way to reduce the likelihood that a video game will be classified as an illegal game of chance. A wide variety of benefits received by players can fulfill the prize element under laws pertaining to games of chance, but a developer can take steps to guard against such a determination. At their heart, those steps often involve reducing or removing to the greatest extent possible any indication that the benefits conferred upon the player, the potential prizes, have any value in real-world dollars.

Returning to the MMO example above, the clearest way to indicate that an in-game benefit has real-world value (which a publisher would typically *not* want to do) is to build in the opportunity for the player to buy or sell that in-game item for real-world dollars. Once a publisher sells or facilitates the player-to-player sale of an epic battle-axe of smiting for actual dollars, it can be difficult for the publisher to argue that said battle-axe has no real-world value. If that battle-axe can then be received in-game by a player as a result of activity that involves an element of chance (e.g., a loot drop or quest reward), then the battle-axe could potentially qualify as the "prize" element in a game of chance analysis.

A publisher has a variety of options for minimizing the possibility of such a determination. The safest of those options is for the publisher to maintain a closed economic system for its game by not providing any mechanisms for players to "cash out" by exchanging in-game items for real currency or real-world goods (e.g., game merchandise). However, if a publisher does not want to completely close their game's economic system, there are other ways to reduce the "prize" element. For example, the publisher can refrain from selling in-game items that can also be received by players in-game through activities that involve an element of chance. This does not mean that a publisher would not sell any in-game items, only that items that a publisher sells to players would be different from items that may be received by players in the game by chance.

To further insulate a game from a possible determination that it constitutes an illegal game of chance, a publisher can take steps to ensure that players are not using real-world dollars to buy in-game items from other players. A publisher could try to prevent such exchanges by prohibiting players from participating in such transactions and taking disciplinary action, potentially including terminating a player's account, if it is determined that they broke this rule. Once such transactions are prohibited, a careful publisher could also make efforts to police and prevent sales of in-game items on unofficial third-party websites (sometimes referred to as "grey markets" for their nebulous position with respect to the game's publisher and the law). Policing the sale of in-game items on third-party websites can help solidify the publisher as the only purveyor of services in connection with its game's brand while simultaneously allowing it to cut off a potential indicator that items received in its game have any real-world value.

## THE DEVIL IS IN THE DETAILS

*Diablo III*, published by Blizzard Entertainment in May 2012, included auction houses that allowed players to buy and sell in-game items for in-game gold or real-world dollars. Prior to the release of *Diablo III*, the Game Rating Board of South Korea (GRB) raised concerns about the rating of *Diablo III* which focused on the auction houses, and reported to the South Korean National Assembly that real currency transactions such as those found in *Diablo III* could violate South Korean gambling law. While GRB subsequently clarified that its report to the South Korean National Assembly was about certain game mechanics in general and did not focus on *Diablo III*, news outlets theorized that GRB's reluctance to rate *Diablo III* or approve the game for sale in South Korea stemmed from GRB's interpretation that exchange of randomly generated in-game items for real-world currency using the auction houses of *Diablo III* too closely resembled online gambling. Blizzard eventually decided to submit a South Korean version of *Diablo III* to GRB for rating that did not include the real currency auction house. GRB subsequently rated and approved *Diablo III* for sale in South Korea with the caveat that the approved game did not include the real currency auction house and would have to be reevaluated if Blizzard decided to add the real money auction houses to the South Korean version of the game at a later date. Blizzard closed all auction houses in *Diablo III* in March 2014, less than two years after the games' release.[5]

## CONSIDERATION

While completely removing consideration from a video game is virtually impossible, it is possible to reduce it significantly. In the typical game of chance, it is very easy to identify the consideration (i.e., "thing of value") that is being offered up in exchange for the possibility of winning a prize. A coin dropped in a slot machine, the ante in a hand of Texas Hold 'Em, and the chips bet in a roll of craps are all consideration in the eyes of the law. Returning to video games, a subscription fee paid to access a game, the initial price to purchase a game, or the incremental cost of purchasing in-game items or activities via microtransactions could also qualify as consideration. Which begs the question: What if there is no charge to play a game?

Making a game that is truly free-to-play, meaning it is not merely a "freemium" experience peppered with DLC power-ups or other microtransaction offers, may not eliminate the element of consideration completely but can significantly reduce its impact. While consideration is most often thought of in terms of dollars and cents, regulators, case law, and certain statutes pertaining to gambling indicate that cold hard cash is not the only "thing of value" that a player can give up.[6] Consideration may include other things invested by the player, including the time, attention, and effort they devote to acquiring or participating in a game. While games that do not cost a player any actual dollars to enjoy are common, they surely cost the player some amount of time and effort to acquire and play, which means some consideration may have been exchanged in the eyes of the law. That being said, all other factors being equal, a truly free game is much less likely to fulfill the consideration requirement of an illegal game of chance than a game that requires an upfront purchase or regular subscription fee.

## FEDERAL RESTRICTIONS

If you are contemplating offering real money gambling, or a game that includes gambling elements that cannot be easily eliminated or minimized, then it is in your best interest to become familiar with the relevant federal laws in this area. The following high-level introduction to several such laws will provide a snapshot of the relevant contours of each, including discussions of their history, applicability, and penalties. This information should be both educational and cautionary, driving home the point that the gambling industry is very heavily regulated and that great care should be taken when introducing its elements into one's game or business.

### The Illegal Gambling Business Act

Enacted in 1970 as part of a larger statutory effort to augment the abilities of federal law enforcement agencies to shut down large-scale criminal operations,[7] the Illegal Gambling Business Act[8] (IGBA) was intended to combat the use of unlawful gambling operations to fund organized crime. Despite the purpose for which IGBA was enacted, no connection to organized crime is required for an activity to be categorized as an illegal gambling operation under the Act. IGBA includes a non-exclusive list of activities that qualify as gambling (e.g., "maintaining slot machines, roulette wheels or dice tables") but the statute relies heavily on the states to define what activities qualify as illegal gambling within their boundaries, most of which adhere to some permutation of the consideration, chance, and prize formula already discussed.

To qualify as an "illegal gambling business" under IGBA, the operation of a game or activity must only (1) violate a law concerning gambling in the state where it is operated, (2) involve five or more persons (not including bettors), and (3) remain in operation for more than 30 days OR take in at least $2000 in any single day. IGBA violations are punishable by up to five years in prison, confiscation of all monies or other property used in the gambling operation, and fines equal to the greater of $500,000 or twice the gain or loss associated with the gambling operation.[9]

IGBA is of particular relevance to operators of games that include real money gambling (or gambling elements) that reach users over the internet because gambling laws in some states dictate that gambling activity is operated where its players reside, instead of where its operator is located. As a result, a game operator may be subject to a federal cause of action based on violation of the gambling laws of a state in which they are not located so long as the game has some players there.

### The Travel Act

Though its enactment predates IGBA by almost a decade, like IGBA, the Travel Act[10] also relies heavily on state statutes and was a part of a larger program to thwart the interstate operations of organized crime. As you may have guessed from its name, the Travel Act focuses primarily on whether tools of interstate or foreign commerce were used in the operation of an unlawful activity or the distribution of its proceeds, with less concern for the specifics of the underlying unlawful activity itself. That said, the Act explicitly prohibits as unlawful the use of interstate commerce in connection with business enterprises involving gambling. As with IGBA, the Travel Act does not contain a definition for "gambling" so it is left to the states to dictate what activities are categorized as illegal gambling. Violations of the Travel Act are subject to the same penalties as IGBA, discussed above.

## The Wire Act

Passed in 1961 to curb organized crime's sports-betting operations, the Interstate Wire Act, as it was officially known, prohibited the use of "a wire communication facility for the transmission in interstate or foreign commerce of bets or wagers or information assisting in the placing of bets or wagers on any sporting event or contest." Despite the statute's explicit reference to sporting events and interstate commerce, until recently the Department of Justice held the position that the Wire Act prohibited any person in the United States from using a telecommunication system (including the internet) to place or receive a bet or wager of any kind.

Following a decision of the Federal Court of Appeals for the Fifth Circuit in 2002,[11] refuting this broad interpretation of the Wire Act, and subsequent requests from several states to the Department of Justice to clarify its position regarding the scope of the Wire Act, the Department changed its position. In a memo released on December 23, 2011,[12] the Department of Justice reversed course, indicating that the Wire Act only concerned interstate sports betting and did not prohibit the use of the internet or other electronic communications to place bets that are unrelated to sporting events and do not cross state borders. In response to this development, several states have begun efforts to legalize and provide licensing for companies to provide certain types of internet gambling to persons located in their state, and potentially also to persons in other states that enact similar laws. Developers contemplating starting up internet gambling operations within the United States would be wise to keep abreast of regulatory developments in states that permit some form of legal online gambling, as well as states where efforts to legalize certain forms of online gambling are already underway or are being contemplated.

## Unlawful Internet Gambling Enforcement Act

The Unlawful Internet Gambling Enforcement Act (UIGEA) is the most recent federal legislation concerning gambling at the time of writing, and because it was enacted to fight foreign internet gambling operations as opposed to large-scale criminal organizations, it takes a different approach than the other regulations we've discussed. Rather than directly targeting the operators of foreign internet gambling websites, many of whom are difficult to prosecute because they are located outside of the United States, UIGEA follows the money by prohibiting U.S.-based payment processors and financial institutions from administering transactions generated by internet gambling websites serving U.S. customers.

Like IGBA and the Travel Act, UIGEA does not contain an independent definition of what activities constitute illegal gambling and defers to existing state and federal law to determine the legality of any particular activity. UIGEA is primarily concerned with whether any U.S.-based entity has participated in any "restricted transactions," which can generally be described as a transfer of funds, electronic or otherwise, in connection with the participation of another person in unlawful internet gambling. A financial institution or money transmission service that engages in restricted transactions faces prosecution under UIGEA that may result in significant fines for the company and potential imprisonment for its principals. In response to UIGEA's passage, operators of several immensely popular online gambling websites stopped accepting wagers altogether from players located in the United States.

## FANTASY SPORTS TOURNAMENTS

Fantasy sports tournaments that offer cash prizes touch upon a number of overlapping legal theories. The operators of these tournaments rely heavily on an exception under UIGEA at the federal level and the dominant factor test at the state level to support the position that their tournaments are legal under U.S. gambling law.

UIGEA excludes "fantasy or simulation sports game(s)" from the gambling activities that it regulates. More specifically, a fantasy sports tournament falls outside of UIGEA if (1) the prizes are established in advance and not based upon the number of participants; (2) winning outcomes reflect the knowledge and skill of participants, based predominantly on accumulated statistics; and (3) winning is not based on score, point-spread, or performance of a real team or teams or an individual athlete in a single event.[13] This carveout appears perfectly suited to modern fantasy sports tournaments.

Looking beyond UIGEA, the majority of applicable federal statutes (discussed in brief above) only prohibit an activity as gambling if it is an illegal game of chance in the state where it occurs. While gambling laws vary from one state to another, many U.S. states apply the "dominant factor" test (discussed above) to determine whether a particular activity is a prohibited game of chance within their borders. At present, tournament operators and legal experts generally agree that the statistical analysis required to win fantasy sports tournaments is a skill and that such skill is a greater factor than the element of chance in determining a participant's success in traditional, season-length fantasy tournaments.[14]

However, these two protections do not completely insulate all fantasy sports tournaments from the law in all jurisdictions. Fantasy sports tournaments in which participants' chances of success are improved based on the final scores of real-world games could lose the protection of the fantasy sports exception under UIGEA because they may fail its third requirement, that is, that winning must not be based on scores or performances of real teams. It is also important to remember that gambling laws vary by state, and that several states categorize activities that involve any element of chance in the awarding of a prize as illegal gambling operations. It is possible that fantasy sports tournaments may be illegal in some of those jurisdictions.[15]

It should also be noted that opinions vary sharply among tournament operators and legal experts as to whether certain variations of the fantasy sports tournament, specifically the shorter "one-day" tournament as opposed to the traditional season-length tournament, provide more or less protection for these activities under U.S. gambling law. Tournament operators have argued that the outcomes of shorter tournaments are less subject to chance because there is a smaller likelihood that an unpredictable event (e.g., a season-ending injury) will impact a selected player during the shorter period.[16] On the flipside, experts have countered that the impact of an unpredictable event is monumentally higher if it occurs during a shorter tournament, effectively obliterating any impact of the participant's analytical skill and leaving chance as the dominant factor for determining the tournament's winner.[17] While it has been definitively established that fantasy sports tournaments do not qualify as illegal gambling in some jurisdictions, the law in this area is still developing and should be watched closely by anyone operating or planning to operate in this sector.

## LEGAL ONLINE GAMBLING

Most of the federal regulations just discussed rely heavily on whether an activity qualifies as an illegal game of chance in the state in which it is played. As a result, states can determine whether certain games of chance, if played within their borders, will run afoul of state or federal law. Most states do not permit the operation of games of chance over the internet, but understanding the rules applied by the few states that do permit some form of online gambling helps in determining where a game that involves gambling may be permissible under the law and what may be required of the game's operator to receive such treatment. At the time of writing, there are at least three states in the United States that allow private companies to operate or participate in the administration of real money online gambling: Nevada, New Jersey, and Delaware.

### Nevada

Historically, Las Vegas and Reno have ensured that Nevada was at the forefront of any legal developments in the United States concerning games of chance, including the discussion surrounding online gambling. In order to ensure that it would be the first to market, Nevada preemptively legalized online gambling in 2001, despite the U.S. Justice Department's interpretation of the Wire Act at that time which prohibited all forms of gambling over the internet.[18] Nevada's foresight was ultimately rewarded following the Justice Department's reversal of its broad interpretation of the Wire Act in 2011 (as discussed earlier in this chapter). Nevada began issuing licenses to companies to offer internet poker within its borders in 2012, and at the time of writing Nevada has issued more than a dozen such licenses.

Upon legalizing online gambling, the Nevada legislature charged the Nevada Gaming Commission with passing regulations that would dictate the limitations and requirements imposed on companies licensed to run online gambling operations within the state. In addition to record keeping, taxation, and dispute resolution rules similar to those placed on brick-and-mortar gambling operations, the Commission's licensing requirements for companies offering internet poker also include significant obligations concerning the prevention of underage users from accessing the services, establishing the real-world location of online players, and protecting players' personal information.[19]

### New Jersey

Since 1976, New Jersey has prohibited by law the establishment or operation of a gambling business outside of Atlantic City, and until recently, provisions of the New Jersey constitution implementing this prohibition have hampered efforts to legalize online gambling in the state. In 2013, New Jersey addressed the Atlantic City issue by legalizing online gambling for a trial period during which only the 12 already-established Atlantic City casinos would be able to operate or advertise online gambling websites. While the New Jersey bill requires that all equipment and personnel of a casino operating an online gambling website be on the casino's premises in Atlantic City, it permits the website to accept players from anywhere in New Jersey so long as their location within the state is verified with each wager and other legal requirements are fulfilled (e.g., the player is over 21 years of age).

## Delaware

While Delaware is not as well known for games of chance as Nevada or New Jersey, passage of the Delaware Gaming Competitiveness Act of 2012 was a big step forward for legal gambling in the Diamond State. Under the 2012 Act, a variety of traditional casino gambling games can be made available over the internet to users that geolocation can verify are within the state, including blackjack, roulette, slots, and poker. Unlike Nevada and New Jersey, where private companies offer online gambling through their own websites, websites offering legal online gambling in Delaware carry the branding of the state's existing racetrack casinos but are operated entirely by the Delaware Lottery Office with technology provided by a few subcontracted firms with online gambling experience. Internet gambling is also heavily taxed in Delaware, with more than 50% of some games' profits being withheld by the Delaware Lottery Office to be split between harness racing breeders and the state.

## THE FUTURE

There is always the potential for states and countries to change the tests that they apply to determine whether an activity qualifies as an illegal game of chance. The video game industry is also constantly developing new game elements, functionalities, and business models, some of which could qualify as gambling in certain jurisdictions depending on the degree to which they involve the elements of consideration, chance, and prize discussed above. For these reasons it is important to keep these factors in mind when reviewing the viability and risk of potential revenue streams for your game going forward.

The next few years could also be transformative for the legal online gambling industry. Legal real money online poker was first offered in Nevada in April of 2013 and a wider variety of traditional casino games became available online in both New Jersey and Delaware later that year. These states and the businesses that operate there are generating real profits from legal online gambling at a time when many states and locales are struggling with significant deficits and cash flow issues. It is expected that in the years to come other states will follow the example of Nevada, New Jersey, and Delaware by legalizing online gambling in one form or another. At the time of writing, regulators in at least eight other states are considering legislation that will allow them to participate in this industry.

It is also worth noting that until very recently the Professional and Amateur Sports Protection Act (PASPA) prohibited most states from licensing companies to accept bets on professional or amateur sporting events.[20] However, in May of 2018 the U.S. Supreme Court decided that the federal restrictions included in PASPA were an unconstitutional commandeering of state legislative power and struck down PASPA in its entirety.[21] The Court's decision freed the states to decide for themselves if betting on sporting events, including potentially placing such bets over the internet, should be legal within their borders. It is too early to say how states will react to being able to license companies to accept wagers on sporting events, but it is likely that at least a few states will begin licensing sports-betting operations. As more states that lack significant brick-and-mortar gambling operations begin to offer legal online gambling or authorize sports-betting, it is expected that there will be greater opportunities for new companies to enter the market and compete with established casinos.

In addition to more states offering legal gambling within their borders, it is anticipated that states that already permit online gambling may begin to enter into compacts with one another concerning the gambling operations authorized within each of their respective states. These agreements could effectively legalize some forms of interstate online gambling (e.g., Nevada residents playing online poker offered by a New Jersey casino) by officially acknowledging that the activity is legal in the separate states where the bettor and casino are located. As of this writing, Nevada, New Jersey, and Delaware have already passed legislation allowing for their states to enter into these kinds of cooperative compacts upon determination that they would not conflict with federal law.

Not to be excluded, Native American tribes in the United States, which are uniquely immune to state rules but closely regulated at a federal level, have also begun to lobby Congress to ensure they have the opportunity to compete in the developing legal online gambling industry. If the legality of Native American casinos offering online gambling is clarified under the Indian Gaming Regulatory Act, then it is expected that a number of established Native American casinos will begin competing directly against state-licensed internet gambling operations.

## NOTES

1. Terms like "game of chance" and "wager" are used throughout this chapter as shorthand for a variety of activities governed by federal and state laws that you or I would commonly refer to as gambling.
2. Elizabeth Erwin (ABC 15), Old School Video Games Making Their Way to Valley Casino Floors, http://www.abc15.com/dpp/news/state/old-school-video-games-making-their-way-to-valley-casino-floors; Kevin Anderton, Casinos Might Replace Slot Machines With Video Game Machines, https://www.forbes.com/sites/kevinanderton/2016/10/15/casinos-might-replace-slot-machines-with-video-game-machines-infographic/#300736714361; Laura Parker, Casinos Look to Video Games as a Draw for Millennials, https://mobile.nytimes.com/2016/07/07/technology/personaltech/casinos-look-to-video-games-as-a-draw-for-millennials.html.
3. A note regarding "gaming" versus "gambling": law enforcement and the gambling industry regularly refer to game of chance activities as "gaming" (e.g., the Nevada Gaming Commission, the American Gaming Association), which can cause confusion when discussing cross-pollination between the "gaming" industry and the video game industry.
4. See State v. Am. Holiday Ass'n, 727 P.2d 807, 812 (Ariz. 1986).
5. Nick Winter, Korean Govt Considers Whether Diablo III is "Gambling," http://pc.gamespy.com/pc/diablo-iii/1197680p1.html; Kwaak Je-yup, Diablo 3 Release Up In the Air, http://koreatimes.co.kr/www/news/tech/2012/01/129_102230.html; Nick Winter, Blizzard Drops Auction House for Korean Diablo III, http://pc.gamespy.com/pc/diablo-iii/1216555p1.html; Kwaak Je-yup, Games Regulator Approves Diablo 3 But Bans Cash Trade, http://www.korea-times.co.kr/www/news/biz/2012/01/123_102801.html.
6. Dale Joerling, Consider this: How do states define "Consideration"? (Florida regulators stated that consideration "need not involve money or anything of monetary value." Rather it "may consist of a benefit to the promisor, or a detriment to the promisor," or if the promisee "does

anything which he is not bound to do" … Iowa defines consideration as "a substantial expenditure of effort." … many common entry activities and requirements must be analyzed on a case-by-case basis to determine whether they require "substantial effort," as defined by the Iowa statute.) https://www.thompsoncoburn.com/insights/blogs/sweepstakes-law/post/2012-01-12/consider-this-how-do-states-define-consideration-; *Seattle Times Co. v. Tielsch*, 495 P.2d 1366, 1368-59 (Wash. 1972) https://law.justia.com/cases/washington/supreme-court/1972/42112-1.html.

7. Organized Crime Control Act of 1970, Pub. L. No. 91-452, 84 Stat. 922 (October 15, 1970). This Act also includes the Racketeer Influenced and Corrupt Organizations Act, commonly referred to as RICO, which was intended to prevent the infiltration of organized crime into legitimate businesses but was drafted broadly enough to encompass a wide range of illegal activities affecting interstate commerce.
8. 18 U.S.C. § 1955. http://www.law.cornell.edu/uscode/text/18/1955
9. 18 U.S.C. §§ 1955, 3571. http://www.law.cornell.edu/uscode/text/18/3571
10. 18 U.S.C. § 1952. http://www.law.cornell.edu/uscode/text/18/1952
11. In *Re Mastercard Intern. Inc.*, 132 F.Supp. 2d 468 (E.D. La), aff'd. 313 F. 3rd 257 (5th Cir. 2002).
12. Virginia A. Seitz, Assistant Attorney General, Whether Proposals by Illinois and New York to Use the Internet and Out-of-State Transaction Processors to Sell Lottery Tickets to In-State Adults Violate the Wire Act, Memorandum Opinion for the Assistant Attorney General, Criminal Division, Dated September 20, 2011, publicly released on December 23, 2011, https://www.justice.gov/file/18341/download
13. 31 U.S.C. § 5362. https://www.law.cornell.edu/uscode/text/31/5362
14. Joshua Brustein, Fantasy Sports and Gambling: Line Is Blurred, http://www.nytimes.com/2013/03/12/sports/web-sites-blur-line-between-fantasy-sports-and-gambling.html.
15. Marc Edelman, A Short Treatise on Fantasy Sports and the Law: How America Regulates its New National Pastime, http://harvardjsel.com/wp-content/uploads/2012/03/1-54.pdf
16. Brustein.
17. Marc Edelman, Will New Lawsuit Help to Clarify the Legal Status of Daily Fantasy Sports? http://www.forbes.com/sites/marcedelman/2013/02/19/will-new-lawsuit-help-to-clarify-the-legal-status-of-daily-fantasy-sports/.
18. The Nevada state legislature meets only once every two years for 120 days, so there was significant fear that if the Justice Department changed its position on internet gambling at a time when the Nevada legislature was not in session and before the state legalized online gambling, then Nevada could lose the opportunity to be the first state offering legal online gambling.
19. Regulation 5a, Nevada Gaming Commission.
20. 28 U.S.C. § 3701. https://www.law.cornell.edu/uscode/text/28/3701
21. Murphy v. National Collegiate Athletic Association, 584 U.S. ___ (2018). https://www.supremecourt.gov/opinions/17pdf/16-476_dbfi.pdf

# CHAPTER 11

# Game Ratings and the First Amendment

## HISTORY LESSON

In 1972, Magnavox released the Odyssey, the first mass-produced console for playing video games at home. To put that release in perspective, *Pong*, the simple tennis simulation game that arguably introduced video games to the public and started the arcade video game industry, wasn't released by Atari until two months later. In the decade to follow, other manufacturers released competing home consoles, including the notable ColecoVision by Coleco and Intellivision by Mattel, which were soon overshadowed by Atari's highly successful Atari Video Computer System (or "Atari VCS," later renamed the Atari 2600). Atari dominated the home console market from the late 1970s through the mid-1980s, due in part to exclusive licenses for home releases of popular arcade games like *Space Invaders* and *Pac-Man*. By the late 1980s, Nintendo had unseated Atari as the market leader in home consoles with the Nintendo Entertainment System (or "NES," first released in Japan as the Nintendo Family Computer or "Famicom"). Games released for the NES included the wildly popular and critically acclaimed *The Legend of Zelda* and *Super Mario Bros.* In the early 1990s, Nintendo followed the NES with the Super Nintendo Entertainment System (or "SNES," released in Japan as the Super Famicom), which competed primarily with the Sega Genesis (also known as the Sega Mega Drive) produced by Sega.

## GAME CHANGER

For the first 20 years following the introduction of video games to the public, there was very little attention paid to the suitability of video game content for younger players. That began to change with the release of "16-bit" home video game consoles, primarily the SNES and the Sega Genesis, which offered developers and gamers significantly better graphics than the systems of the previous generation. A rough timeline of the development of graphics in the game industry might help illustrate this change from the consumer perspective. In 1981, a young couple might play *Pac-Man* at a bar on their first date, controlling a circle eating dots and avoiding ghosts rendered in simple 2D shapes. Seven years later, in 1988, that same couple might remember that date fondly while watching their young child play *Super Mario Bros.*, controlling a plumber breaking bricks and stomping on toadstools, rendered in cartoon-like 2D animation. Fast forward only five years to 1993, and that couple might be surprised when they find their preteen child playing *Mortal Kombat*, controlling a ninja that freezes their opponent solid before tearing off its head, complete with dripping blood and a dangling spine, rendered using pixelated images of real people.

While the advances in video game graphics in the 1990s were impressive, some parents and advocacy groups were less than thrilled about young children viewing some of the content that this cutting-edge technology was being used for. At a time when regulation of purportedly violent and anti-social content on television and in hip-hop and heavy metal music was still fresh in the minds of the public, it was only too easy for certain people to take up the same fight against the video game industry. Newspaper editorials, television interviews, and calls for boycotts and regulation eventually culminated in hearings before the United States Senate in 1993 and 1994, led by Senators Herbert Kohl of Wisconsin and Joe Lieberman of Connecticut.

The Senate hearings included testimony from advocacy group representatives as well as from video game companies. While Sega and Nintendo traded barbs at one another, they also described the processes that each company already had in place to address the concerns that were the subject of the hearings. Specifically, Nintendo's strict internal policies concerning game content had already prevented several games that included graphic content from being released for Nintendo consoles, and Sega had recently developed and introduced a rating system of its own that was intended to inform parents about the ages of players for which a game might be appropriate. Despite these points, the message from the senators leading these hearings was clear: the government would take steps to require and participate in the establishment of a rating system for video games if the video game industry did not establish its own rating system and begin rating video game content. As a warning shot, Senator Lieberman even introduced a draft bill, the Video Game Ratings Act of 1994, which would establish a government commission tasked with establishing a rating system for the video game industry.

Less than a year after the first Senate hearings focusing on video game content, representatives from the video game industry appeared again before the Senate to indicate that several video game publishers (including Nintendo, Sega, Acclaim, Atari, and others) had begun developing a regulatory body for the video game industry. The regulatory body that the industry was creating would design a rating system that was easy to understand, would require the display of assigned ratings on video game packaging and advertising materials, and would educate the public and retail outlets regarding what the ratings mean and how they could inform parents about the content of rated games. The ratings body that the video game publishers discussed before the Senate and subsequently established was the Entertainment Software Rating Board (ESRB).

## ENTERTAINMENT SOFTWARE RATING BOARD

In 1994, a group of video game companies came together to establish the Interactive Digital Software Association (IDSA), a trade organization that would represent the interests of video game developers, publishers, and manufacturers in North America. Only a few months later, the IDSA (subsequently renamed the Entertainment Software Association, or ESA) formally established the ESRB, which would assign age-based ratings to video games published in North America in order to inform consumers, particularly parents, about the content of the video games available for purchase, and to address concerns about mature video game content recently raised by parents and advocacy groups and reviewed by the United States Senate. The ESRB is an independent, non-government agency that assigns ratings to video games and apps that are displayed throughout the United States, Canada, and parts of Central and South America.

To receive an ESRB rating for a game that will be distributed through physical retail outlets, the game's publisher must apply for a rating from the ESRB by completing an online questionnaire discussing the pertinent content of the game. Pertinent content is a term of art that refers to the content of a game that may be relevant to a game's content rating. Most pertinent content falls into one of several broad content categories (e.g., violence, language, sexuality, drug use), but pertinent content may also include structural elements of the game, including the game's reward and advancement system, and the level of player involvement in relevant activities (e.g., does the player only observe violence in the game or do they control or participate in violent acts). The publisher must also provide a video file for the ESRB to review that includes all content disclosed in the online questionnaire, representative examples of regular play of the game, and the most extreme examples of content included in the game in relevant content categories. As part of the rating process, the publisher must enter into a contract with the ESRB which requires that the publisher honestly disclose to the ESRB all pertinent content that the game contains.

The completed questionnaire, video file, and any other materials and information provided by the game's publisher during the submission process are then reviewed by at least three raters, each of which have been hired by the ESRB from the general public for their educational, occupational, and/or parental experience with children. Once the raters agree on the appropriate rating category and content descriptors to be assigned to a game, and a parity review is conducted by ESRB staff (if necessary) to ensure consistency in ESRB ratings, an official rating is assigned to the game and a certificate bearing that rating is issued to the submitting publisher. If the publisher does not accept the rating that its game has received from the ESRB, then the publisher may revise the game and submit the revised game to the ESRB for rating again using the same process. Following a rated game's release to the public, the game may be play-tested by full-time play testers employed by the ESRB to ensure that the publisher disclosed all pertinent content included in the game during the submission process. The ESRB performs a high number of in-depth play tests of rated games each year, some of which involve games about which the ESRB has received inquiries from consumers or the news media, or which have been heavily or uniquely marketed or sold.

Ratings generated by the ESRB can have up to three parts, depending on the platform, content, and functionality of the game being rated. The primary and most recognizable part of an ESRB rating is the rating category (e.g., Everyone, Teen, Mature), which indicates the age of players for which a game is rated as appropriate and is communicated using the rating icons displayed above. Next are the content descriptors, which are short phrases that indicate the type and degree of content (e.g., Intense Violence, Partial Nudity) present in the game relative to the assigned rating category or content that may be of interest to a consumer making a purchase decision. The final part of an ESRB rating is the interactive elements, which are short phrases indicating functional and/or interactive aspects of certain games (e.g., Shares Location, In-Game Purchases) or that certain content accessible through a game has not been rated by the ESRB (e.g., Users Interact, Unrestricted Internet). Consumers that want to know more about rated games can access rating summaries, which are brief descriptions of content that resulted in the rating assigned to the game and are available from the ESRB website or mobile app.

As part of the ESRB's commitment to ensuring that rated games are appropriately marketed and advertised, publishers that have submitted physical games to the ESRB for rating are contractually obligated to comply with a set of rules and requirements that have been adopted by the video game industry concerning the packaging of rated games and advertising materials and campaigns promoting rated games. The Advertising Review Council ("ARC") is the full-time ESRB department tasked with ensuring compliance with those requirements. ARC works directly with video game developers, publishers, and advertising agencies to review and discuss advertising and marketing materials for rated games, and monitors those materials across television, print, in-store, mobile, and online channels to ensure that publishers abide by the requirements adopted by the video game industry.

The rules and requirements adopted by the industry can generally be found in the ESRB's Principles and Guidelines for Responsible Advertising Practices and the ARC Manual. The Principles and Guidelines contain a set of general requirements that publishers must follow when advertising rated games (e.g., advertisements must accurately reflect the game being promoted and may not be directed to consumers for whom the promoted game is not rated as appropriate), and a more detailed list of content that publishers should avoid when advertising rated games (e.g., fatal injuries, sexual activity, hate speech). The ARC Manual contains a much more detailed set of rules and requirements that publishers and advertising agencies must follow when creating marketing and advertising materials promoting rated games, including how rating information must appear on packaging and advertisements, how audience compositions can impact when games with certain ratings may be advertised, and where publishers must age-gate or age-restrict certain advertisements.[2]

The agreement that a publisher enters into with the ESRB in order to receive a rating for a physical game provides the ESRB with several options if the publisher fails to comply with ESRB requirements concerning the rating process or advertising a rated game. The ESRB works closely with publishers to prevent these issues before they arise, which may include answering questions and participating in one-on-one conversations with developers and marketing staff, or reviewing draft advertisements that publishers or their advertising agencies have voluntarily submitted to the ESRB for review. When an issue of non-compliance arises, the ESRB may begin an enforcement action and request background materials and information from the publisher regarding the infraction. Depending on the details and severity of the issue, the ESRB may require that the game's publisher complete corrective measures to address or mitigate any potential harm caused (e.g., correction of non-compliant advertisements, stickering of mislabeled physical units). In matters involving more serious infractions, or if a publisher commits the same type of offense repeatedly or refuses to correct an infraction that has been identified, the ESRB may also levy monetary fines upon the publisher. In extreme cases, the ESRB may even revoke a product's rating and/or halt the rating of future products from the publisher until the publisher corrects the issues that the ESRB has identified.

Submitting a game to the ESRB for rating is voluntary and receiving a rating is not required by law. However, in addition to providing consumers with more detailed information about a game, there are significant financial incentives to having a game rated by the ESRB. Video game console manufacturers (e.g., Microsoft, Sony, and Nintendo) will not typically license a game to be released on their platforms if the game has not been rated by the ESRB. Also, most large video game retailers in North America will not carry a game that has not been rated by the ESRB. It is worth noting that despite there being no laws prohibiting the sale of video games with more restrictive ratings to minors, many retailers, including most of the larger chain stores, have adopted policies prohibiting the sale of games that have been rated Mature to consumers below the age of 17 without the permission of a parent or guardian. The ESRB works directly with retailers to educate staff about the rating system, encourage and test the efficacy of store policies concerning the sale of rated games, and provide signage with information about the ESRB system that store staff can reference when discussing available games with customers.

Additional information concerning the ESRB can be found at http://www.esrb.org.

## THE GOVERNATOR TAKES ON VIDEO GAMES (*BROWN V. EMA*)

Harking back to the public controversy and senate hearings focusing on video game content from the early 1990s, the public debate on whether violent video game content has a detrimental impact on young players continues to crop up from time to time. Several state legislatures in the United States have attempted to regulate video games on the basis of their content since the early days of the medium, but none of those efforts have been discussed more widely or resolved more conclusively than *Brown v. Entertainment Merchants Association* (originally filed as *Schwarzenegger v. Entertainment Merchants Association*), which the United States Supreme Court ruled upon in 2011.

In *Brown*, trade groups representing the video game industry filed a lawsuit to overturn a California state law passed in 2005 that would have prohibited the sale or rental of violent video games to persons under the age of 18 and created labeling requirements for video games in addition to and separate from the rating display requirements enforced by the ESRB. Both the United States District Court for the Northern District of California and the

Ninth Circuit Court of Appeals held in favor of overturning the law on grounds including that the law violated rights protected by freedom of speech under the First Amendment. The Governor of California, Arnold Schwarzenegger, sought an appeal of each loss and the Supreme Court of the United States granted certiorari to hear the case in April 2010.

In June 2011, the Supreme Court held in favor of the Entertainment Merchants Association, definitively striking down the 2005 California law as unconstitutional. Early in his opinion for the seven-to-two majority, Supreme Court Justice Scalia indicated without equivocation that, like plays, books, and films, video games are artistic expressions protected by the freedom of speech afforded by the First Amendment. Justice Scalia then demonstrated how the California law failed each of the three prongs of the "strict scrutiny" test historically applied to laws that restrict freedom of speech on the basis of its contents, any one of which would have been dispositive of the laws' unconstitutionality.

Regarding the first prong, whether the law serves a compelling government interest, Scalia concluded that the various reports and studies presented by California did not demonstrate that violent video games were harmful to children, which undercut California's position that the law served the compelling interest of protecting children from harm. Scalia next indicated that the law was not the least restrictive means of accomplishing its goal, as required by the second prong, highlighting that the industry's voluntary system of the ESRB issuing ratings and retailers restricting the sale of products with Mature and Adults Only ratings already largely accomplished the goal of preventing the sale of violent video games to minors. Regarding the third prong, that the law be narrowly tailored, Scalia opined that the California law was both under-inclusive by singling out video games and ignoring violent content in other forms of media, and over-inclusive by restricting all children from buying violent video games, even if some parents didn't mind if their children purchased such games.

A concurring opinion by Justice Alito agreed that the California law was unconstitutional, but primarily due to the vagueness of its drafting as opposed to a conceptual inability to withstand the strict scrutiny test applied by the majority. Dissenting opinions by Justices Thomas and Breyer focused, respectively, on purported limitations of the First Amendment relating to parental authority over children, and a lack of justification for treating depictions of violence in the present case differently from depictions of nudity in previous cases.

Additional information about *Brown v. Entertainment Merchants Association* and selected other cases relevant to the regulation of the video game industry can be found at http://www.theesa.com/public-policy/legal-issues.

### LAWMAKER TO LAWBREAKER

Several years after the U.S. Supreme Court's decision in *Brown*, Leland Yee, the California State Senator that sponsored the law at issue in *Brown*, was arrested on multiple criminal charges relating to international weapons trafficking, bribery of a public official, and racketeering. Yee later pleaded guilty to a federal racketeering charge and was sentenced to five years in prison. As of this writing, Yee is serving that sentence in a federal correctional facility in Fort Worth, Texas. It is unknown whether Yee or his criminal associates regularly played violent video games, or whether Yee is permitted to play them in federal prison.

## FOREIGN RATING AUTHORITIES

Publishers and developers contemplating distributing their games outside of North America may also be interested in learning more about authorities that issue ratings for video games in other parts of the world. The following sections provide relevant information about a few rating authorities and regimes in foreign territories.

## EUROPE: PAN EUROPEAN GAME INFORMATION

As its name implies, Pan European Game Information (PEGI) is a single organization that issues video game ratings that are used throughout Europe. The PEGI rating system was founded and developed by the Interactive Software Federation of Europe (ISFE), an association which represents the interests of the video game industry in Europe, which has entrusted operation of the PEGI rating system to PEGI S.A., an independent but wholly-owned subsidiary. The PEGI rating system has been officially adopted by most European nations, including Austria, Belgium, Bulgaria, Cyprus, the Czech Republic, Denmark, Estonia, Finland, France, Greece, Hungary, Iceland, Ireland, Israel, Italy, Latvia, Lithuania, Luxembourg, Malta, the Netherlands, Norway, Poland, Portugal, Romania, the Slovak Republic, Sweden, Switzerland, Slovenia, Spain, and the United Kingdom. Some publishers also display PEGI ratings on the packaging of video games shipped to non-PEGI nations in Europe, Asia, and other regions.

In order to receive a PEGI rating, a publisher must first complete a two-part online content assessment and declaration form that asks about the content included in the game and addresses legal provisions of certain PEGI countries. Based on the responses to that form, PEGI generates a provisional (i.e., temporary) rating for the game and submits the game to one of two agencies for evaluation. Games for which the online form generates a provisional rating of PEGI 3 or PEGI 7 are reviewed by the Netherlands Institute for the Classification of Audio-Visual Media (NICAM) and games that receive provisional ratings of PEGI 12, PEGI 16, or PEGI 18 are reviewed by the Video Standards Council (VSC). The appropriate agency then applies PEGI's rating criteria to determine whether the game's provisional rating should be confirmed or adjusted based on a hands-on review of the game and an examination of the completed online form and any other information and materials provided by the publisher. Following examination, the Publisher receives the official rating for its game in a license from PEGI which authorizes them to use that rating in connection with the marketing, promotion, and sale of the game. A publisher that disagrees with the rating that PEGI has assigned to its game can submit a complaint to NICAM or VSC, depending on which agency performed the hands-on review of the game. If the publisher and the reviewing agency cannot come to a mutually acceptable resolution, then the complaint can be submitted to an independent Complaints Board organized by

PEGI and composed of members of the public and experts in child protection and psychology for a final decision on the PEGI rating of the game.

Video game console manufacturers like Microsoft, Nintendo, and Sony require PEGI ratings for games for their consoles, which is a strong motivator for publishers operating in Europe to voluntarily submit their video games to PEGI for rating. As a self-regulatory agency, PEGI is not backed by the force of law in most countries, but the combination of co-regulation in some countries and many publishers' pan-European distribution models make PEGI the de facto market standard for most of Europe. Furthermore, publishers that receive ratings from PEGI are contractually obligated to comply with the PEGI Code, which is a set of guidelines and requirements for the labeling, marketing, and advertising of video games. A publisher that has had a game rated by PEGI but does not adhere to the PEGI Code may be subject to penalties and required corrective actions that are determined by an Enforcement Committee organized by PEGI. In addition, a few countries have formally implemented aspects of the PEGI rating system in national legislation and some nations may subject video games to laws and government action that are independent of PEGI ratings and requirements.

Additional information concerning PEGI can be found at http://www.pegi.info.

## BRAZIL: CLASSIFICAÇÃO INDICATIVA/DEPARTMENT OF POLICIES OF JUSTICE

Classificação Indicativa (ClassInd) is a rating system administered by the Department of Policies of Justice (DPJUS) of the Ministry of Justice of the Federative Republic of Brazil. DPJUS assigns ClassInd ratings according to the Brazilian Federal Constitution of 1988, the Statute of the Child and Adolescent of 1990, the Manual of the New Rating System published by the Ministry of Justice in 2006, and Ordinance no. 368/2014 of the Ministry of Justice.[5] Under the ClassInd rating system, DPJUS applies the same rating criteria, categories, and descriptors to most audiovisual works, including television programs, motion pictures, and video games. While the Ordinance delineates the broad categories of ratings that DPJUS may assign, the Brazilian National Secretariat of Justice has prepared a practical, plain-language guide that contains detailed guidance concerning the content and boundaries of the rating categories (pictured above) and content descriptors of the ClassInd system.[6]

Every video game must receive a ClassInd rating from DPJUS before it can be legally sold online or in physical retail outlets in Brazil. In order to receive a rating, the game's publisher or its representative must submit an application to the DPJUS office of Content Rating Coordination (COCIND), which includes a recommended rating and support for that recommendation. Once an application has been submitted, the rating process does not typically involve conversation or coordination between the submitter and DPJUS unless the submitted materials are inconsistent or incomplete. If the application is complete, DPJUS will assign a ClassInd rating to the video game within approximately 30 days and the submitter can learn the rating category and descriptors assigned to the video game when the rating is published in the Brazilian Official Journal (DOU).

While a ClassInd rating is required by law in Brazil, DPJUS does not have the authority to deny a video game a rating, or to ban the sale of a game which has been properly submitted and received a rating. The ClassInd rating system is intended to be informational for consumers, primarily parents, and Brazilian law includes requirements concerning how assigned ratings must be displayed on game packaging and communicated in advertising and marketing materials. While DPJUS does not have the authority to enforce requirements or levy sanctions if they discover inconsistencies in the submission of a game for rating or in the compliance of publishers or distributors with applicable requirements (e.g., display of assigned ratings on game packaging), they can refer such issues to the courts or the appropriate prosecutors to enforce the law and (potentially) impose penalties.

Additional information concerning DPJUS and the ClassInd rating system can be found at http://justica.gov.br/seus-direitos/classificacao.

## JAPAN: COMPUTER ENTERTAINMENT RATING ORGANIZATION

    [7]

The majority of video game ratings in Japan are issued by the Computer Entertainment Rating Organization (CERO). CERO was established by the Computer Entertainment Supplier's Association (CESA), the primary organization representing and promoting the video game industry in Japan, and has since become an independent, non-profit corporation.

After CERO receives a rating request from a game publisher, a group of raters trained in rating by CERO who are not otherwise associated with the game industry evaluate the product's content in a series of expression (content) categories (e.g., "Sex-Related," "Violence," and "Anti-Social" content) delineated in the CERO Code of Ethics[8] and scaled to the CERO rating categories (depicted above). CERO then determines a rating for the game based on the evaluations of the raters and communicates the rating to the game's publisher. Once a publisher has received a rating from CERO it is obligated to display that rating on the game's packaging and before purchase on any website selling the game.

The CERO rating system is a self-regulatory system adopted by the Japanese game industry and CERO rating categories are advisory only. However, CERO may deny a rating to a product if the product includes content that exceeds an "upper limit" set by CERO for an expression category. There are no laws or regulations in Japan limiting the freedom of expression with respect to content of video games. Publishers releasing a game in Japan are not obligated to receive a rating from CERO, but the major console manufacturers will not publish a game in Japan if it has not received a rating from CERO. Individual Japanese prefectures may also require by regulation that physical retailers in their region check official ID to confirm that a purchaser is over the age of 18 before selling them a game that has received a "Z" rating from CERO.

Additional information concerning CERO can be found at http://www.cero.gr.jp/e.

### Ethics Organization of Computer Software (EOCS)

The Ethics Organization of Computer Software (EOCS) is a rating organization that focuses on the rating of certain games and interactive entertainment products for the personal computer, which can include visual novels, dating simulators, and "eroge" (erotic games). Some computer games that cannot receive a rating from CERO due to expressions that exceed CERO's upper limit for sexual content may be able to receive a rating from EOCS. Retailers in Japan are legally prohibited from selling games rated "R" or "18" by EOCS to persons under the ages of 15 and 18, respectively.

Additional information concerning EOCS can be found at http://www.sofurin.org/.

## GERMANY: UNTERHALTUNGSSOFTWARE SELBSTKONTROLLE

[9]

The German rating system is administered by Unterhaltungssoftware Selbstkontrolle (USK), a subsidiary of Freiwillige Selbstkontrolle Unterhaltungssoftware GmbH, a non-profit jointly owned by Bundesverband Interaktive Unterhaltungssoftware/the Federal Association of Interactive Entertainment Software (BIU) and Bundesverband der Entwickler von Computerspielen/the Federal Association of Computer Game Developers (GAME), which together represent video game developers, manufacturers, and distributors in Germany. While USK operates as an independent, self-regulatory body established by the German video game industry, all German ratings for games distributed on physical media are issued by representatives of the German supreme youth protection authorities, working closely with USK in a co-regulated system using rating categories delineated in the Children and Young Persons Protection Act of 2003.

Once a publisher has applied to USK to receive a rating for a video game, USK thoroughly tests the game and reviews materials submitted by the publisher in order to prepare a neutral report and presentation of the game for a classification committee. Each committee is comprised of four appointed experts in the protection of children and young persons from various fields (e.g., education, social sciences) and one permanent representative of the German supreme youth protection authorities. For each rating, the youth protection experts and the permanent representative of the supreme youth protection authorities agree on a rating category based on the USK tester's detailed report and other criteria adopted by USK. The committee then informs USK of its decision and USK transmits that decision to the publisher. Unless the publisher appeals the committee's decision, a representative from the supreme youth protection authorities issues the rating to the game.

Under the Children and Young Persons Protection Act, each video game sold in Germany on physical media must display a rating assigned via the rating process administered by USK. The Act also prohibits physical and online retailers in Germany from selling video games to young persons for whom they are not rated as appropriate, violation of which carries a fine of up to €50,000. While USK takes steps to educate the public and retailers regarding these requirements, their enforcement and the levying of attendant fines are the responsibility of local police and judicial authorities.

Please note that, for a small portion of games, USK classification committees may refuse classification based on a determination that such games include highly objectionable or illegal content that cannot be legally and securely sold in Germany. Bundesprüfstelle für jugendgefährdende Medien/the Federal Department for Media Harmful to Young Persons may subsequently place such games on an index of media deemed unsuitable for young persons, which makes it illegal to advertise or display such games publicly or to sell them to anyone other than an adult in Germany. Most physical and online retailers in Germany will not carry a game that has been "indexed."

Additional information concerning USK can be found at http://www.usk.de/en/.

## AUSTRALIA: CLASSIFICATION BOARD/CLASSIFICATION BRANCH

[10]

The Classification Board is an independent body operated by the Commonwealth of Australia that assigns ratings to video games sold in Australia. The Board assigns ratings according to the Classification (Publications, Films and Computer Games) Act of 1995,[11] which established the Classification Board, the Guidelines for the Classification of Computer Games,[12] and the National Classification Code,[13] which together delineate the key characteristics and differences among the rating categories that the Classification Board assigns (pictured above). The Act also makes receiving a rating from the Board mandatory before a video game can be sold in Australia. Following a rating decision by the Classification Board, a game's publisher or distributor may appeal the rating that its game has received by submitting a formal application for review by the Classification Review Board, a separate body comprised of completely different members, which meets only to review decisions of the Classification Branch following a valid application for review.

Of the rating categories that the Classification Board can assign, the G, PG, and M classifications are only advisory and are not accompanied by legal restrictions on the sale of video games assigned those ratings. In contrast, it is illegal in Australia to sell a video game assigned an MA 15+ classification to persons under the age of 15 unless they are accompanied by a parent or guardian, or a video game assigned an R 18+ classification to persons under the age of 18. The Classification Board may also designate a video game as "Refused Classification," which makes it illegal to sell, advertise, or import the video game in Australia.

While the Classification Board assigns ratings to video games distributed in Australia, the Australian rating system is managed primarily by the Classification Branch, which is a division of the Department of Communications and the Arts of the Commonwealth of Australia (previously of the Attorney General's Department, and originally of the Office of Film and Literature Classification). The Classification Branch administers all applications for video game ratings, fields and responds to complaints from the public concerning ratings, and works with Australian states and territories to promote compliance with assigned ratings and educate the public about the rating system. Individual states and territories are responsible for enforcing classification decisions and have each adopted their own legislation which sets requirements concerning to whom video games with certain ratings may be sold and advertised and also sets the criminal penalties for failure to comply with such requirements.

Additional information concerning Australia's Classification Board and Classification Branch can be found at http://www.classification.gov.au.

## OTHER FOREIGN RATING AUTHORITIES

### Argentina

The National Council of Children, Youth and Family, working with the National Institute of Cinema and Audiovisual Arts (both of which are agencies of the Argentinian government), is responsible for rating video games in Argentina using rating categories set by Argentinian law. Rating and labeling are mandatory for games sold in Argentina. Additional information concerning the National Institute of Cinema and Audiovisual Arts can be found at http://www.incaa.gov.ar, and an unofficial English translation of the law that established the rating requirement and the required rating categories can be found at https://goo.gl/9ZfFdt.

### Indonesia

The Indonesia Game Rating System (IGRS) is a recently established system for the rating of interactive entertainment products sold in Indonesia. IGRS, and the rating categories which it assigns based on game content and user age, were established by Regulation of the Ministry of Communication and Informatics of the Republic of Indonesia, Number 11 Year 2016, on the Classification of Interactive Electronic Games. Additional information concerning IGRS can be found at https://igrs.id.

### Iran

In 2007, the Iran Computer and Video Games Foundation, a quasi-governmental non-profit agency which operates under the supervision of the Iranian Ministry of Culture and Islamic Guidance, established the Entertainment Software Rating Association (ESRA), a self-regulatory organization which assigns age-based rating classifications to video games for Iran. Rating and licensing by ESRA are mandatory in order for a publisher to sell a game in Iran, and ESRA may deny permission to sell a game based on factors that may include cultural and religious considerations. Additional information concerning ESRA can be found at http://www.esra.org.ir.

## New Zealand

The Office of Film & Literature Classification (OFLC) is responsible for rating video games in New Zealand. The OFLC applies the same rating categories to video games that it applies to films, books, and other publications. In addition to General, Parental Guidance, and Mature rating categories, the OFLC rating system includes several "restricted" rating categories, each of which designates a minimum purchaser age for the sale of that product. Video games that are likely to receive a restricted label if rated are required to be submitted for rating and it is a crime to sell or supply a game that has a restricted rating to a child below the age designated by the rating. Additional information concerning the Office of Film & Literature Classification can be found at https://www.classificationoffice.govt.nz.

## Russia

The Russian Federation has promulgated a law, Federal Law of December 29, 2010 No. 436-FZ "On Protecting Children from Information Harmful to Their Health and Development" (as subsequently amended), that requires the rating of video games and establishes rating categories for such ratings but does not designate any agency or group responsible for assigning ratings. In the absence of a rating authority, game developers and publishers self-apply ratings to their games based on the qualitative criteria set forth in the law, general guidance provided by the government's limited interactions with previous games, and established industry practices. The text of Federal Law of December 29, 2010 No. 436-FZ can be found at http://kremlin.ru/acts/bank/32492 or https://goo.gl/4ubCvc.

## South Korea

The Game Industry Promotion Act of 2006 (as subsequently amended) makes submission of a game for rating and receiving a rating mandatory before a game can be sold or distributed in South Korea. The responsibility for rating video games in South Korea is divided between two agencies established and supported by the South Korean government: the Game Content Rating Board (GCRB), which can issue All, 12+, and 15+ ratings for online, mobile, and console video games, and the Game Rating and Administration Committee (GRAC), which rates all games that require an 18+ (Adult Only) rating and all arcade video games. These agencies may require that a game developer or publisher have an office or representative in South Korea before issuing a rating for its game. Additional information concerning GRAC can be found at http://www.grac.or.kr/english.

## Singapore

Since October 2016, the Info-Communications Media Development Authority (IMDA), a government board under Singapore's Ministry of Communications and Information, has been responsible for all rating of video games for Singapore. Before being sold in Singapore, video games must be declared to the IMDA using an online declaration system and games that include content in categories generally described in the IMDA's classification guidelines (e.g., violence, nudity, drug use) must be submitted to the IMDA for rating. A game is not required to display classification information in Singapore unless the IMDA has assigned the game a rating of "Age Advisory—Suitable for 16 and Above" or "Mature 18." The Mature 18 rating is enforced by retailers. The IMDA may also ban a game by classifying it as NAR (Not Allowed for All Ratings), in which case it may not be sold or distributed in Singapore. Additional information concerning the IMDA can be found at https://www.imda.gov.sg.

## South Africa

Under the Films and Publications Act of 1996, all video games must receive a rating from the Film and Publication Board (FPB) before being sold in South Africa and must display such rating and related information on their packaging. FPB rates games according to classification guidelines that are released for public comment each year and are updated on a regular basis. If FPB refuses to classify a game or classifies the game as "XX," then the game may not be sold and is essentially banned in South Africa. Retailers are required by law to register with FPB, to submit to FPB for rating any games in their possession that have not been rated, and to restrict the sale of any game rated "X18" to only persons 18 or older. FPB monitors retailers, and failure to comply with applicable requirements is a criminal offense subject to fines and/or imprisonment. Additional information concerning FPB can be found at http://www.fpb.org.za.

## Taiwan

In 2006, the Taiwanese government promulgated the Game Software Rating Management Regulations (subsequently amended), which established rating categories; provided general descriptions of content that should result in a game receiving each rating category; and obligates publishers, developers, and retailers to self-rate and label games in accordance with the specifications and requirements of such regulations before such games can be sold in Taiwan. Once a company has self-applied a rating to a game as required, they must register that rating with a searchable database established by the Industrial Development Bureau of Taiwan's Ministry of Economic Affairs. Additional information concerning the Game Software Rating Management Regulations can be found at http://www.gamerating.org.tw.

## INTERNATIONAL AGE RATING COALITION

For several years, the authorities that issue ratings for video games in many of the largest geographical regions in the world had discussed developing a shared system that could generate age-classification ratings for all of their territories. In 2013, a group of rating authorities that had participated in those discussions formed the International Age Rating Coalition (IARC), which manages and administers a system which does exactly that for mobile and digitally distributed games and apps.

Working with rating authorities, game publishers, and digital storefronts, IARC has developed and operates a system that uses a single electronic questionnaire to automatically generate age-classification ratings for mobile and digitally distributed games for all of the rating authorities participating in IARC. Rather than creating a new set of rating icons and descriptors to be generated by IARC and used across the world, IARC generates ratings using existing rating icons that are already recognized and trusted by consumers in regions that have a rating authority participating in IARC. IARC can generate multiple ratings using a single set of questions because the software underlying those questions has been programmed with unique algorithms that embody the proprietary ratings logic for each of the rating authorities participating in IARC. By running publisher responses to a single questionnaire through multiple algorithms that apply the rating logic developed by each participating rating authority, IARC allows each rating authority to apply the distinct standards that it has developed for rating video games for its own region(s), thus preserving the unique attitudes and concerns toward different types of content in each of those regions.

The process also creates a single, streamlined solution for publishers. Once a publisher has completed the IARC questionnaire for their mobile or digitally distributed game, the IARC system generates ratings for that game for all of the rating authorities and regions participating in IARC. As of this writing, IARC includes the ESRB issuing ratings for the Americas, PEGI issuing ratings for Europe, USK issuing ratings for Germany, ACB issuing ratings for Australia, ClassInd issuing ratings for Brazil, GRAC issuing ratings for South Korea, and Russian ratings based on applicable Russian law, plus a generic rating for all other regions, with more rating authorities expected to join over time. To further simplify the process for publishers, the IARC questionnaire is implemented as a part of the process that publishers must already complete in order to submit their game for distribution on any storefront that is participating in IARC. As of this writing, participating storefronts include Google Play, the Microsoft Store, the Nintendo eShop, and the Oculus Store. Once the publisher completes the IARC questionnaire, the ratings generated are also automatically communicated to the storefront that the publisher is submitting to, and can typically be reused by the publisher if it submits the same game to any other storefront participating in IARC.

The following diagram provides a simple illustration of the process:[14]

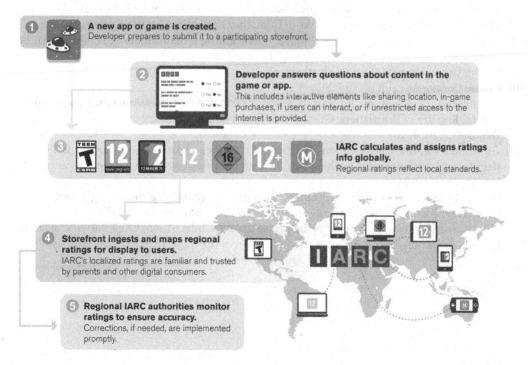

Additional information concerning IARC can be found at https://www.globalratings.com.

## GOING FORWARD

The video game industry is always evolving and efforts to rate and regulate video game content, both by governments and industry participants, develop and evolve in parallel. The organizations and government bodies that rate games several years from now may be different or operate differently from the organizations of today. New organizations or regulations may arise where none existed before, or may replace those that already exist. This chapter offers an introduction to video game ratings and regulations throughout the world, but it is always in your best interest to learn more and to continue to refresh your knowledge of the regulatory frameworks that your games may be subject to.

## NOTES

1. The ESRB rating icons are trademarks of the Entertainment Software Association.
2. The Principles and Guidelines for Responsible Advertising Practices can be found online at http://www.esrb.org/ratings/principles_guidelines.aspx. The ARC Manual is available upon request to publishers that have submitted games to the ESRB for rating.
3. The PEGI rating icons are trademarks of PEGI S.A.
4. Credit: Federative Republic of Brazil.
5. Manual of the New Rating System, Ministry of Justice of the Federative Republic of Brazil, 2006; Ordinance no. 368/2014, Ministry of Justice of the Federative Republic of Brazil, 2014; both of which can be found online at http://www.justica.gov.br/seus-direitos/classificacao/legislacao.
6. Content Rating Practical Guide, Brazilian National Secretariat of Justice, 2012; which can be found online at http://www.justica.gov.br/seus-direitos/classificacao/guia-pratico.
7. The CERO rating icons are trademarks of Computer Entertainment Rating Organization.
8. CERO Code of Ethics, Computer Entertainment Rating Organization, 2011; which can be found online at http://www.cero.gr.jp/en/publics/index/18/.
9. Credit: Unterhaltungssoftware Selbstkontrolle.
10. Credit: Commonwealth of Australia.
11. Classification (Publications, Films and Computer Games) Act of 1995, Australian Government Federal Register of Legislation; which can be found online at https://www.legislation.gov.au/Details/C2017C00267.
12. Guidelines for the Classification of Computer Games, Australian Government Federal Register of Legislation, 2012; which can be found online at https://www.legislation.gov.au/Details/F2012L01934.
13. National Classification Code, Australian Government Federal Register of Legislation, 2005; which can be found online at https://www.legislation.gov.au/Details/F2013C00006.
14. The "How IARC Works" graphic is the property of the International Age Rating Coalition, Inc. and the rating icons it includes are trademarks of the respective rating authorities.

# CHAPTER 12

# Welcome to Tortious Games

T HE CONTENT ISSUES THAT arise when creating video games are as varied as the experiences that video games provide and no book (or series of books) can fully prepare you to navigate all the problems that could come up. This chapter provides a few hypothetical situations that highlight content issues sometimes faced by video game developers in order to illustrate concepts that are valuable to keep in mind when creating games.

## YOU'RE HIRED

Tortious Games is a mid-size independent video game developer that has just hired you to help produce its first solo AAA video game for consoles. Tortious has some experience with assisting in the development of console games for larger developers and also making smaller PC and mobile games of its own. As Tortious has grown, they have reached a critical mass of staff with experience and interest in making AAA games for consoles so they have decided to take a shot at making one for themselves. The following are a few circumstances which come up over the course of creating that game.

## EARLY CONCEPTS

You have joined Tortious only a week or so after they have decided to develop a AAA game and the heads of the studio are still trading ideas about what the game should be. You receive the following initial bullet points about the game's potential design from the first few people you speak to at Tortious:

- The tone of the game will be serious, with some social commentary and satire.

- The game will use a third-person perspective.

- The setting will be a fictional version of New York City, currently referred to as "Freedom City."

- The protagonist will be a recent European immigrant with a violent and mysterious past.

- The protagonist is chasing a shadowy man who wronged him that may be involved in a criminal organization in Freedom City.

- The protagonist receives help in his quest from entertaining family members and new friends that he meets in Freedom City.

- The protagonist takes to crime easily due to his checkered past and uses it in his quest to find the man who wronged him.

- The player completes selectable missions in order to advance the story.

- Missions include a variety of legal and non-legal activities, including deliveries, robberies, assassinations, and kidnappings.

- The game will also feature driving elements, including car chases and races.

Looking at these concepts and discussing them with the team leads at Tortious, it becomes clear that a few staff members at Tortious are very interested in creating a game that is similar to some pre-existing games, perhaps one very successful game in particular. You also collect the following alternative ideas and feedback from other members of the team:

- Some team members are interested in creating a game with more sci-fi elements, potentially involving robots.

- Some teams feel that New York City has been the setting of too many games in the last few years and would like to place the game in a different locale.

- A few developers would like for the game to include more mini-games and puzzles to leverage Tortious' experience and success with these elements in previous projects.

Looking at both collections of bullet points, you may be concerned that copying elements that appear in other games can be legally risky, but also unsure how to determine which elements create risk of a lawsuit and which are safe to use. The concept of "scènes à faire" may help with this analysis. Scènes à faire refers to elements which are common or obligatory in stories of a certain type which precludes them from being protectable elements that can only appear in a single creative work like a book, film, or video game. For example, multi-level criminal organizations are almost a requirement for urban crime stories so including such an organization in a new urban crime game does not by itself create much risk of legitimate lawsuits from the creators of other urban crime games. For a video game, scènes à faire may also refer to game mechanics that are common across a variety of different games or types of games (e.g., third-person perspective). There is no bright line rule that separates elements that are scènes à faire from elements that are protectable under intellectual property law and legally risky to copy. That is why it is useful to picture game elements as existing on a spectrum from inarguably scènes à faire and safe to use (e.g., selectable missions, mini-games) to the other extreme of very specific elements of a game or franchise that are protectable by their creators and may result in a lawsuit if copied (e.g., a tight-clothed brunette that spends her free time raiding exotic tombs).

After discussing the concept of scènes à faire versus protectable elements with the team at Tortious and reviewing the bulleted lists you've collected, the decision-makers have settled on the following general concepts for the game that integrate new ideas with scènes à faire elements and avoid more specific protectable elements from other games:

- The tone of the game will be serious with strong sci-fi elements.

- The game will use third-person perspective.

- The game will take place in a fictional version of Chicago called River City.

- The protagonist will be a morally ambiguous, recently-created, human-looking android that does not know the details of its creation.

- The protagonist is on a quest to uncover its unknown past which may involve tracking down a nefarious scientist working for a criminal organization.

- The protagonist will receive help in its quest from new friends that it meets in River City, including neighbors, hackers, and technophiles.

- The protagonist chooses from selectable missions, including normal activities like introducing itself to new people and delivering pizza, and criminal activities like robbing electronics stores and kidnapping scientists.

- The player learns how to complete activities required for missions through "artificial intelligence" and "machine learning" themed mini-games and puzzles.

Comparing the initial list of game elements to the final list, you'll see that some of the unchanged elements are scènes à faire that did not require changing (e.g., third-person perspective, selectable missions, criminal organizations, the protagonist making allies), some of the more specific elements from other games have been removed (e.g., the European immigrant chasing a shadowy man from his past), and other changes may have been made for largely creative reasons (e.g., adding robot and sci-fi elements, setting the game in a version of Chicago instead of New York City).

## CHARACTERS WITH CHARACTER

Fast forward a few months. The game's writers and art department have been working together for a few months to design interesting and memorable characters for the game. There's the protagonist android that starts out emotionless but eventually develops endearing quirks and character over time based on the player's decisions, but there is also a supporting cast of allies, various neighborhood folk that live in the area near the android's home base, plus engineers and hackers that the android has befriended or coerced into cooperating with its mission, and there are villains, a good mix of low-level criminal lackeys, some mini-bosses in both science and organized crime themes, and a few impressive high-level bosses. In going over scripts and initial character designs for some of the villains, you begin to have some concerns about one particular mini-boss, tentatively named "Crusher McFist."

Based on the limited scripts and character background that have been prepared thus far, you can piece together that Crusher is a former boxer-turned-mob enforcer with a history of particularly brutal wins in the ring and a variety of violent altercations outside of the ring that make him an intimidating presence in any situation. Regarding the appearance of the character, Crusher is dark-skinned and bald with a muscular build, he has an unusually high-pitched voice with a bit of a lisp, and he also has a large tribal tattoo on one side of his face. Despite Crusher's comical name, it is clear to you that similarities between the character of Crusher McFist and a certain famous former boxer may create too much risk of a lawsuit for McFist to exist unchanged in the final game. So what options do you have?

It is not unheard of for celebrities to appear in video games, so there is always the option of reaching out to a celebrity to see if they are interested in appearing in your video game. The likelihood of such a pitch succeeding can vary widely based on many factors, including the prestige of the project, the status of the celebrity, and the compensation that your company is willing to pay the celebrity in order for them to appear in the game. It's likely that the celebrity will also want some level of approval over their portrayal in the game, potentially removing or toning down negative or criminal elements that might cast them in a bad light, which could limit what your writers and art department can do with the in-game character.

There is also a significant risk in reaching out to a real person about appearing in your game that may not be immediately obvious. By reaching out to someone about appearing in your game, you indicate to that person and the attorneys and business people that work for them that you are considering including a character that may be similar to them in your game. If they refuse to be included in your game, it makes it very risky to use a character that shares any similarities with that person in your game because doing so may result in the famous person filing a lawsuit against your company claiming that you have infringed upon their rights in their own likeness and related rights by including them or a version of them in your game without permission. In such a case, the fact that you reached out to the celebrity about appearing in the game could be used against your company. Ultimately, before reaching out to a notable person about appearing in your game, a wise developer would be prepared to avoid including any character in the game that arguably resembles them if they refuse.

Alternatively, if Tortious is not interested in working with the famous inspiration for Crusher McFist, then they should definitely not reach out to that person and should revisit the design of that character instead. The individual elements of the Crusher character bring to mind a specific real-world person, so changing some of those elements can go a long way toward differentiating the character and protecting Tortious from a potential lawsuit. The options for such changes are as varied as the creative team can imagine; for example, Tortious' designers could change Crusher's complexion, facial features, or ethnicity; they could also change Crusher's former profession from boxing to football. The creative team should use this as an opportunity to create something new rather than relying on something that already exists.

It may also be a good idea for Tortious to avoid using the actual tattoo that appears on a famous person on their Crusher McFist character. Recreating a real-world tattoo in a video game can present multiple issues that a game developer may prefer to avoid. Reusing an actual tattoo as it appears on an would be a significant element of similarity between the in-game character and that person, which could be used against Tortious in a potential lawsuit by that person. Perhaps less obvious but just as problematic, multiple tattoo artists have brought lawsuits in recent years alleging that recreating their tattoos in creative works like films and video games infringes upon their intellectual property rights in the artwork of those tattoos. While the law is far from settled in this area and the outcome of lawsuits involving these issues will be heavily dependent on the circumstances of each case, it is almost always better to avoid a lawsuit than to win one. Creating a new tattoo for an entirely fictional in-game character is almost always safer than rolling the dice by copying or reusing an existing tattoo in a game.

## BRAND (VS.) NEW

The creative departments at Tortious have come to you with a disagreement about whether to include brands in the game. There are some on the team that would like to include existing real-world brands and products in the game to make the game world feel more real, while others would prefer to create their own in-game brands and products so they can exercise more creative freedom and take advantage of opportunities to poke fun at some products and industries. While there are certainly creative aspects of this decision that you would prefer the creative teams to agree upon, you are concerned that there may also be legal factors to consider when deciding whether or not to include real brands in a video game.

Including real-world brands and branded products can be more complicated in a video game than in other mediums like film and television. As a threshold matter, for a branded automobile or soft drink bottle to appear in a game, the game's developer must first create an in-game version of that object which approximates the appearance and potentially the functionality of the real-world branded object. This may require copying or duplicating protected elements of the branded object, for example, logos that appear on the product that may be registered trademarks of the company that owns the brand. This is a noteworthy difference from what is required for a branded product to appear in a film or television show. Specifically, the studio or production team for a film or television show need only buy or rent a product to be used during filming, which does not require copying or recreating the branded product and actually supports a stream of revenue that flows to the product creator.

Returning to video games, there are arguably some benefits to having brands and branded products in a game. The principal benefit from a creative perspective is that brands and branded products appear in the real world, so properly integrating them into an in-game world may make that world seem more real. This is especially true with respect to real-world locations that feature a significant amount of branded advertising, such as

Times Square in New York City, Piccadilly Circus in London, and most professional sports stadiums. While in-game recreation of brands and advertising may be out of place in some locations, its absence would be more jarring in locations like these. Recreating real-world brands and branded products in a game can also provide enjoyable wish-fulfillment for players (e.g., street racing in an expensive sports car). On the other hand, including real brands in a game can have drawbacks, including that some players feel that seeing real brands in a game space can feel too much like advertising, breaking the illusion and pulling them out of the game's narrative.

There are also some potential risks in recreating existing branded objects in a game. There have been a number of lawsuits and legal threats by manufacturers of real-world products like cars, guns, and other objects that players regularly interact with in video games, which claim that the recreation of their products in a game infringes upon their intellectual property in those products. There is a strong argument to be made that a video game developer that includes real brands or branded products in a game may be shielded by the First Amendment protection of the game as an expressive work. However, at the time of writing few of these cases have resulted in reliable legal precedent and some have yet to be finally adjudicated, so there remains some risk that a game developer that includes branded products in their game may be contacted by the owner of those brands demanding compensation or potentially other corrective measures (e.g., recalling the game). The risk of such claims may be lessened (although, unfortunately, not entirely eliminated) by minimizing the use of brands or branded products to only the amount necessary to establish the world in which the unrelated story of the game takes place, and by not focusing on or featuring brands or branded products in the game (or in the game's advertising materials) in such a way that might lead players to think that the owner of the brand was the source of the game or involved with its creation.

A developer that does not want to include brands or branded products in a game without the brand owners' permission may be able to negotiate with brand owners and license rights to include their brands in a game. For example, game developers making sports games may license brands that appear in advertisements in in-game stadiums, and potentially even the athletic gear that the in-game players wear and use. The economic terms of these licenses can vary widely, from a developer paying the brand owner to include a brand in a game, to the brand owner and the developer agreeing on a no-cost ("gratis") license on the basis that featuring the brand in the game would be beneficial for both parties, to a brand owner or advertiser paying the game developer to include their products or advertisements for their products in the game ("in-game advertising"). In recent years, some game developers have even entered into arrangements with brand owners that combined in-game use or game-related promotion of a brand with real-world promotion of the game by the brand owner, which is why it is not out of the ordinary to see a video game property appear on the packaging of a soft drink.

While working directly with brand owners may seem like the safest way to include brands and branded products in a game, it may not always be an option and may raise other issues for a game's development team. For instance, brand owners do not typically want their products associated with dangerous or criminal behavior, which can make it difficult or impossible to license real-world brands to feature in games that include criminal or violent elements. Brand owners may place limitations on how their products can appear in a game, for example, a car licensor may prohibit their cars from being damaged or destroyed in a game, which may be unacceptable to the game's creative team. A developer may also just not have the time or budget to negotiate and pay for the licenses required by brand owners in order to include branded products in the game.

If Tortious decides not to include real-world brands or branded products in their game, then instead of recreating existing brands and products they can create generic, non-brand products that blend into the game world, or create their own brands and branded products for the game. Creating generic products can be as simple as using nondescript labels and designs for typically branded objects (e.g., not duplicating well-known bottle designs or labels for drinks, or creative flourishes of famous sneakers or cars). These kinds of in-game objects typically won't tell the player much about the game world, but they also won't draw attention away from the narrative elements and activities of the game.

On the other hand, creating your own brands for a game can emphasize aspects of the game or the game world. For instance, if the game is intended to have a serious tone, then the original game brands can sound rough and foreboding. If the game's tone is lighter, then the game's original brands and advertising could be sillier or make jokes at the expense of real-world brands (while being careful not to copy too much from them). In addition to offering another avenue to flesh out the game world, if a game becomes popular, original in-game brands offer the game's developer an opportunity to create and sell real-world game merchandise (e.g., shirts, hats, etc.) bearing the logos or imagery of popular in-game brands similar to what real-world brands do to promote their products.

When creating in-game brands, it is always important to perform a thorough search of real-world brands for the same or similar products to ensure that you are not accidentally infringing on someone else's intellectual property. Also, it is wise to avoid including licensed real-world brands and products in the same game as original developer-created brands and products. The reason being that if a game includes both and the developer is later sued by a third party who claims that one of the developer-created brands infringes on their real-world brand, the third party may allege that, because the game includes some real-world brands, players may be led to the mistaken belief that the developer-created brand is actually a licensed version of their brand.

## SKIN-DEEP TROUBLE

The player-controlled character in the game that Tortious is developing is an android that looks like a fairly average adult human. However, a few members of the creative team have been toying with the idea of offering alternate skins for the main character that look more like typical robots and androids. The designs and skins that they have already begun working on include some very recognizable robots and androids from popular films and television series. While you agree that initial demos of game-play using these alternate skins are very entertaining, and you do not want to impede the team's creativity, you are concerned that creating in-game versions of characters from famous pop culture properties could land Tortious in hot water. Thankfully, Tortious has a few options that should look somewhat familiar if you've read the previous sections discussing characters and in-game brands.

The first option is to license the appearance of existing characters directly from the owners of the properties that those characters are from. For the present situation, this might include contacting and working with Valve to license the appearance of the Atlas and P-Body androids from *Portal 2*, Disney to license the appearance of *Star Wars* droids C3-PO and R2-D2, Marvel characters like Ultron and the Vision, or even cute little Wall-E from the Pixar film of the same name. Tortious could contact whoever currently owns the rights to the Terminator franchise in order to try to license the appearance of the famous silver T-800 endoskeleton, and even contact and negotiate with Arnold Schwarzenegger's people about whether they can include a skin of the actor's likeness in the game. The process of licensing the appearance of these characters will not be easy, and it is likely that some of the property owners will not be interested in having their character(s) appear in Tortious' game, even as an optional skin. However, licensing the appearance of these characters from the owners of the underlying properties is the safest way to include them in a video game.

As previously discussed with respect to basing in-game characters on real people, Tortious should keep in mind that contacting the owner of a pre-existing character in order to potentially license the appearance of that character puts the owner of that character on notice that Tortious' game may include content that infringes on their rights. This means that Tortious should only contact character owners if it is very serious about negotiating with them for such a license, which could entail creative limitations, financial requirements, and other terms which Tortious may be reluctant to agree to.

If Tortious does not have the time, money, or interest in working directly with third-party licensors to include alternative android and robot skins in the game, then its next best option is to get a lot more creative with those skins. More specifically, the artists at Tortious should work on creating skins that are recognizably robots and androids in a style that they want in the game, but that are not so similar to well-known robots and androids from famous pre-existing franchises that including them in the game creates a risk that Tortious will be sued. Exactly what changes will be needed to make each skin its own, original non-derivative character that still evokes "killer android" or "clumsy, helpful robot" in the mind of the player will vary from skin to skin, but generally speaking, replacing copied elements (e.g., chassis color, limb shape, facial features, build) with original or alternative options can make a new skin less likely to infringe on a pre-existing character owned by a third party. If Tortious has contacted the owner of an existing character without entering into a license, then Tortious may want to take extra care in making significant changes to any skin or other game content that arguably features significant elements from that existing character, in order to avoid a potential legal claim by the owner of that character in the future.

## SOFTWARE AND HARD PROBLEMS

In talking with some of the teams working on the game that Tortious is developing, you occasionally hear the names of software companies and programs being used to create the game or being included in the game. You've heard of some of these companies and utilities before, but some you're hearing about for the first time. Having been involved in discussions with the accounting department regarding invoices for some software being used to create the game, you realize that some of the companies and tools that the development and creative teams have mentioned have not come up in accounting conversations. When you asked the members of those teams for more information about the sources of the software that they've mentioned using or adapting for the game, they indicate that some they had from previous projects, some they got from other developers, and some they downloaded from various sources on the internet for free or for nominal fees. Regarding whether the creators or owners of the software gave Tortious permission to use it to develop a game or include it in a game, the staff members that you spoke with didn't know and only had vague, unhelpful answers, some of which mentioned that the software was "just available for free" or "it shouldn't be a problem." You are now concerned that Tortious may be using software to create the game or including software in the game without the permission of the owners of that software, and that if the software owners find out what Tortious is doing, they may sue for infringement of their intellectual property rights in that software.

The software that is used to develop a game or included in a game can have an enormous impact on how that game functions and looks. This software can include everything from complex 3D modeling software and physics engines to simpler audio codecs and lighting plugins, all the way down to basic texture packs and font files. Some of these tools are classified as development or art tools, some are commonly referred to as "middleware," and some go by various other names. Which software falls within each category can vary depending on who you ask and is not terribly important for our purposes. What's important to remember is that, regardless of its level of complexity, all software was created by someone and unless there is some kind of agreement between Tortious and that someone, using that software in Tortious' game or to create Tortious' game could infringe on that someone's legal rights and result in that someone suing Tortious.

Game development can be extremely complex, and the amount of third-party software that may be involved in that process can be truly mind-boggling. One way to keep track of all of that software and Tortious' rights and licenses with respect to using it or including it in a game is to create a spreadsheet that tracks all of those elements in one place. Columns of that spreadsheet might list the name of the software, the company that created or owns the software, how the software is being used to create the game or included in the game, the relevant terms controlling how the software may be used or included in the game, and whether using the software or including it in a game places any requirements on Tortious with respect to that game (e.g., a credit or logo on screen or on packaging).

While some information about a piece of software may be easy to determine and fill in, like the name of a piece of software and who created or owns it, some information can be more difficult to nail down, like the terms that control how the software can be used or included in a game. For these terms, you usually have to look through the license agreement for the software, which can take many forms. For robust software suites like physics engines there may be signed contracts that will include payment requirements and other terms that will help you fill in the more detailed parts of the software chart. For smaller pieces of software, like individual files or apps downloaded from the internet (and not always directly from the owner or creator), the terms controlling their use may be found in an end-user license agreement (EULA) or terms of service or use (TOS/TOU) that you or someone at Tortious agreed to with a click before downloading, or may be posted in a "Legal" or "Licenses" section of the download site. Sometimes license terms are even found in a "Readme" or other text file that's included when a file or piece of software is downloaded.

Reviewing software that is used to create a game or included in a game can be daunting, particularly for larger projects, so it can be useful to set priorities. One of those priorities may be that it is more important to determine that Tortious has all of the necessary rights to software that is being included in the game than to software that is only being used to create the game (but will not actually be included in the game). The reasoning behind this distinction is that, while use of an unlicensed piece of software may constitute copyright infringement and is not a good business practice, that infringement is small-scale and can typically be remedied by purchasing one or more desk licenses. Also, knowledge of that infringement is confined to the office and is unlikely to halt production or sale of a game if it gets out. On the other hand, if a game includes a piece of unlicensed software, every copy or download of the game likely infringes on the software creator's intellectual property rights which makes the game developer's infringement on the software owner's rights much larger in scale and much more likely to be discovered since the game is distributed publicly, which could result in a lawsuit that could stop the sale of that game temporarily or permanently.

As you review the terms controlling how each piece of software on the list can be used to create a game or included in a game, the first thing you want to confirm is that those terms permit Tortious to use or include the software in the way that Tortious is doing or plans to do. If the uses that Tortious is making or has planned are not mentioned at all, even in a general sense (i.e., the terms don't mention integrating the software in to a product for sale, never mind a video game), or worse, are expressly prohibited, then the safest next steps for Tortious may be to cease use or scrap plans to include that software in the game. Alternatively, Tortious could reach out to the creator or owner of the software and attempt to negotiate a license for the right to use the software or include it in Tortious' game.

Once you have determined that the license terms applicable to a piece of software permit Tortious to use or include the software in the way that Tortious intends, the next step should be to review the rest of that license to ensure it does not include any other terms that Tortious cannot accept. Terms that licenses may include can be extremely varied, but there are a few to always look out for. You should always be sure to confirm that any terms involving payments, royalties, or other fees are acceptable within the scope of the game's development budget, and that any time limitations of the license will not prevent Tortious from fully exploiting a product for its entire commercial life (which could be very long). As a general rule, you should be wary of any terms that require, limit, or prohibit future actions by Tortious. Also, terms that require the input or approval of the owner or creator of the software for any action by Tortious or use of the software can prove to be problematic, both in the present and down the road.

Regarding license obligations, it is worth noting that a game developer like Tortious should exercise extreme caution when using or integrating into its game any piece of software that is referred to as "open source" or is licensed under an open-source license. Developers occasionally find themselves wanting to use open-source software because many open-source applications are developed and supported by robust online communities and are available to download and use for free. However, that "free" software may come at a cost that is not immediately obvious to Tortious' development staff. Specifically, open-source licenses are generally known to include terms that may be antithetical to the production of commercial projects. For example, some open-source licenses include requirements where, if the software is included in a game or other product, the creator of that game or product must then license the resulting game or product (or at least its underlying code) to the public for free. While not all open-source licenses include terms this extreme, and some open-source licenses can be more business-friendly than others, the potential for a free distribution obligation, which could significantly harm a commercial project, should make developers like Tortious very cautious about using open-source software or including it in their games.

## PROCEED WITH CAUTION

These examples are just a very small sampling of the extremely varied content clearance and intellectual property issues that can arise when developing a video game. As with the rest of this book, this chapter is no substitute for consulting an attorney when facing these or other legal issues. However, having more information about potential legal pitfalls involving your game's content can help you identify issues like those discussed herein and determine when it may be a good idea to call a lawyer.

# Index

Printed in the United States
by Baker & Taylor Publisher Services